Eva Gross
THE EUROPEANIZATION OF NATIONAL FOREIGN POLICY
Continuity and Change in European Crisis Management

Sebastian Krapohl
RISK REGULATION IN THE SINGLE MARKET
The Governance of Pharmaceuticals and Foodstuffs in the European Union

Katie Verlin Laatikainen and Karen E. Smith *(editors)*
THE EUROPEAN UNION AND THE UNITED NATIONS
Intersecting Multilateralisms

Esra LaGro and Knud Erik Jørgensen *(editors)*
TURKEY AND THE EUROPEAN UNION
Prospects for a Difficult Encounter

Paul G.Lewis and Zdenka Mansfeldová *(editors)*
THE EUROPEAN UNION AND PARTY POLITICS IN CENTRAL AND EASTERN EUROPE

Ingo Linsenmann, Christoph O. Meyer and Wolfgang T. Wessels *(editors)*
ECONOMIC GOVERNMENT OF THE EU
A Balance Sheet of New Modes of Policy Coordination

Hartmut Mayer and Henri Vogt *(editors)*
A RESPONSIBLE EUROPE?
Ethical Foundations of EU External Affairs

Lauren M. McLaren
IDENTITY, INTERESTS AND ATTITUDES TO EUROPEAN INTEGRATION

Philomena Murray *(editor)*
EUROPE AND ASIA
Regions in Flux

Daniel Naurin and Helen Wallace *(editors)*
UNVEILING THE COUNCIL OF THE EUROPEAN UNION
Games Governments Play in Brussels

David Phinnemore and Alex Warleigh-Lack
REFLECTIONS ON EUROPEAN INTEGRATION
50 Years of the Treaty of Rome

Sebastiaan Princen
AGENDA-SETTING IN THE EUROPEAN UNION

Frank Schimmelfennig, Stefan Engert and Heiko Knobel
INTERNATIONAL SOCIALIZATION IN EUROPE
European Organizations, Political Conditionality and Democratic Change

Angelos Sepos
THE EUROPEANIZATION OF CYPRUS
Polity, Policies and Politics

Marc Weller, Denika Blacklock and Katherine Nobbs *(editors)*
THE PROTECTION OF THE MINORITIES IN THE WIDER EUROPE

Palgrave Studies in European Union Politics
Series Standing Order ISBN 978–1–4039–9511–7 (hardback) and ISBN 978–1–4039–9512–4 (paperback)

You can receive future titles in this series as they are published by placing a standing order. Please contact your bookseller or, in case of difficulty, write to us at the address below with your name and address, the title of the series and one of the ISBNs quoted above.

Customer Services Department, Macmillan Distribution Ltd, Houndmills, Basingstoke, Hampshire RG21 6XS, England

The Europeanization of National Foreign Policy

Continuity and Change in European Crisis Management

Eva Gross

Senior Research Fellow for European Foreign and Security Policy
Institute for European Studies, Free University Brussels, Belgium

palgrave
macmillan

Contents

List of Tables and Figure   vii

Acknowledgements   viii

List of Acronyms   ix

Introduction   xi

1 **The Europeanization of National Foreign Policy?**   1
   The choice for (or against) CFSP and ESDP   1
   The role of member states: Britain, France and Germany   3
   International Relations theory and EU foreign and
     security policy   7
   Hypotheses generated from the conceptual
     approaches: some definitions   24

2 **Continuity and Change in European Crisis Management**   29
   Baptism by fire: European crisis management in FYROM
     and Afghanistan   29
   Plus ça change? European crisis management in
     Lebanon and DRC   46
   From 'European' to 'Europeanized' crisis management?   61

3 **Britain: Balancing European and Transatlantic
   Commitments**   63
   Introduction: Britain and European foreign and
     security policy   63
   2001: FYROM and Afghanistan   63
   2006: Lebanon and DRC   83
   Conclusion   90

4 **France: Exporting National Preferences**   91
   Introduction: France and European foreign and
     security policy   91
   2001: FYROM and Afghanistan   91
   2006: Lebanon and DRC   112
   Conclusion   121

5   **Germany: From Bystander to Participant**   122
    Introduction: Germany and European foreign and
      security policy   122
    2001: FYROM and Afghanistan   123
    2006: Lebanon and DRC   145
    Conclusion   153

6   **From Continuity to Change: an Emerging European**
    Crisis Management Policy?   154
    The Europeanization of national foreign policy? Comparing
      member states' reactions   154
    Europeanization of foreign policy: preliminary assessments   155
    Changing priorities for ESDP   170
    Towards the Europeanization of crisis management?   171

Notes   173

Bibliography   175

Index   192

List of Tables and Figure

Tables

1.1	Operationalizing governmental politics	13
1.2	Operationalizing Europeanization	21
1.3	Operationalizing alliance politics	24
6.1	Decision-making in FYROM	158
6.2	Decision-making in Afghanistan	162
6.3	Decision-making in Lebanon	166
6.4	Decision-making in DRC	167

Figure

1.1	Europeanization	16

Acknowledgements

This book has profited from the intellectual and social environment of the London School of Economics Department of International Relations. Dr Karen Smith in particular deserves special thanks for her support and intellectual input during various stages of the research that forms the basis of this book – as do Professor David Allen and Professor Michael Cox for their useful comments.

In the course of my field research I have enjoyed the hospitality of two research institutes. The Centre d'Etudes et de Recherches Internationales (CERI) Science Po hosted me in Paris during the summer of 2005 and the Centre for European Policy Studies (CEPS) in Brussels hosted me for much of 2006; thanks to Professor Renaud Dehousse at CERI and to Michael Emerson at CEPS for making this possible. I would also like to thank Professor Jolyon Howorth, who was instrumental in helping me with the interviews during my stay in Paris and who has continued to offer his support when needed ever since.

I thank all the diplomats in Berlin, Brussels, London and Paris for taking the time to talk to me during the various stages of this research, and for being generally very supportive and interested in this project. Most have requested to remain anonymous, but I am happy to acknowledge their collective input. As befits the subject of this book, the final part of the manuscript was completed in Brussels and Paris (and sometimes somewhere between the two) while carrying out research in the framework of a visiting fellowship at the EU Institute for Security Studies.

Last but certainly not least, thanks go to family and friends who have contributed in so many ways to the research and writing of this book. I would also like to thank my mother and my sister for their support.

This research would have been a lot more difficult to carry out had it not been for the financial support from a number of sources, and I gratefully acknowledge the support of the VolkswagenStiftung for a generous grant in the framework of the 'European Foreign and Security Policy Studies Programme'; the European Social and Research Council for a +3 grant; the LSE Department of International Relations; and the University of London Central Research Fund for supporting my field research.

List of Acronyms

AIA	Afghan Interim Authority
CDU	Christian Democratic Union
CFSP	Common Foreign and Security Policy
CSU	Christian Social Union
DFID	Department for International Development
DPKO	Department of Peacekeeping Operations
DRC	Democratic Republic of Congo
ECHO	European Commission Humanitarian Aid Office
ENP	European Neighbourhood Policy
EPC	European Political Cooperation
ESDP	European Security and Defence Policy
ESS	European Security Strategy
EU	European Union
EUBAM	European Union Border Assistance Mission
EUFOR	European Union Force
EUPOL	European Union Police Mission
EUSEC	European Union Security Sector Reform Mission
EUSR	European Union Special Representative
FDP	Free Democratic Party
FHQ	Force Headquarters
FYROM	Former Yugoslav Republic of Macedonia
GAERC	General Affairs and External Relations Council
IDF	Israeli Defence Forces
ISAF	International Security Assistance Force
KFOR	Kosovo Force
MOD	Ministry of Defence
MONUC	United Nations Mission in the Democratic Republic of Congo
NATO	North Atlantic Treaty Organization
NLA	National Liberation Army
OEF	Operation Enduring Freedom
OHQ	Operations Headquarters
OSCE	Organization for Security and Cooperation in Europe
PDS	Party of Democratic Socialism
PSC	Political and Security Committee
RRM	Rapid Reaction Mechanism

SACEUR	Supreme Allied Commander Europe
SPD	Social Democratic Party
SG/HR	Secretary General/High Representative
SSR	Security Sector Reform
UN	United Nations
UNIFIL	United Nations Interim Force in Lebanon
UNPREDEP	United Nations Preventative Deployment Force
UNSC	United Nations Security Council
WEU	Western European Union

Introduction

Giving the EU a voice in international affairs has been a key concern for EU member states at least since the creation of the European Political Cooperation (EPC), the precursor of the Common Foreign and Security Policy (CFSP). Strengthening the EU's political influence took on added urgency after the end of the Cold War in light of the violent disintegration of Yugoslavia and on account of concerns over weakening transatlantic commitments to European security. A united European position and a visible role for the EU in international crisis management thus became a political priority even among member states that had previously not been as supportive of equipping Brussels-based EU institutions with decision-making powers and eventually also military capabilities under the European Security and Defence Policy (ESDP). Continued institutional improvements to European foreign policy structures foreseen in the Lisbon Treaty further attest to the growing consensus in favour of a growing role of the EU in the world.

The period since the launch of the first ESDP operation in 2003 has witnessed rapid developments in the number of crisis missions launched, their geographical reach, as well as in the variety of tasks for which ESDP operations have been employed. Despite the number and the geographical range of the missions deployed over the past five years, however, the performance of the EU in reacting to international crises as well as the incidence of EU member states deciding on an ESDP format for either a military or a civilian crisis response has been uneven. The Balkans and sub-Saharan Africa from the beginning were regarded as a European responsibility, and the eventual launch of ESDP missions in the Balkans hinged on cooperation between the EU and the North Atlantic Treaty Organization (NATO) and transatlantic concerns rather than member states' disagreements on the matter. Reactions to the wars in Lebanon in 2006 and in Afghanistan in 2001 painted a very different picture, however. Member states either did not privilege the EU platform and/or shied away from deploying military forces under the ESDP label. The creation of CFSP and ESDP has enabled the EU's performance in crisis management, but it has not turned the EU into a crisis manager in the sense that the EU has become a privileged institution in the formulation of member-states' foreign policy responses to international and regional crises.

Recent European leadership under the French EU Presidency following the August 2008 war in Georgia shows that European crisis management, not only through launching ESDP missions but also through formulating and implementing common policies in response to international crises, has matured considerably since the policy's beginning in 2001 and the first discussions over launching an ESDP operation. In Kosovo, however although member states did reach a decision to launch a rule of law mission (EULEX KOSOVO), divided positions with respect to Kosovo's international recognition have come to negatively affect the EU's capacity to act. Most recent developments in the way the EU and its member states respond to international crises, then, continue to raise important and enduring questions over the role of member states in the formulation and implementation of EU foreign policy, as well as member states' commitments to the EU CFSP and ESDP.

Straddling domestic, European and transatlantic commitments: the role of member states

The increasing role of Brussels-based institutions in the formulation of foreign policy notwithstanding, the intergovernmental nature of EU foreign policy means that the role of member states remains crucial in the formulation and implementation of policies elaborated under CFSP and ESDP. Member states have a choice in whether they pursue foreign policy through the EU, through other international institutions, or whether they rely on bilateral channels or even unilateral moves in pursuit of their national interests. Which member state holds the EU Presidency at any given time continues to matter as larger member states easily eclipse smaller ones, and as member states may choose to reinforce their own position through the EU, including their position as the EU Presidency, or may choose to rely on other ways to do so. Similarly, member states can continue to choose to either strengthen or eclipse Brussels-based institutions and personalities, including the Secretary General/High Representative (SG/HR) Javier Solana but also the broader EU foreign policy machinery.

The position of individual member states in formulating and implementing European foreign policy, therefore, continues to matter – particularly when it comes to formulating reactions and policies in response to international crises, the concern of this book. They also matter with respect to the broader question implicit in research on European crisis management: how much space do individual member states afford 'Europe' in their foreign policy, to what extent have they developed 'European' preferences as a result of EU foreign and security policy institutions, and to what extent have they adapted to the growing European foreign policy machinery – in other words, to what extent have member states' positions been Europeanized in favour of a greater EU role?

This book explores this question by analysing national responses to international crisis situations in order to draw broader conclusions as to the role of the EU CFSP and ESDP in national foreign policy, and the degree to which national positions have evolved over time. It takes as a starting point the assumption that EU member states straddle three potentially conflicting commitments that have to be continuously negotiated in the formulation of foreign and security policy. The first is domestic politics, and the specific domestic political circumstances in terms of the composition and strength of a given government as well as governmental opposition. This category also includes particular national circumstances such as the need for parliamentary approval of sending troops abroad, or traditionally held attitudes towards the use of force, transatlantic commitments and commitments towards a multi-polar world order.

The second is transatlantic relations, which includes both states' commitments to NATO but also their bilateral relations with the United States (US). US hegemony post-World War II and the security guarantee issued by NATO throughout the Cold War mean that transatlantic relations have been (and to a large extent remain) a key element in the formulation of national foreign policies, a fact that is compounded by individual bilateral ties through historical connections based on European migration as well as past colonial ties. For its part, the US through its military presence in Europe as well as its political and economic assistance in Europe's post-World War II reconstruction, has had a key stake in European political affairs throughout the Cold War, and continues to influence EU policy as well as European and member states decision-making.

European commitments, finally, are placed between or alongside these domestic and transatlantic commitments. Although the creation of the EU, and efforts to equip the EU with foreign and security policy instruments, bear witness to European foreign policy ambitions, for the duration of the Cold War moves towards creating European foreign policy institutions took place under the political and security shield of the US. The challenge of coordinating a set of diverging foreign policy positions in an intergovernmental framework presented (and continues to present) a further challenge to member states' European commitments.

Since the creation of CFSP and ESDP, member states have an institutional choice as far as foreign and security policy is concerned.

As a result of the growing role for the EU in foreign and security policy, there is added potential for friction between domestic, transatlantic and European commitments; a fact that individual foreign policy choices with respect to the EU CFSP and ESDP, and the decision-making process that precede them, bear out. This makes the analysis of European commitments in national foreign policies both timely and salient. Given the growth of EU security institutions, member states increasingly have to take into account these institutions when making foreign policy – either because they present a useful platform from which to launch foreign policy initiatives or because member states have to bear European institutions in mind when making foreign policy choices. The European dimension, in other words, has become of increasing importance over the past decade in particular.

In order to analyse the conflicting pressures acting on member states and to account for when and why they choose to privilege domestic, transatlantic or European institutional venues, this book employs three separate analytical lenses: Europeanization, alliance politics, and governmental politics. Chapter 1 outlines these approaches in depth and formulates hypotheses as well as guiding questions for the analysis of decision-making that is presented in subsequent chapters. These questions also serve as a way to structure the narrative as well as the research findings that are presented in Chapter 6. Governmental politics, an approach rooted in foreign policy analysis (FPA) that was first conceptualized by Graham Allison (1999) in his seminal work *Essence of Decision*, serves as the basis for analysis. Enquiring into governmental processes, preferences and bargaining games among key decision-makers, bureaucracies and parliaments highlights assumptions and domestic constraints as well as transatlantic and European preferences and biases in national governments. The study then applies two additional lenses, those of Europeanization and transatlantic politics, in order to delineate the at times conflicting commitments by national governments. Europeanization in particular inquires about the nature of European influences and distinguishes between the EU as a platform through which to export and magnify national preferences and one that exerts adaptation pressures on individual governments. Tracing European preferences allows for conclusions as to the place of Europe in national foreign policies: either one of an instinctive preference that may be helped or hindered by the presence or absence of transatlantic pressures; or that of a secondary consideration, with instinctive foreign policy orientations remaining transatlantic or rooted in particular domestic circumstances. The transatlantic politics framework, finally, serves to inquire into the role of NATO and the US in national foreign policies and their respective commitments and preferences towards the crises in question. This is especially important with a view to highlighting tensions between transatlantic and European commitments, a fault line that this research assumes to be crucial in the commitment to a growing role for the EU, particularly when it comes to military crisis management under ESDP and implicit or explicit competition with NATO; and when it comes to contested geographical areas where the US claims a political lead, such as Afghanistan or the Middle East. It is the assumption of this research that these three pressures – domestic, European and transatlantic – act on each individual member state and that they are crucial for explaining member states' European choices (or the absence thereof).

Keeping research manageable necessitates choices of which member states to analyse. This book focuses on those member states that were most crucial in the development of CFSP and ESDP and that remain crucial for both policies to succeed based on their size as well as their potential and actual political and military commitments. Britain and France were the two member states whose positions with respect to ESDP diverged the most; and it was only once their respective positions aligned in the course of the 1990s that the creation of ESDP was made possible in the first place. Germany, lastly, had to adjust much of its foreign policy posture with respect to the use of force to play a significant political role in CFSP and ESDP. Its size and its historical role in Europe, but also its traditional balancing act between transatlantic and European commitments make the analysis of German foreign policy relevant – and the Europeanization of German foreign policy crucial for the advancement of EU foreign, security and defence policy.

A second selection concerns the choice of international crises to be analysed. The 2001 crisis in the former Yugoslav Republic of Macedonia (FYROM) and the war in Afghanistan recommend themselves as ideal cases. Both represented almost simultaneous regional and international crises that required a European response, and crises that involved transatlantic interests with respect to the role of NATO in FYROM and with respect to bilateral relations with the US in Afghanistan. The two crises also provoked very different reactions in one key aspect. Whereas an ESDP mission was suggested and eventually realized in FYROM, despite significant member state contributions to both Operation Enduring Freedom (OEF) and the International Security Assistance Force (ISAF) and despite a European lead in commitments to ISAF, member states were divided as to whether these contributions should be termed 'EU', 'European' or national contributions, which suggests significant constraints on the use of an EU label.

The analysis of two additional crisis responses in 2006 serves to highlight the ways in which national positions have evolved since the early days of ESDP. The fact that by 2006 the EU had undertaken 16 ESDP missions in particular suggests that the role of the EU in international crisis management had grown considerably. Reactions to the war in Lebanon but also French initiatives towards launching an ESDP mission in the Democratic Republic of Congo (DRC) in support of the United Nations Mission in the Democratic Republic of Congo (MONUC), the UN peacekeeping operation, illustrates the changing role of the EU in crisis management. Even if the case of DRC is not a case of an international crisis per se, its juxtaposition with reactions to the war in Lebanon highlights the extent to which constraints on utilizing ESDP have remained in place – or evolved.

The analysis shows clearly that, although the EU and Brussels-based European institutions have come to play a more substantial part in international politics, and although the value of an ESDP mission in DRC was uncontested, member states remain reluctant to deploy ESDP missions in international crises and do not necessarily rely on the EU for multilateral decision-making. In Lebanon, the UN proved to be the more influential platform for negotiations and the more appropriate institutional framework for the launch of a peacekeeping operation. The EU is thus not automatically privileged as a key institutional platform, even where transatlantic constraints do not act on individual member states or EU institutions. Reactions to the war in Lebanon thus illustrate that member states are still some ways away from a 'Europeanization' of foreign policy, or from advocating 'European' in the sense of 'EU' crisis management.

Analysing crisis decision-making: the structure of the book

Having outlined the conceptual framework in Chapter 1, Chapter 2 presents a detailed analysis of the international crisis situations in FYROM, Afghanistan, Lebanon and DRC to provide the background for the analysis of British, French and German foreign policy decision-making in Chapters 3–5. Its purpose is also to highlight the most important aspects of decision-making where tensions between domestic, European and transatlantic choices were the most apparent. In FYROM, and the negotiations that led to the signing of the Ohrid Framework

Agreement in August 2001, the EU for the first time played a significant and highly visible role through Javier Solana, EU–NATO cooperation and intensive shuttle diplomacy that took place between March and August 2001. Debates over a continuation of the NATO peacekeeping operation formed the nucleus for what was later to become the first ever ESDP military operation. In Afghanistan, on the other hand, military aspects of decision-making, particularly participation in OEF, were heavily over-shadowed by transatlantic commitments. The institutional anchoring of ISAF, the international peacekeeping force that was largely European-led, revealed transatlantic and inner-European tensions between those member states that advocated a common 'European' and perhaps also a ESDP contribution, and those that chose to highlight national commitments instead. Only when it came to Afghanistan's political and economic reconstruction could the EU and its member states claim some lead. The two crises in 2001, therefore, show a mixed picture with respect to European crisis management. The EU was very visible in FYROM, where a European-led NATO force eventually morphed into an ESDP operation. In the case of Afghanistan, on the other hand, EU member states made significant military, economic and political contributions, but this did not translate into political weight or visibility for the EU – a trend that has continued to this day.

With respect to transatlantic commitments, the particular historical circumstance of a US administration largely dismissive of international institutions and one that preferred to rely on coalitions of the willing in its military pursuits – but also one that lost some of its international credibility on account of the war in Iraq in 2003 – meant that European crisis management in 2006 was less restricted by transatlantic reservations than it had been in 2001. The crisis that erupted in Lebanon in 2006 subsequently saw a European pillar emerge around the French position in the political responses to the crisis and efforts to achieve a ceasefire, even if the UK and Germany stuck close to the US position. Despite a European lead in assembling the peacekeeping force, however, member states decided not to launch an ESDP mission. While Brussels-based institutions, particularly the Political and Security Committee (PSC), played a substantial role in negotiating national military commitments, member states were reluctant to launch an ESDP military operation in the Middle East. In the case of DRC, lastly, French initiatives to reinforce an existing UN peace-keeping mission led to the launch of EUFOR RD Congo in 2006. Although the nature and purpose of the mission was not contested among member states, there were some reservations on account of the nature of decision-making in this case and reservations on the part of Germany over the size of military commitments requested. European crisis management in 2006, therefore, suggests that reluctance to utilize ESDP stems not necessarily from transatlantic tensions but from reservations over high-risk operations and the need for making significant military contributions that preclude contributions to ESDP missions.

These conflicting positions vis-à-vis ESDP are highlighted in the analysis of individual countries' foreign policy decision-making. The analysis of British decision-making in Chapter 3 highlights the extent to which Britain has reneged on European commitments that had been visible in 2001. Europe in 2006 matters less than in 2001, and while the UK is more amenable to consenting to ESDP operations, it does not make military contributions to those missions. In FYROM, Britain insisted on an inter-institutional agreement between the EU and NATO before consenting to an ESDP mission but also invested diplomatic efforts in aiding EU negotiations by practically supporting Javier Solana in FYROM and in resolving Turkish reservations with respect to the Berlin Plus agreement. Reactions to Afghanistan but also to the war in Lebanon, on the other hand, highlight the extent to which Britain privileges transatlantic over European commitments, a trend that has been reinforced rather than lessened. Rather than playing an active part in either ESDP or European crisis management in general, London's position is one of giving consent to the launch of particular missions but without making military or financial commitments. The case of Britain in particular shows that Europeanization is not a linear process, but one that is reversible in favour of domestic or transatlantic commitments.

The fact that most initiatives with respect to ESDP and European crisis management in 2001 and 2006 were taken by French national and EU officials confirms arguments of France exporting national preferences on the EU but also the UN agenda. Chapter 4 shows the extent to which France has shaped the European agenda in FYROM, DRC and, to a lesser extent, Lebanon where France privileged the UN as a coordination mechanism also on account of its permanent seat in the UN Security Council. Foreign policy initiatives by the French EU Presidency under President Sarkozy in response to the war in Georgia in August 2008 were, therefore, entirely consistent with French positions vis-à-vis European crisis management that are analysed in this book. The case of Afghanistan also highlights, however, that this is not a universal position. Paris responded to transatlantic pressures and even exhibited transatlantic preferences, highlighting that NATO and transatlantic commitments have a firm place in the French foreign policy agenda.

Chapter 5, finally, analyses German decision-making. From the three countries analysed Berlin shows the most marked departure in the frequency but also in the nature and the volume of its military deployments, even if this was not all done in pursuit of EU political objectives but rather with the goal of being able to influence or determine international political agenda-setting. Historical taboos were broken, not just with respect to sending German troops to Afghanistan, but also to the Middle East. With respect to Europeanization, German decision-making shows preference for a stronger and more visible role for the EU in FYROM but also in Afghanistan. When it came to military commitments but also its position in the war in Lebanon Berlin's position was closer to that of the US. Germany, therefore, continues to straddle transatlantic and European commitments, orienting itself equally on the position of the US and the objective to strengthen the European foreign policy platform. At the same time, its participation in ESDP has significantly increased since the policy's early days, which shows both a European preference but also adaptation in order to pursue future agenda-setting goals.

Towards the Europeanization of foreign policy?

The analysis of member states' decision-making in the four crises yields a somewhat mixed picture. Although transatlantic constraints no longer preclude ESDP operations, transatlantic relations and European commitment continue to be mutually exclusive in areas where there are either strong national transatlantic leanings to begin with, such as in the case of the UK, or where member states concur with US views or align with an overarching US position, such as Germany did in the case of Lebanon. The comparison of the two time periods also shows that the basic national positions of France, Britain and Germany – pushing the EU agenda in pursuit of a multi-polar world order; privileging transatlantic relations; and fence-sitting by simultaneously privileging transatlantic commitments but also pushing for greater European involvement in world affairs – remain in place, increasing adaptation pressures emanating from the European level notwithstanding.

These growing adaptation pressures, however, also indicate that these basic national positions and a growing European profile increasingly coexist, and that this does not prove necessarily conflictual: British consent to ESDP missions it does not have a stake in and does not intend to participate in nevertheless increases the reach and operational experience of the EU even without active British participation. In addition, the outgoing Bush administration has also proved less engaged internationally, which has allowed and at the same time demanded from the EU a greater political and in some parts also military commitment in international crises. This was evident in the war in Lebanon in 2006 but also more recently in the war in Georgia in August 2008. Growing EU experience as well as growing external demands on the EU, therefore, stand to further increase adaptation pressures on member states to equip the EU with the necessary institutional and personnel contributions.

In this respect, however, the analysis presented in the pages that follow show that at least in one case, Lebanon, it is the EU itself rather than external opposition, that prevent the EU from playing a greater role in international crisis management. Here, it is not about transatlantic conflicting with European commitments but rather about reservations that have their roots largely in domestic inhibitions against launching crisis missions under an EU label, the reluctance to test a 'new' instrument and to possibly incur European casualties. This means that, at the end of the day, the Europeanization of foreign and security policy is about more than merely achieving autonomy for EU instruments from those of NATO or easing political reservations against ESDP. It is also about changing domestic member states' attitudes with respect to the use of military force in the name of Europe, and under a EU label, and that of taking a decisive political stance in the name of Europe. It is here that the EU and its member states have some way to go before the EU develops into a crisis manager in its own right.

1
The Europeanization of National Foreign Policy?

The choice for (or against) CFSP and ESDP

Since the end of the Cold War, and informed in part by the experience of the conflicts in the Balkans throughout the 1990s, EU member states have created European security institutions in order to be able to act independently from NATO and the US. Two countries in particular, Britain and France, have adjusted their national positions in order to make possible the creation of the EU ESDP in the first place. While there is more than one institutional tool at EU member states' disposal in matters of international security, this book addresses the circumstances, national preferences and crisis situations that determine the choice and the extent of the use of political and military instruments located in the EU CFSP and ESDP as opposed to other institutional venues or bilateral initiatives – and the extent to which these preferences have evolved since ESDP was declared partly operational in 2001. The chapters that follow analyse British, French and German policies with respect to the EU CFSP and the ESDP in crisis decision-making, and shows the extent to which national considerations over EU instruments have evolved since the creation of ESDP in particular. This research is motivated by the observation that, although the EU is in possession of foreign, security and defence policy instruments, the application of these instruments has been selective (Biscop, 2006). This in turn potentially contradicts conclusions over the ongoing Europeanization of national foreign policy, including security and defence policy (Wong, 2006; Miskimmon, 2004; Irondelle, 2003).

This study traces the evolution of national preferences towards the use of EU CFSP and ESDP instruments by analysing decision-making in two crises occurring in the early days of ESDP in 2001, and by contrasting these findings with the analysis of two more recent case studies in 2006. The crisis in the former Yugoslav Republic of Macedonia (FYROM) and the war in Afghanistan in 2001 were the first two crises to occur after the creation of ESDP in 1999 that prompted significant political and military involvement on the part of EU member states. However, national responses towards the two crises with respect to the involvement of instruments located in EU CFSP/ESDP were very different. Whereas the EU CFSP in the persona of EU High Representative Javier Solana was very active in the political mediation of the crisis in FYROM, initial suggestions for an ESDP takeover of the NATO Operation were rejected by EU member states. It was not until March 2003 that the first ever military ESDP mission, Operation Concordia, took over from NATO. In Afghanistan, on the other hand, the EU CFSP and ESDP both appeared to be eclipsed by the national considerations of member states, prompting concerns over a renationalization of foreign policy after 11 September (see Hill, 2004). The suggestion by then-Belgian Foreign Minister Louis Michel that EU member states' contributions to ISAF constituted 'EU' rather than national contributions was rejected. Moreover, NATO – not ESDP – assumed ISAF command in 2003. It was not until June 2007 that an ESDP mission – a civilian police mission rather than a military operation – was launched.

By 2006, ESDP instruments had rapidly evolved and the EU had undertaken 16 ESDP operations. This signalled not only a fast and impressive evolution of EU crisis management capabilities but also by implication a growing preference of EU member states in favour of utilizing ESDP instruments. Yet, responses and policy choices in two crises occurring in 2006 exhibited a similar puzzle as in 2001: during the war in Lebanon, although an ESDP mission was discussed as a possibility, an existing UN mission was (re-)launched instead; in DRC, on the other hand, the EU launched a military operation – EUFOR RD Congo – in support of the United Nations Organization Mission in the Democratic Republic of the Congo (MONUC) during the election process. This means that a question relevant in 2001 – what is the role afforded to the EU CFSP/ESDP in national foreign policy decision-making, and when does it stop short of a military operation under the EU ESDP – has retained its relevance despite the fact that ESDP has evolved to a considerable extent since its early days. Focusing on decisions taken with regard to the EU CFSP and ESDP in these cases promises to shed light on the underlying attitudes towards the European security institutions when it comes to the application of available crisis management instruments – and how they have evolved. It will also allow for drawing broader conclusions on the role of CFSP/ESDP in national decision-making, and help determine whether and to what extent national foreign policies exhibit evidence of Europeanization in the sense that existing EU security institutions exert influence on individual governments to adapt their decision-making in favour of a larger role for the EU – or whether other considerations, such as the position or preferences of the US and the transatlantic alliance are more pertinent to explain specific policy outcomes. The inclusion of the US in addition to NATO as determining factors can be justified both on account of the US' central role in the management of the crisis in FYROM, the war in Afghanistan and the war in Lebanon, as well as on account of the fact that the US 'has a privileged position in terms of access to European decision-making, with some particularly "special" relationships with member states and individuals [...] it often succeeds in dividing and ruling the Europeans, as well as over-shadowing them in high politics' (Hill and Smith, 2005: 394). The analysis of national decision-making with respect to the crisis in Lebanon and the ESDP operation in DRC will reveal to what extent these constraints acting on foreign policies of individual member states in 2001–03 continued to be valid in 2006.

The role of member states: Britain, France and Germany

For scholars of international relations in general and of European foreign relations in particular, the question of how to analytically approach the role of individual member states in the EU decision-making process and how to best capture the nature of this interaction has been a contentious one. Theoretical approaches found in the mainstream International Relations literature have not always been entirely useful in addressing or explaining the processes of European foreign policy-making more generally. Similarly, CFSP (and ESDP) is too intergovernmental to fit comfortably within the framework of integration theories (Øhrgaard, 2004). Because of the intergovernmental nature of decision-making in the EU CFSP and ESDP, the policies and attitudes of national governments towards CFSP are relevant as they are crucial not only for the institutional evolution of CFSP and ESDP but also for its application: if CFSP is sidelined by national policy priorities, it cannot be expected to be an effective policy instrument. This research therefore proceeds from the assumption that member states' policies and preferences are crucial in the formulation of policies adopted under CFSP. This in turn warrants a study that focuses solely on the national decision-making processes and the resulting policy outcomes.

The positions of Britain, France and Germany are of particular relevance in explaining policy outcomes in European crisis management due to their substantial political and military involvement in the crisis management operations analysed, their size and influence in the EU setting, and their contrasting preferences and approaches towards the EU foreign and security institutional framework. Changing preferences of Britain and France but also Germany towards the evolution of European security institutions were crucial in the evolution of CFSP and ESDP instruments as well as their future application. Throughout the Cold War, efforts at creating mechanisms for coordination in the areas of security and defence stalled on account of the lack of support for a European foreign policy independent of NATO among atlanticist member states – Britain in particular; and French unwillingness to consider foreign policy cooperation that excluded defence issues (Smith, 2004). This makes this particular research endeavour of dual interest: for one, it analyses the positions of those member states that had been furthest apart from one another with respect to the creation and purpose of the EU ESDP; with one (France) rooted in the Europeanist camp and the other (Britain) in the Atlanticist camp – and with the third (Germany) situated somewhat uneasily between the two.

The end of the Cold War presented a strong impetus for improving European security and foreign policy coordination. Although the European Political Cooperation (EPC) that was created in 1970 had the aim of establishing the EU as a foreign policy actor, policy means available were of a declaratory nature, and policy implementation took place using Community instruments, such as aid programmes or economic sanctions. Defence and military security issues were explicitly excluded. A second strand of European foreign policy, security politics, included the creation of the Western European Union (WEU) in 1954, even if the WEU was throughout the Cold War neglected in favour of the transatlantic defence structure (Duke, 1999). The 1993 Treaty of Maastricht institutionalized EPC mechanisms in the new Common Foreign and Security Policy (CFSP). The wars in the Balkans starkly underlined the EU's shortcomings in the field of foreign and security policy (see Howorth, 2005; Lucarelli, 2000), although the first Gulf War in 1991 had already demonstrated the degree of dependence of the participating EU states on the US and NATO, further underlining the need for the incorporation of a security and defence component to the EU structures (Duke, 1999). Reforms outlined in the (1999) Treaty of Amsterdam included the provision for a High Representative, and the establishment of a CFSP Policy Planning and Early Warning Unit.

The election of a Labour government under Tony Blair in 1997 proved to be a key factor for the future development of the European foreign and security policy (see Whitman, 1999). Along with Blair's commitment to a greater British role within Europe to counterbalance French-German dominance and the recognition that European autonomy did not have to mean emancipation from NATO but the improvement of European capabilities inside the alliance, London dropped its objections to an autonomous European defence for the first time and made possible the creation of ESDP (Howorth, 2000: 377–96).

In contrast, German attitudes to the use of force have undergone a significant transition since the end of the Cold War. This makes Germany an interesting case on purely domestic grounds: Germany's international engagement since the end of the Cold War had been guided largely by the principles of German post-World War II foreign policy – multilateralism and a culture of restraint with regards to the use of military force (Maull, 2000). However, the historical taboo against the use of force increasingly eroded in light of post-Cold War realities, starting with allies' expectations in the first Gulf War, and increasing doubts over whether Germany could remain a credible partner in the transatlantic alliance without military participation. On a normative level, the humanitarian catastrophe unfolding in the Balkans raised the question of whether pacifism was the only, and the most appropriate, historical lesson to draw from the experience of World War II (Janning, 1996). The conflict in Kosovo crystallized these conflicting pressures, and German reactions to the crisis marked a watershed in post-war German policy as Berlin for the first time since the end of World War II took part in offensive military operations against a sovereign state. In addition to a changing view on the use of military force, Germany also moved from its traditional post-World War II transatlanticist orientation to one that increasingly accommodated the emergence of CFSP/ESDP.

For France, the end of the Cold War and changed geopolitical realities raised the issue of the EU's role in European security and the preservation of France's status, particularly in light of a reunified Germany and resulting concerns over the geo-strategic marginalization of France. Bosnia demonstrated to France that its European partners not only lacked the political will but also the confidence for Europe to act alone in security matters (Treacher, 2001: 33). To avoid marginalization in Europe, France modified its vision of the European security architecture, particularly with regard to NATO. Although this did not mean the abandonment of the idea of building an autonomous European defence structure (see Howorth, 2000), it did signal a more pragmatic approach. At the Anglo-French summit at St Malo in December 1998 Britain and France issued a 'Joint Declaration on European Defence' that called for the establishment of 'autonomous' capacities backed by credible military force.

During the German EU presidency in the first half of 1999 the British-French bilateral initiative at St Malo became a European reality with the creation of the EU ESDP. At the European Council of Cologne in 1999, Javier Solana was appointed as the first CFSP Secretary General/High Representative, and leaders agreed to limit the defence capacity of the EU to the 'Petersberg Tasks' that include humanitarian and rescue tasks, peace-keeping tasks, and tasks of combat forces in crisis management, including peacemaking. The WEU as an organization was considered to have completed its function, and its assets were transferred to the EU (Gnesotto, 2004). At the European Council of Helsinki 10–11 December 1999, EU leaders agreed on the Headline Goal (60,000 troops by 2003, deployable within 60 days and sustainable for one year), to set up a new institutional structure, and to agree on the modalities for cooperation between the EU and NATO (Gnesotto, 2004). At the Laeken European Council 14–15 December 2001, finally, EU leaders declared the EU capable of conducting some crisis management operations.

The EU ESDP represents a new security institution that has moved the EU into a policy realm previously reserved for NATO. The purpose of ESDP is to complete and strengthen the EU's external ability to act through the development of civilian and military capabilities for international conflict prevention and crisis management. Although the idea of a European foreign and defence policy preceded the end of the Cold War, the creation of corresponding institutions was precluded by conflicting positions of member states on the purpose and the existence of European security and defence institutions.

Given the evolution of EU foreign and security policy instruments since the creation of CFSP and ESDP, and the increasing demands placed on the EU and its member states in matters of external relations and international security, the 'big three' member states occupy a central position in the formulation and the putting into practice of EU foreign and security policy. Britain and France enjoy a foreign policy lead based on the size of their military contributions and engagements worldwide. Together with Germany, although it is not on par with Britain and France in the military arena, the three are indispensable in diplomatic terms (Everts, 2000:19). The substantial change in all three countries' national positions vis-à-vis the development of ESDP in particular but conflicting positions when it came to questions of these instruments' application in the four cases makes the analysis of the foreign policies of the three countries highly topical. The crises analysed highlight differences among the three member states with respect to the EU's global and regional role and different national positions over where the instruments located in the EU CFSP/ESDP should be applied.

International Relations theory and EU foreign and security policy

Although the EU CFSP since its inception has been criticized for its incoherence and ineffectiveness (Stavridis, 1997; Zielonka, 1998), EU member states have made continuous efforts to create effective institutional structures and to formulate common policies. This challenges realist assumptions about the limits of cooperation. A European foreign policy not only exists but is a dynamic and ongoing process in which EU member states play a defining role.[1] What is more, the creation of CFSP and ESDP has also raised expectations of further foreign policy activities on the part of the EU, and the increasing application of these instruments provide evidence that the Capabilities-Expectations Gap (CEG), identified some years ago by Christopher Hill, is diminishing (Hill, 1993 and 1998). This makes the impact and the interaction between the national and the European level a fruitful line of inquiry – and raises the question of the conceptual approach best suited for explaining the nature of these interactions.

For mainstream IR theory, the creation of CFSP/ESDP presents a challenge as it puts into question the notion of state sovereignty – the European Union is 'neither a state, nor a traditional alliance, and [...] presents a heterodox unit of analysis' (Andreatta, 2005: 19); and is unique in the nature of its international cooperation and integration (Wallace, 1994), even if the area of foreign and security policy is intergovernmental and likely to remain so. Theories and concepts found in the literature on European integration generally have not been applied to foreign and security policy,[2] but have instead concerned themselves with the problem of economic and political integration. Existing theories of both IR and European integration are ill-equipped to explain either the emergence of the EU CFSP/ESDP, the process under which policies are adopted, or the nature of the impact and influence of the European on the national level and vice versa – even if existing research on the interaction between the EU CFSP and national foreign policies has yielded some results that point towards change in national foreign policy practice (Nuttall, 1992) as well as policy outcomes (Tonra, 2003). This research locates potential explanations for national decision-making in three separate levels of analysis (see Singer, 1961). The impact of European institutions on national foreign policies as a result of Europeanization privileges the regional level of analysis and therefore regional institutions. Alliance politics, and the enduring relevance of NATO and US preferences to European security locates the explanation primarily at the systemic level; whereas a focus on domestic politics based on a governmental politics approach focuses on the domestic level of analysis and assumes that domestic preferences and policy processes involving government agencies and ministries, elected government officials as well as the elite public sphere, determine policy outcomes. An analysis of the underlying preferences and bargaining games among the different domestic actors is to draw conclusions on the explanatory power of Europeanization or alliance politics with respect to national decision-making.

Europeanization focuses on the impact of the EU institutions on national politics, both as a potential platform to export policy preferences and as a constraint that influences national foreign policy-making. The Europeanization approach conceptualizes EU institutions as exerting influence on national foreign policy through separate processes: the projection of national preferences, the adaptation of national policies, or the emergence or change of national preferences that privilege a European approach (Wong, 2005). Alliance politics and the preferences and attitudes towards and relations within the transatlantic alliance, on the other hand, assumes that the role of NATO along with US hegemony as a broader response to an anarchical international system plays a central role in the decision-making process that leads states to seek the preservation of existing alliances. Central within this alliance framework, of course, is also the role of the US in European – and global – security. The model of governmental politics, lastly, focuses on the domestic political conditions in the individual countries, and the way key participants in the political process bargain successfully to implement their policy preferences. In this context, the perception and preferences of key officials and bureaucracies, as well as the elite public sphere are important in assessing the choices for or against a larger role of the EU CFSP and ESDP. This in turn permits drawing some conclusions over which approach, Europeanization or Alliance politics, is more appropriate for explaining national foreign policy choices.

The contribution of this particular research is two-fold. First, it applies two analytical approaches, Europeanization and alliance politics as well as an FPA approach that focuses on domestic policy processes, to member states' foreign policies to analyse the influence exerted by the EU CFSP/ESDP on policy decisions taken during two crises. And, it does this in a case that involves 'hard' politics: foreign security and defence policy, the bastion of state sovereignty (Howorth, 2005). If it can be shown that even in this area integration mechanisms are at work in the sense that existing EU institutions result in policy adaptation on the national level, this would weaken state-centric, liberal intergovernmentalist analyses (see Moravcsik, 1993) that argue that outcomes of bargaining between member states are determined by the preferences and bargaining power of states. Applied to the EU CFSP/ESDP, this approach attributes the major decision-making power to the member states, and assumes that domestic preferences are fixed and unaffected by normative concerns and interstate bargaining processes.[3] Alternatively, if there is no or only weak evidence of Europeanization, then this would strengthen the state-centric approaches located in the IR paradigm. Lastly, both approaches would be weakened if it were to be shown that specific domestic political considerations that do not point towards systemic or regional preferences conditioned policy responses in these four crises.

Governmental politics

The governmental politics model, which is to provide a basis from which to draw conclusions as to the validity of the alliance politics and Europeanization frameworks, is located in the Foreign Policy Analysis (FPA) paradigm. FPA in general aims at formulating middle-range theories, which offer explanations of particular, limited phenomena rather than more general explanations of state behaviour (Merton, 1957). The advantages of an FPA approach for this project are that it 'enquires into the motives and other sources of the behaviour of international actors, particularly states ... by giving a good deal of attention to decision-making, initially so as to probe behind the formal self-description (and fictions) of the processes government and public administration' (Hill, 2003: 10). The particular approach adopted in this project is closely modelled on Allison's governmental politics model (Allison, 1999), which seeks to open the 'black box' of policy-making in order to identify the chain of decision-making and the different players involved policy decisions. It stands to offer a detailed explanation of the decision-making process, and will make it possible to draw conclusions over whether considerations that would point towards Europeanization or alliance politics drove policy decisions.

Although a potentially fruitful line of inquiry, FPA approaches have been criticized for their state-centric outlook and the exclusive focus on US foreign policy (Smith, 1994; Brown, 2001). More generally, and partly as a result of these criticisms, the FPA approach itself has suffered from neglect as a separate field of investigation even if it has generated a large body of scholarship (Light, 1994). However, the criticism of state-centrism can be effectively countered by the argument that FPA itself grew out of reactions to realist assumptions of the state as a unitary actor, and is fundamentally pluralist in orientation (Hill, 2003). An analytical focus on the state itself, and policy processes that take place at the domestic level promises a more nuanced analysis of policy decisions and outcomes than structuralist theories can provide. It is also a promising approach in the context of foreign policy making in the CFSP/ESDP context. There is a gap in the scholarship on the EU's impact on member states' foreign policies, which also points towards the applicability of FPA in a European context. Accordingly, it has been argued that the existing foreign policy literature has 'under-explored the distinctiveness of the foreign policies of European states who are members of the EU and the issues that this membership raises' (Manners and Whitman, 2000: 3).

Governmental politics in the EU CFSP/ESDP framework

The framework and application of governmental politics[4] was conceptualized by Graham Allison in *Essence of Decision*, his influential study of the Cuban Missile Crisis, and focuses on the 'competing preferences and processes for aggregating among them' (Allison, 1999: 11). Originally published in 1971, Allison's study built on the work of first-generation foreign policy analysts who focused on the 'political process' approach to foreign policy (Huntington, 1960; Neustadt, 1960; Schilling et al., 1962). The governmental politics model conceives of government behaviour and policy outputs as the results of bargaining games among decision-makers and departs from assumptions of states as unitary actors and of government actions as partially coordinated by leaders. The players in this model include in the first instance political leaders as well as officials occupying positions on top of major bureaucracies. In addition, other actors might play a role, including lower level officials, the press, NGOs, and the public. The model assumes that policy-makers' positions derive from the department or agency they represent; that their preferences and beliefs are related to the different organizations they represent; and that their analysis accordingly yields conflicting recommendations (Allison, 1999: 256). Another basic and crucial assumption underlying this approach is that power is shared, and that the foreign policy process is inherently a political one. As a result, policy outcomes are not guided by a rational course of action, but according to the power and performance of proponents and opponents of the action in question. Allison suggests that the organizing concepts of the governmental politics model can be arranged along four interrelated factors: who plays; the factors that shape players' perceptions, preferences, and stance on a particular issue; determinants of a player's impact on results; and the combination of players' stands, influence and moves to yield governmental decisions and actions (Allison, 1999: 390).

While there has been a continuing interest in the influence of governmental politics that has gone hand in hand with increased attention to the impact of domestic politics on foreign policy more generally (Light, 1994), the governmental politics model has also met with significant criticism. Governmental politics has been criticized for underestimating the power of the executive in the context of US politics (Art, 1973; Rosati, 1981); the failure to specify assumption and formulate testable hypotheses (Art, 1973; Wagner, 1974); for being inapplicable to the non-US setting (Wagner, 1974; Caldwell, 1977); for assuming too close a fit between roles and positions and for ignoring the images and beliefs that are shared across role positions (Art, 1973; Krasner, 1971; Steiner, 1977; Welch, 1992); and for being ineffective as a model because it requires researchers to analyse too much detailed information about a foreign policy decision in order to draw conclusions – and therefore does not simplify the task of analysis (Ripley, 1995). Allison himself conceded that while his model stands to yield a detailed and nuanced picture of decision-making, the amount of detail the data collection and analysis required to carry out a study on government decisions means that accurate accounts of the bargaining processes involved pose a challenge for the researcher (Allison, 1999). Much of the necessary information must be obtained from the participants themselves. This in turn can pose a problem as memories of past events are not only unreliable, but access to the players in question may not always be possible. The model also presupposes a level of knowledge and familiarity of governmental processes that is difficult to obtain for an outside observer who has not been able to immerse him- or herself in the government process, either as a practitioner or as a participant observer.

As a result of these criticisms, but also of other trends in social science research that include the apolitical bias in foreign policy scholarship and the focus on grand theory and its emphasis on parsimony and hypothesis testing, relatively little theoretical progress has occurred since the mid-1970s (Kaarbo, 1998: 72). At the same time, the enduring finding of the model, that policy makers are influenced by ingrained bureaucratic habits even under extraordinary circumstances, continues to apply to present day conditions. As a result, despite the criticisms and despite the lack of theoretical development of this approach (Welch, 1992), the governmental politics model remains a useful analytical approach. It also continues to be applied in FPA scholarship, albeit with modifications. The governmental politics model has been adjusted by combining it with new theoretical development in FPA that includes research on organizational culture and social cognition (Ripley, 1995). A second approach that argues in favour of the relaxation of assumptions in the original model focuses on the more general notion of political power as dispersed and of conflict as deriving from incentive structures (Kaarbo, 1998: 91). It therefore advocates dropping overly strict assumptions and predictions in favour of using governmental politics to inform a research question – as is the case in this research – and of taking the concepts of power, conflict and institutional structures as a backdrop for the investigation of specific questions in foreign policy. Taken together, the suggested modifications result in an explanatory approach or perspective rather than a strict model, and include the individual players' views and beliefs on their role in the decision-making process, the appropriate behavioural structures, and their views on appropriate behaviour.

As for criticism that the model is not applicable in a non-US setting, the model is not inherently US-centric but can be amended to explain non-US policy outcomes (Allison, 1999). It is thus possible to apply the governmental politics model in the European setting and to specify the key players and identify the relevant policy processes that lead to a policy decision. Policy-making in the area of the EU CFSP/ESDP is distinct because of the ongoing growth in this particular policy field. Beyond specific governmental processes and the beliefs and preferences with regard to the EU CFSP/ESDP that may span across bureaucracies, the model should therefore be mindful of the wider governmental process, such as the role of parliaments, political parties and the elite public sphere as far as they impact decision-making. Applied to the European context, and to this particular research, the governmental politics approach yields the guiding questions shown in Table 1.1 around which to structure the analysis:

Table 1.1: Operationalizing governmental politics

Organizing concept	Operationalization
Who are the participants?	Who were the individuals and departments within the relevant ministries (Foreign and Defence) involved in this issue area?
	Who were the executive decision-makers involved in these crises?
	Who were the relevant actors in the wider governmental process (members of parliament, think tanks, press)?
What shapes participants' perceptions, preferences and stance?	What, if any, were the priorities of the participants with regard to CFSP/ESDP, the transatlantic alliance and the role of the US in European security?
	What were the participants' conception of how the national interest would be served by the application of CFSP/ESDP or NATO instruments (or lack thereof)?
What determines their impact on results?	What was the formal authority and responsibility of the participants in question?
	What was their degree of control over resources in order to carry out a mission?
	What was their access to players with bargaining advantages?
What combination of stands, influence and moves result in decisions and actions?	What was the decision structure?
	What were the rules of the game, in terms of constitutional limitations, executive orders, or conventions?

Europeanization

The concept of Europeanization has been increasingly used to study aspects of European integration and to analyse the way in which 'Europe matters' in a specific policy field (Börzel, 2003; Caporaso et al., 2001; Dyson and Goetz, 2003; Knill, 2001; Featherstone and Radaelli, 2003; Schimmelfennig and Sedelmeier, 2005). Europeanization has been conceptualized as an historic phenomenon, transnational cultural diffusion, institutional adaptation, or the adaptation of policies and policy processes – reflecting the interdisciplinary nature of the use of the concept (Featherstone and Radaelli, 2003). The broad usage of the term thus poses a number of challenges for researchers wishing to employ the concept. First, 'Europeanization' must be properly defined in order to delineate Europeanization from related processes and concepts, in particular that of European integration. This is also important with a view to establishing relevant indicators of Europeanization for the analysis of empirical data collected. More fundamentally, the concept's applicability in the area of foreign and security policy must also be established, as foreign and security policy differs from other policy areas because of the intergovernmental nature of decision-making. In addition, decision-making in matters of foreign and security policy tends to be entrusted to the national executive with less domestic parliamentary oversight than in other policy areas.[5] As a result, any influence of the EU on the formulation on national foreign policy is not immediately apparent. And, the intergovernmental nature of EU foreign and security policy does not generate the type of legally binding adaptation pressures policy areas in the first pillar do.

Apart from the problem of defining Europeanization, another frequently voiced concern regarding the utility of research on Europeanization is that it is an analytical concept rather than a theory. These are certainly valid reservations. However, it has been argued that Europeanization, rather than serving as an explanatory concept or theory, can be useful 'as an attention-directing device and a starting point for further exploration' (Olsen, 2002: 943). Thus, the potential contribution of the application of the concept of Europeanization is that it helps the understanding and the analysis of the impact of the EU on the national level. It also helps focus on processes of change (Radaelli, 2004). Europeanization thus allows the researcher to focus on puzzles beyond the cause of European integration or the nature of EU decision-making, and to inquire into the nature of the 'reciprocal relationship' between the European and the national level (Börzel, 2002: 195).

Applying 'Europeanization' to foreign and security policy

Due to the intergovernmental nature of the EU foreign policy process in the area of foreign policy, pressures emanating from the EU level are not as strong or direct as in areas of economic and social policy where research has established modifications occurring in national policies and institutional structures in policy areas located in the first pillar (Börzel,

1999; Bulmer and Burch, 1999; Cole and Drake, 2000). With regard to foreign policy, therefore, the delegation of policy competences in foreign affairs has been said to have had a limited impact on domestic policy choices (Hix and Goertz, 2000). On the other hand, EU membership has resulted in adaptation processes for new and for founding EU member states, both in terms of their policies towards previously external states as they join the EU, as well as policies towards third states in order to align it with existing EU policies (Manners and Whitman, 2000). Through the institutionalization of EPC and later CFSP and ESDP, foreign policy and security policy have become part of the integration process, despite its intergovernmental decision-making, and cooperation within the EU CFSP has been shown to reinforce shared norms of behaviour (Ginsberg, 2001).[6]

Although the effects of Europeanization on national foreign policy are weak in comparison with policy areas located in the first pillar, there do exist a number of documented changes in states' foreign policy as a result of national and European interactions, even if those changes are not always explicitly referred to as 'Europeanization'. Research has shown that repeated interactions and the quantity and quality of information available has changed working patterns among the diplomats of EU member states (Nuttall, 1992; Forster and Wallace, 2000), resulting in a coordination reflex going beyond calculated exchanges of information (Tonra, 2003) and pointing towards a socializing dimension of Europeanization where changing practices can be expected to change preferences and interests. With the evolution of EU foreign policy coordination, some scholars have used a Europeanization approach to document changes in national foreign policy: in his study of Irish foreign policy, Keatinge (1984) referred to the 'Europeanization' of foreign policy to label the reorientation of Irish foreign policy as a result of EC entry, whereas Torreblanca some years later identified such a shift in the case of Spanish EU membership (2001). More recently, Tonra has analysed Europeanization in the cases of Holland, Denmark and Ireland (2001), Wong in the case of France (2006) and Miskimmon in the case of Germany (2004). In applying the concept to national decision-making under CFSP and ESDP, therefore, one can reasonably expect to find evidence of some degree of Europeanization even in the field of security and defence.

Defining Europeanization

One commonly cited definition of Europeanization focuses on domestic change caused by European cooperation and defines Europeanization as 'an incremental process reorienting the direction and shape of policies to the degree that EC political and economic dynamics become part of the organizational logic of national politics and policy making' (Ladrech, 1994: 69). In addition to a process of domestic change, however, analysts adopting a bottom-up perspective understand Europeanization as 'the emergence and development at the European level of distinctive structures of governance' (Caporaso et al. 2001: 3). But, because member states initiate these EU policies that they later adapt to, the two dimensions of Europeanization are linked in practice, suggesting that Europeanization is a mutually constitutive process of change at the national and the European level (Radaelli, 2002; Börzel, 2003). In addition, socialization mechanisms and cognitive change also suggest a third dimension of Europeanization, where changes come about through the transfer of norms or ideas.

Building on the broad definitions of Europeanization presented above, Wong (2005) subsequently suggests that three conceptions of Europeanization in particular can be useful in explaining possible changes taking place in foreign policy-making in EU member states: national adaptation (a top-down process), national projection (a bottom-up process), and identity reconstruction (changing interests and identities). Figure 1.1 illustrates the interaction between the national and the European level.

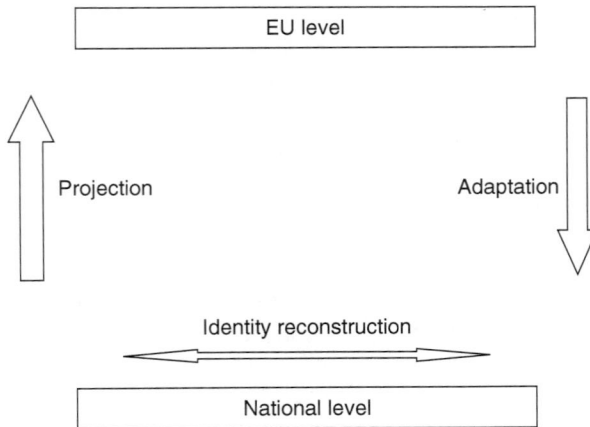

Figure 1.1: Europeanization

National adaptation understands Europeanization as a reactive, top-down process that introduces change from the European level to the national level of policy decision-making. Europeanization as national adaptation can be defined as 'the process of change at the domestic level (be it of policies, preferences or institutions) originated by the adaptation pressures generated by the European integration process; a process of change whose identity and character depend on the "goodness of fit" of domestic institutions and adaptation pressures' (Torreblanca, 2001). This definition extends to institutional processes as well as informal structures. In the context of foreign and security policy, this understanding of Europeanization runs counter to liberal intergovernmentalist conceptions of CFSP/ESDP as a forum where states try to push through individual objectives, and outcomes are the lowest common denominators (Moravcsik, 1998). It conceptualizes participation in CFSP as a reciprocal relationship. It is more congruent with domestic structure approaches found in international relations and comparative politics and fits into what has been termed 'the second image reversed' (Gourevitch, 1978), or the international (in this case, European) sources of domestic change.

Following Smith (2000), one can expect to observe changes in one or more of the following as a result of Europeanization as national adaptation: bureaucratic reorganization, constitutional change, elite socialization and shifts in public opinion. In addition, adaptation can be expected to result in a more general change in policies, preferences and institutions, increased salience of the European agenda, and adherence to common policy objectives, policies agreed to for the sake of EU unity (high price of defection) and the relaxation of traditional policy positions to accommodate progress of EU projects. In the context of decisions taken in crisis situations, or decisions that concern the application of a policy instrument located in CFSP/ESDP in a specific instance, bureaucratic reorganization and constitutional change are less likely to be observed as these constitute changes as a long-term response to events and the institutional evolution of CFSP/ESDP. One could expect to find, however, a high degree of salience of the European agenda, the adherence to common objectives, and the relaxation of national policy positions in order to accommodate the progress of EU policy and institutions. 'Salience' can be understood as a general importance or prominence of the EU CFSP/ESDP in national foreign policy. 'European agenda' here refers to the development of EU security institutions. In practice, this means that an increased importance of the EU CFSP/ESDP in the minds of decision-makers leads to advocating increased application of CFSP/ESDP instruments.

Europeanization as national projection (a bottom-up process), on the other hand, can be regarded as a process where states seek to export domestic policy models, ideas and details to the EU (Bulmer, 1998). The concept of politics of scale (Ginsberg, 1989), and the benefits of collective action in conducting foreign policy actions at lower costs and risks than member states acting alone applies here as well. States are not just passively reacting to changes at the institutional level but are the primary actors in the process of policy change, and pro-actively project preferences, policy ideas and initiatives to the European level. By 'Europeanizing' previously national policies and generalizing them onto a larger stage, a dialectical relationship between the state and the EU level is created, which in turn feeds back to the national level. The benefits of national projection are first, that the state increases its international influence; second, that it reduces the costs of pursuing a controversial policy against an extra-European power; and third, that a strong European presence in the world is potentially beneficial to all EU members as it increases individual states' international influence (Regelsberger, 1997). Policy outcomes of national projection could see states taking advantage of the EU to promote specific national interests, states attempting to increase national influence in the world by participating in or initiating EU policies, and states using the EU as cover to influence foreign policies of other member states.

In practice, these top-down and bottom-up processes are interlinked, rendering Europeanization not just a result or a consequence of policy, but also an ongoing and mutually constitutive process as the responses of member states to the EU integration process feed back into EU institutions (Börzel, 2003, Radaelli, 2002). This creates a methodological problem as far as EU policies and institutions can be regarded both as modifying policy preferences at the national level while at the same time originating at the national level, and therefore can potentially serve as a dependent or an independent variable. Nevertheless, the empirical analysis of member states' foreign policies presented in later chapters shows that it is possible to analytically distinguish between the impact of the institution on a member states' policy as well as moves of policy projection, especially when analysing a particular policy decision, as is the case in this research project.

The third conception of Europeanization, that of changing policy preferences, moves the definition of Europeanization closer to notions of integration and suggests the possibility of eventual convergence of national foreign policy. It evokes the concept of security communities (Deutsch, 1957), and that of elite socialization previously referred to (Smith, 2000) as well as the broader literature on national identity. Such readings of European identity also focus on the redefinition and negotiation of identities within EU institutions as well as national citizenry, mirroring a neo-functionalist reading of a gradual transfer of identity and affiliation towards a new supranational Europe (Haas, 1960), even if it should be quite obvious that Europe as an identity category is far from replacing national identity and that Europe does not enjoy the same level of legitimacy that the individual nation-states do. In the context of Europeanization, 'Europe' as an identity category co-exists and can be incorporated in a given nation-state identity, depending on the degree of resonance. The question then becomes how much space there is for 'Europe' in collective nation-state identities and how these identity constructions of 'Europe' relate to given nation-state identities and ideas about the European political and economic order (Risse, 2001). Evidence of conceptions of identity towards Europeanization includes the emergence or existence of norms among policy-making elites, shared definitions of European and national interests, increase in public support for European political cooperation, shared or overlapping definitions of the state's and Europe's role in the world, and of Europe's security parameters. Identity construction also suggests convergence, and in the context of EU foreign policy 'prolonged participation in the CFSP feeds back into EU member states and reorients their foreign policy cultures along similar lines' (Smith, 2000: 614).

However, Europeanization should not be regarded as synonymous with convergence or integration, even if it can lead to aspects of both. Adaptation pressures and simultaneous policy projection are both filtered through national preferences and strategic cultures. This means that it is equally likely that national foreign policy cultures, although changing as a result of CFSP, remain significantly distinct from one another. This can be expected to negatively impact the emergence of a truly common European interest, identity or foreign policy – as research on the emergence of a European strategic culture has documented (Meyer, 2006; Giegerich, 2006). The conceptual questions aside, conceiving of Europeanization as identity formation also points towards long-term processes of change that are not necessarily captured in single policy-decisions, as is the focus of this research. This does not mean, however, that norms and more generally the value attached to a 'European approach' cannot impact on national decision-making. Potential indicators for Europeanization as a result of identity formation can be expected to include the recourse to the European option as an instinctive choice, and the value attached to a European approach in a particular policy decision – in other words, similar to the indicators one would expect to observe as a result of Europeanization conceptualized as national adaptation.

Operationalizing Europeanization

Europeanization promises to be a useful analytical approach as it allows for a conceptualization of the parallel processes of adaptation and national influence exerted on the institution, as well as the potential for long-term changes in policy preferences. In the context of this particular research project, the first two definitions – national adaptation and the projection of policy preferences on to the EU level – are most directly relevant for the purposes of this particular research. Following from the discussion on the various potential observations as a result of Europeanization, the indicators and questions that result from them are suggested (see Table 1.2 opposite) that allow for an operationalization of Europeanization.

Alliance politics

The third and final conceptual approach locates a potential explanation in the role of alliances in international politics, in this particular case NATO and transatlantic relations more generally, and the way in which they influence national foreign policy. It locates the explanation primarily at the systemic rather than the regional level and assumes that states' interest in the preservation of the transatlantic alliance and/or the continued involvement of the US in European security conditions their policy responses. NATO's survival after the end of the Cold War and its evolving role since the 1990s suggest that the transatlantic alliance continues to play a role in national foreign policies, even if NATO's original purpose – the defence of Western Europe against a possible attack from the Soviet Union – has disappeared. This explanatory approach thus places weight on the preferences and role assigned to NATO, as opposed to the EU CFSP/ESDP. The following sections will analyse the literature on theoretical approaches towards the existence and purpose of alliances; apply this theoretical framework to the context of the EU member states in the context of the post-Cold War era, and discuss ways to assess the role of NATO and US preferences on national foreign policy.

Alliances in international politics

Studies of the role of alliances in international politics are generally grounded in realist thinking. This approach assumes that states are unitary actors in world politics, and that states form alliances in order to

Table 1.2: Operationalizing Europeanization

Indicator of Europeanization	Operationalization
The salience of the EU CFSP/ESDP in national foreign policy (adaptation)	Was the EU CFSP/ESDP suggested as the appropriate institution?
	Was the application of CFSP/ESDP instruments in the decision-making process considered important, or a priority, on the part of national governments?
The adherence to EU policy objectives, especially over other considerations and preferences (adaptation)	Did the member state compromise its national preferences in order to accommodate the use of CFSP/ESDP instruments?
The use, or advocating the use of the EU CFSP/ESDP in an attempt to increase national influence (projection)	Did the EU CFSP/ESDP represent a vehicle for the member state to increase their influence in this particular policy case?
The use of the EU CFSP/ESDP to push through policies on either the domestic or international level (projection)	Did the member state pursue national policy preferences through the EU CFSP/ESDP in this particular case?
The existence of shared definitions of national and European preferences among policy makers (changing preferences)	Did the member state equate national with European preferences in this particular case?
The existence of norms and preferences among elites that favours the application of EU instruments over other available possibilities (changing preferences)	Did policy elites, including the elite public sphere, favour the application of CFSP/ESDP instruments?
Increase in public support for the EU CFSP/ESDP (changing preferences)	Was there public support for the use of CFSP/ESDP instruments?
The relaxation of traditional policy positions to accommodate progress of EU projects (adaptation/changing preferences)	Was the EU CFSP/ESDP suggested as the appropriate institution in this case despite previously held preferences to the contrary that would have suggested the adoption of a different course of action?

protect themselves against threats in an anarchical system. Alliance formation is thus a product of systemic anarchy, inequality of strength, and conflicts and common interests among states (Snyder, 1977). The belief that states form alliances to prevent stronger powers from dominating them lies at the heart of balance of power theory, which holds that states join alliances to protect themselves from states or coalitions whose superior resources could pose a threat (Bull, 2002; Waltz, 1979; Morgenthau, 1948). The tendency to balance will increase if a powerful state is nearby, especially if it appears to have especially dangerous intentions, such as territorial ambitions or an expansionist ideology (Walt, 1987). Shifts in the level of threat will alter the nature of existing alliances, and the alliances formed to protect against a state that is weakened are less necessary and more likely to resolve (Walt, 1997). The absence of an overarching threat makes the disappearance of an alliance likely: thus, the end of the Cold War and the emergence of a unipolar system prompted predictions that the US and Europe would drift apart and security competition would return if the US were to withdraw from Europe (Layne, 1993; Mearsheimer, 1990).

NATO since the end of the Cold War

While the conceptual literature on the formation of alliances explains the origins and persistence of NATO throughout the Cold War, the collapse of the Soviet Union in 1991 posed a significant challenge not only to NATO, but also to theorists of alliances who were faced with having to explain NATO's persistence in view of the disappearance of the Soviet threat. For one, it was argued that traditional balance of power theory in itself does not predict the disappearances of alliances but rather their becoming less coherent and more fragile (Walt, 1999). Others attribute a certain type of stability to the current unipolar system that leaves the US so powerful that other states are unlikely to challenge it. As long as the US remains willing to remain actively involved (even if its vital interests are no longer at stake), NATO is likely to persist in the future (Wohlforth, 1999; Mastanduno, 1999). From an institutionalist perspective, on the other hand, institutions encourage cooperation through reducing transaction costs and facilitating compliance with existing agreements (Keohane, 1984), and are therefore likely to endure. NATO's highly institutionalized character and the transatlantic network of an elite community consisting of former NATO officials, defence intellectuals, military officers and researchers is more likely to keep the institution alive, even more so since NATO's capabilities and assets have been demonstrated to be useful in the post-Cold War world during the Gulf War 1990–91 and in the Balkans (Walt, 1999). But, this point of view is most applicable in cases where states have common interests – and when common interests decline and the number of potential points of conflicts is growing it can be expected that it is more likely that Europe and the US drift apart, with negative implications for the future of NATO.

The fact that NATO did survive the end of the Cold War reinforces the argument that approaches rooted in the rationalist tradition do not suffice in explaining the creation and participation in an alliance, as they cannot account for underlying themes of institutional identity, and the socialization effect that participation in an institutions has for members of an alliance (Williams and Neumann, 1996). Constructivist approaches that understand NATO as a security community (Deutsch, 1957) focus on norms and identity issues similar to those raised in the context of the creation and participation in the EU CFSP/ESDP. From a social constructivist perspective, NATO did not fragment because of the shared norms and identities of its members. NATO, therefore, represents an 'institutionalization of the transatlantic security community based on common values and a collective identity of liberal democracies' (Risse-Kappen, 1996: 395). In addition to having persisted, however, NATO has also embarked on a process of enlargement – demonstrating that the end of the Cold War instead of terminating led to an extension of the concept of a 'democratic security community' (Risse-Kappen, 1996; Schimmelfennig, 1998/99). Accordingly, NATO has since the end of the Cold War changed its identity from purely that of a military alliance to that of an organization of cooperative security: whereas NATO during and immediately after the Cold War was tied to the maintenance of an 'overall strategic balance' (Ciutã, 2002: 51), it has shifted towards 'cooperative security' and regards as its fundamental security tasks the creation of partnerships, along with crisis management (NATO, 23/24 April 1999).

Although NATO has undergone significant changes since the end of the Cold War both with regards to membership as well as the definition of its main tasks, it remains a significant fixture in national foreign policy. This is both for the continuing involvement of the US in European affairs as well as for its political purpose as a permanent forum for diplomatic exchanges between member states. Arguments exist for both sides: that NATO is kept together by a shared recognition that the solution of common problems are best found through cooperation (Keohane, 1984) or that the transatlantic relationship is one essentially dominated by the US. In this reading, the creation of ESDP itself can be regarded as a response to US hegemony: even if ESDP does not quite constitute a balancing project it is certainly an effort to develop an alternative security supplier (Posen, 2004). Either position in this debate, however, assigns a significant place to the role of NATO but also the US, in national foreign policy.

Operationalizing alliance politics

Applied to this research, a framework informed by alliance politics yields the indicators shown in Table 1.3.

Table 1.3: Operationalizing alliance politics

Indicator of alliance politics	Operationalization
States align with NATO or the US in order to keep the US involved in European security concerns	Was US involvement deemed crucial in this particular case by the member states, and did this result in alliance behaviour?
US preference leans towards the use of NATO	Did the US prefer (or insist) on NATO involvement, and did this result in the decision on the part of member states to use NATO in this particular case?
Preference is given to NATO as an institutional forum, or to US policy preferences, out of a clear transatlantic preference	Did the member state in question exhibit a preference towards NATO over other institutional settings?
	Did the member states regard NATO as the primary forum for the solution of the crisis?
	Did the member states regard the crisis as a platform for NATO to prove NATO's continued relevance in the post-Cold War era?
	Did the member state regard the use of NATO as a means to express solidarity with another member of the alliance?
Preference is given to NATO for utilitarian reasons: military instruments are in possession of NATO, NATO is more capable/ acceptable to do the job at hand	Were necessary military tools available only through NATO?
	Was NATO considered the more appropriate resource for reasons of prior involvement in the region or case?
	Was NATO the preferred option for the host country?

Hypotheses generated from the conceptual approaches: some definitions

Having briefly introduced the conceptual approaches that will be used to analyse national policy decisions, and having provided the historical

institutions; as the potential for policy projection and the export of national preferences on to the European level; or a reflexive preference for the utilization of policy instruments located within the EU CFSP and ESDP. These can arise from the nature and location of the conflict as well as the EU's past involvement in a geographic area; the existence of EU political and military instruments that have yet to be put to use; the desire to maximize national influence on a given policy area by means of the EU; or an inherently strong European orientation in national foreign policy. 'Small' influence by contrast can be expected to manifest itself as the opposite: weak or nonexistent adaptational pressures; no potential or perceived advantage to export national preference on to the European level; and the absence of preferences for the utilization of policy instruments located within the EU CFSP and ESDP.

'Significant' influence of considerations of alliance politics on national policy decisions, by contrast, is taken to mean that US involvement is deemed crucial by policy makers; that the US objects to the application of instruments other than those located in NATO; or that policy makers regard NATO as the most appropriate forum for the resolution of the crisis, either out of a transatlantic preference or because the necessary military tools are located in NATO. A 'weak' influence of alliance politics considerations, on the other hand, is defined to mean the absence of US objections or that policy makers do not view NATO as the only or most appropriate forum for the resolution of the crisis.

Having defined the terms, as well as the dependent and independent variables in this research endeavour, it is now possible to formulate a number of hypotheses that will be tested in the empirical chapters. The governmental politics approach is concerned with analysing the decision-making process in a particular instance rather than with the formulation of a grand theory. Two competing assumptions can nevertheless be derived from this approach that tie together the analysis of Europeanization versus alliance politics:

(1) If key government officials, bureaucrats and/or the elite public sphere favour the utilization of EU CFSP/ESDP over other institutional venues, and if they succeed in implementing their preferences, this results in a significant role for the EU CFSP/ESDP and points towards evidence of Europeanization; whereas:

(2) If the reverse is true – that key officials either do not favour the utilization of the EU CFSP/ESDP, or favour the utilization but do not succeed in implementing their preferences, then this results in a small role for

the EU CFSP and ESDP and disproves the Europeanization hypotheses that are formulated below.

The *Europeanization approach* generates the following hypotheses:

(1) If there is a significant influence of EU security institutions on national foreign policy, then one would expect to find national governments to advocate a significant role for the EU CFSP/ESDP in both crises.

(2) If there is little evidence of an influence of EU security institutions on national foreign policy, then one would expect to find a small role afforded to the EU CFSP/ESDP in both cases.

(3) If there is significant influence of EU security institutions but this influence is weighed against other factors, then one would expect to find a role afforded to the EU CFSP/ESDP in specific cases only, or only a partial role afforded to policy instruments located in CFSP/ESDP.

According to the *alliance politics* approach, one can formulate these hypotheses:

(1) If there is significant influence of the transatlantic alliance, both in terms of US preferences against an EU role, or other pressures to keep NATO in play and adjust policy preferences accordingly, then one would expect to find a small role afforded to the EU CFSP/ESDP.

(2) If there is little influence of the transatlantic alliance on member states, or if there is little interest of (or perceived threat towards) the alliance in a particular region or conflict, then one would expect to find a significant role afforded to the EU CFSP/ESDP.

Lastly, with regard to military operations in particular there is also a utilitarian argument to be derived from alliance politics that focuses on the availability of military assets:

(3) If NATO assets are required for carrying out an operation that are not available to the EU, then one can expect to find a small role afforded to the EU CFSP/ESDP.

To restate the hypotheses in more specific terms, significant evidence of Europeanization – manifested either as policy responses as a result of adaptational pressures, or the export of national preferences on to the European agenda – can be expected to result in a significant role for the EU CFSP/ESDP in the resolution of both crises. However, evidence of Europeanization may not necessarily result in a significant role for the EU CFSP/ESDP if alliance politics play a bigger role in national decision-making. National member states may prefer the use of NATO either for utilitarian reasons, for reasons of solidarity with another member of the alliance, out of preference for the involvement of the US and NATO, or because of US pressures or concern over possible negative consequences for transatlantic relations. In this case, one would not expect a significant role afforded for the EU CFSP/ESDP, even if some evidence of Europeanization is present in both cases. Focusing on governmental politics, lastly, will open the black box of policy making and reveal what impact the preferences and influence of the individual agencies, key participants and the elite public sphere had on policy outcomes. Governmental politics will disaggregate the broader concepts of Europeanization and alliance politics by identifying preferences and bargaining positions within the national governments. In applying these conceptual approaches to the individual country case studies, this research will be able to arrive at a nuanced analysis of policy decisions taken both from the domestic as well as the international level.

The remainder of this study is structured as follows: Chapter 2 analyses the crisis case studies and identifies aspects of the political response that crystallize tensions between European, domestic and transatlantic commitments. Chapters 3, 4 and 5 consist of the empirical study of British, French and German policies. Chapter 6 draws conclusions from the evidence established in Chapters 3 through 5, particularly with a view to the explanatory power of the Europeanization hypotheses and its evolution.

2
Continuity and Change in European Crisis Management

Baptism by fire: European crisis management in FYROM and Afghanistan

The creation of ESDP, made possible by a sea-change in British foreign policy that was informed both by the conflicts in the Balkans and the end of the Cold War, led to a further institutionalization of not only foreign but also security and defence policy. This institutionalization was to lead to gradual acceptance for ESDP to be deployed in theatre – and in theatres beyond the Balkans. Member state consensus was that 'ESDP was born in the Balkans' and the Balkans, provided that a prior agreement with NATO could be arrived at, constituted a natural theatre for the EU to act in foreign, security and defence policy. Deployment beyond the Balkans, however, was met with nervousness about moving too soon on the part of some member states. This is evident from member state reluctance to lend political approval, let alone military contributions, to Operation Artemis in 2003 – with one member state stating that not only was ESDP 'born in the Balkans – it should stay in the Balkans'. Apart from the nervousness about moving too soon, conflicting views on the applicability of both CFSP and ESDP instruments also show that the purpose of having ESDP had not quite been worked out on the part of the member states. Reactions towards the two crises in 2001 – FYROM and Afghanistan – in particular crystallized conflicting pressures acting on member states, and show the extent to which they had to re-evaluate their stance not just vis-à-vis CFSP/ESDP but also the EU's relationship with NATO and the US. Both crises came about suddenly and had not been foreseen; and represented a simultaneous regional and systemic shock that required a re-evaluation of entrenched policy positions.

FYROM and EU foreign policy

The crisis in FYROM represents a success story for the EU in crisis management. Although smaller in scale than the conflicts in the former Yugoslavia during the 1990s, the crisis in FYROM nevertheless posed a significant threat to regional security because of the potential for a spillover of the conflict into neighbouring Kosovo and the destabilization of the entire region. Another failure to act on the part of the EU would also have been quite damaging to EU credibility in the region and beyond, a threat that was taken very seriously by the EU and the individual member states (Interview with French official, 8 September 2005). The crisis in FYROM thus had a strong symbolic character for EU crisis management, and was 'a first' in several respects: the first time the EU made use of crisis management tools located in CFSP and ESDP; the first time NATO and the EU worked together on a practical level; and the first time a military mission for the EU was suggested and eventually realized under the EU ESDP framework. Operation Concordia, the first ever ESDP military mission, put into practice the Berlin-plus agreements and was high on symbolism even if it was a relatively small mission (Interview with EU official, 21 June 2005). This particular case, therefore, appears to validate the Europeanization hypothesis as far as the policy decisions of member states were concerned. However, the involvement of NATO in the conflict, differences among member states with respect to the application of instruments located in the EU CFSP/ESDP, the timing of an ESDP takeover from NATO, and US interests in the region suggest that alliance politics considerations played an important part in this case as well.

Due to its geographic location at the southern border of Kosovo and the eastern border of Albania, and because of persistent interethnic tensions and the resulting potential for escalating violence that could result in the destabilization of the entire region, FYROM holds an important position in the security in the Western Balkans. One of the poorest republics of the former Yugoslavia, FYROM is a country over which Serbs, Greeks and Bulgarians have historically asserted and maintained cultural and geographic claims. As part of the Yugoslav Federation, FYROM worked to create its own cultural identity; at the same time, the concerns of the Albanian population were not high on the agenda. Albanian nationalism thus took root and began to grow predominantly in Kosovo, as well as in FYROM (Liotta, 2003).

Following the declarations of independence by Slovenia and Croatia in June 1991, FYROM held a referendum on 8 September 1991 and declared independence on 17 November 1991. Whereas Serbia agreed to Macedonian independence and Bulgaria also quickly recognized the new state (although not its language), Greece blocked the recognition of the country. In addition to these external problems, internal challenges included the need for democratic institutions and legal and economic reforms in a bankrupt state with the potential for multiethnic tensions. In light of the fighting in Croatia and Bosnia-Herzegovina, then President Gligorov asked the UN for an observer force that would enhance FYROM's sovereignty and international recognition, and keep the conflicts away from FYROM's borders. The mission, which was subsequently known as the United Nations Preventive Deployment Force (UNPREDEP), had as its objectives to monitor the border areas and to report any developments that could pose a threat to FYROM; to deter such threats from any source and help prevent clashes between external elements and Macedonian forces, and to use good offices to contribute to the maintenance of peace and stability in the republic (Sokalski, 2003: 102). The US also deployed troops in support of UNPREDEP in order to contain the fighting south of Bosnia and to signal to Milosevic that the US considered both Kosovo and FYROM of interest. In 1999, as the situation in Kosovo was becoming increasingly unstable and the potential for spillover of the conflict into FYROM increased, UNPREDEP lost its mandate on 25 February 1999 due to China's veto in the Security Council (United Nations, 25 February 1999). US elements remained in FYROM initially under national control with the mission to maintain, protect and preserve US infrastructure but came under NATO jurisdiction and remained in the country under a more precisely defined force protection mission and a logistical support base for NATO's Kosovo operation (The White House, Office of the Press Secretary 26 March 1999).

Smuggling along the border between FYROM and Kosovo by ethnic Albanians further complicated interethnic tensions in an economic climate where unemployment was as high as 32 per cent (Liotta and Jebb, 2002: 73). The end of the UN mandate, coupled with NATO's apparent lack of interest in internal Macedonian stability on account of an exclusive focus on the situation in Kosovo in turn created a window for ethnic Albanian extremists to radicalize the political agenda. Stability began to unravel as members of the ethnic Albanian National Liberation Army (NLA) led by Ali Ahmeti, many infiltrating from the US sector in Kosovo, staged several attacks along the ill-defined Kosovo–Macedonian border during 2000 and increasingly frequent as of January 2001 (International Crisis Group, 2001a).

Negotiations leading to the Ohrid Framework Agreement

As the nature of international intervention changed from preventive diplomacy to third-party mediation that focused on crisis management and containment and later to a post-peace agreement intervention (Ackermann, 2005: 105–19), the involvement of NATO and the EU increased considerably. For the EU in particular, the crisis in FYROM presented an opportunity to act early and decisively to absorb the lessons from Bosnia and Kosovo and demonstrate its credibility as a global actor. With respect to the negotiations leading to the Ohrid Framework Agreement the EU quite successfully managed to do so, eclipsing the OSCE as a political actor in the crisis. However, the presence of the revived Contact Group and NATO in the negotiations also raises the question of the importance attached to the EU CFSP given the commitment among member states to NATO, and the Contact Group as forums for coordinating positions and conducting negotiations.

The EU was active in FYROM early on in the crisis, and successfully employed economic as well as political incentives in the resolution of the conflict and the eventual signing of the Ohrid Framework Agreement on 8 August 2001. To be sure, the initial discussions on the possible steps to stop the violence and to seal the border between Kosovo and FYROM to prevent the NLA from using the safety zone in Kosovo as a base from which to launch its attacks and to store weapons, had taken place between NATO and the Macedonian government. However, member states discussed the crisis for the first time in the General Affairs Council on 19–20 March 2001, and confirmed support for Javier Solana's efforts in managing the crisis (Council of the European Union, 19–20 March 2001). Javier Solana was due in Skopje on 19 March 2001, a visit that marked the beginning of a rather intensive shuttle diplomacy, often in conjunction with NATO Secretary-General Lord Robertson and/or Chris Patten, the Director of the Commission's Directorate General of External Relations (DG Relex). This was the first time that NATO and the EU joined forces, announcing on 19 March 2001 that the two organizations would coordinate their efforts in order to prevent FYROM from sliding into a civil war (*Le Monde*, 21 March 2001). Cooperation between NATO and the EU on the crisis in FYROM thus took place in the context of increasingly institutionalized relations between the two organizations, including the first formal NATO–EU meeting at the level of foreign ministers on 30 May 2001, where the NATO Secretary-General and the EU Presidency issued a joint statement on the Western Balkans (NATO, 29 July 2004).

The role of the EU consisted in diplomatic and economic support for the Macedonian government, combining both CFSP (pillar 2) and Commission (pillar 1) policy tools. Javier Solana played a very visible and effective role in managing the crisis through frequent visits to Skopje to put pressure on the government as well as the Albanian side to arrive at a political solution to the conflict. In turn, the Foreign Minister of FYROM visited Brussels several times and President Trajkovski attended the EU Goethenburg summit in 2001 at the suggestion of France and Germany. Solana, in conjunction with NATO Secretary-General Lord Robertson, played a crucial role in mediating ceasefires, establishing a government of national unity and bringing political leaders – Albanian as well as their Macedonian counterparts – to the negotiating table to work out a political agreement. Both acted as 'trouble shooters' keeping on track the pursuit of a negotiated settlement by softening entrenched positions and mending internal divisions within the different political parties (Ackermann, 2005: 105–19).

Importantly, Javier Solana was proactive not only in the negotiation of the crisis but also in carving out a role for himself in the negotiations in the first place. He was thereby acting as what may be termed a policy entrepreneur (Roberts and King, 1991; Sabatier, 1999) in defining his role as HR/SG of the EU CFSP as well as his action radius vis-à-vis the member states. His role and stature also indicates the Europeanization of national foreign policy with respect to the support of the member states for an increasingly visible role for the EU CFSP.

In the emerging division of labour NATO brokered security arrangements between the NLA and the government security forces and generally provided the military deterrent, whereas the EU and US encouraged political dialogue and confidence-building measures (Eldridge, 2002: 65). The urgency of the situation and the need for demonstrating unity also proved an additional incentive for member states to act in support of EU unity. As the crisis worsened under the Swedish EU Presidency, which did not have an Embassy in FYROM and thus could not represent the EU, British Ambassador Mark Dickinson represented Sweden's interests. The UK thus acted as the local presidency on the ground (Interview with UK official, 29 June 2006). The need for a continuous EU presence forged a consensus to create the position of an EU Special Envoy to FYROM – Mark Dickinson was appointed on 6 March 2001. In accordance with French interests (Interview with French official, 8 September 2005), François Léotard, a former French Defence Minister, was subsequently appointed as EU Special Representative (EUSR) on 25 July 2001. The appointment of a US negotiator, James Pardew, three days after Léotard's appointment (Interview with French official, 8 September 2005) in turn highlighted the interest on the part of the US to maintain its influence on the outcome of the negotiations.

In early May 2001 Solana played an important role in negotiating the creation of a government of national unity consisting of all political parties. Solana and Robertson were also actively involved in negotiating several ceasefires and, importantly, were twice able to prevent Prime Minister Ljubco Georgievski from proclaiming a state of war, a move that would have led to a considerable escalation of the conflict (International Crisis Group, 2001b). The negotiations in Ohrid, in South-Eastern FYROM close to the Albanian border, took place between the leaders of the four major political parties (two Slav, two Albanian) in the presence of President Trajkovski as well as François Léotard and US negotiator James Pardew. Léotard also met with Russian Foreign Minister Igor Ivanov for support of the EU's and NATO's initiative in FYROM. In response to diplomatic pressure from the international community, the ethnic Slav and Albanian political leaders began negotiations on 2 April 2001. Upon the signature of the Ohrid Agreement on August 13, the EU pledged an additional $42 million in aid to push the parliament to back the reform plan and ratify the Agreement – the precondition for NATO Operation Essential Harvest, which began on 27 August 2001 (NATO, 15 August 2001).

Britain, France and Germany thus played an active role in the solution in the crisis and the support for the EU platform in supporting and/or endorsing Solana and the use of EU CFSP instruments. The UK acted as the EU local presidency, whereas Germany and France used the EU platform to invite President Trajkovski to the Goethenburg Summit; France, lastly, lobbied for the appointment of a EUSR. This potentially underlines the European hypothesis as the EU appears to have been suggested and perceived as an appropriate and salient platform. But the EU was not the only institution active in the negotiations, and broader geostrategic issues were of salience as was the credibility of NATO on the ground. First, the crisis in FYROM coincided with the advent of a new US administration and doubts on the part of the EU whether the US would continue to be engaged in the Balkans. Although the US allayed fears of withdrawal from Kosovo and Bosnia at the US–EU summit in Goetenburg in June and James Pardew, the US negotiator, acted side by side with Solana, lending weight to the European effort – this also signalled that the US was not yet confident that the Europeans could manage this conflict on their own (Interview with French official, 8 September 2005), and suggesting that the role of the US in member states political considerations had important weight. Another highly salient actor in the negotiations was the Contact Group, which was resurrected and first met on the crisis in FYROM in April 2001. Although the Contact Group ended up endorsing the EU's political mediation in the crisis in FYROM and included Javier Solana or his representative Stefan Lehne, its resurrection for coordinating policy nevertheless questions the extent to which alliance politics considerations by the member states took precedence over those of Europeanization in the case of the negotiations leading to the Ohrid Accords.

NATO Operation Essential Harvest

Although the need for a NATO presence was not contested among EU member states, NATO Operation Essential Harvest and its follow-up operations serve as a precursor to considerations of an eventual ESDP takeover. Since the end of the conflict in Kosovo, about 4,000 NATO troops (KFOR rear) were based in FYROM, in addition to intelligence and training personnel stationed there since the early 1990s when NATO and FYROM signed the Partnership for Peace (PfP) agreement (*Financial Times*, 7 August 2001). For NATO, a peace accord in FYROM was important as instability potentially could negatively impact the logistic lines to Kosovo. NATO had been active in FYROM on one prior occasion when the Extraction Force (XFOR) was assembled in 1999 to protect the first elements of KFOR in the area. Upon the first signs of crisis, President Trajovski made an immediate request to NATO to help secure borders (NATO, 20 June 2001). This shows that NATO, and in particular the US, were necessary for Western credibility in FYROM (Interview with French official, 8 September 2005), although there was no desire to extend KFOR's mandate to FYROM. Active in the political negotiations – apart from Lord Robertson – was Pieter Feith, NATO special envoy, and Senior Civilian Representative to Skopje, Ambassador Hanjorg Eiff (NATO, 20 June 2001). A NATO presence was also necessary because NATO was already in the area and had a degree of political credibility both with the Albanian as well as the Slav part of the population (Interview with EU official, 21 June 2005). The conclusion of the Ohrid Agreement was the precondition for a NATO peace-keeping operation.

Operation Essential Harvest was deployed 'in order to collect weapons and ammunitions, on a voluntary basis, from those who have been fighting government forces' (NATO, 17 August 2001). Key tasks were the collection of weapons and ammunition from the insurgents; transportation and disposal of weapons which are surrendered; and transportation and destruction of ammunition that is turned in (NATO, 16 December

2002). Britain, France and Germany contributed sizeably to the force. Soon after the launch of the NATO mission it became apparent that an international military presence would be required beyond the term of Operation Essential Harvest. About 50 EU and OSCE observers, a number that was intended to double, had entered FYROM in late August and early September 2001, and their mandate extended beyond that of Operation Essential Harvest. EU foreign ministers soon expressed security concerns for the safety of the monitors. There was still potential for conflict: two further parliamentary votes were needed to pass Albanian rights into law, and rebels were still occupying areas of the country, and armed Slav Macedonian paramilitary groups were unhappy with the peace deal (International Crisis Group, 2001c). NLA commanders warned that they would remobilize and the Interior Minister, Ljube Boskovski, said he would launch a security crackdown on them (*Independent*, 7 September 2001). Operation Amber Fox, the follow-on operation to protect OSCE and EU unarmed monitors that entered FYROM to oversee the settlement after Operation Essential Harvest ended, began with a three-month security mandate that was extended until 15 December 2002 (NATO, 31 July 2003). The next mission began 16 December 2002 – Operation Allied Harmony – which was eventually taken over by the EU ESDP.

The politics of the ESDP takeover from NATO

Success in political mediation and EU–NATO cooperation prepared the groundwork for a ESDP takeover from NATO and the first ever EU military mission. In the case of FYROM, the risk of failure was low because the demands of the KLA – a multiethnic state where Slav and Albanian Macedonians enjoyed equal rights rather than secession – were regarded as reasonable on the part of the West (Garton Ash, 2001), and because the threat of full-scale civil war had receded with the signing of the Ohrid Agreement. Accordingly, the EU and member states expressed interest in a takeover early on, and according to EU officials and outside observers it was not so much a question of if but of when the EU would assume a more central role in the military and political process (Interview with EU official, 21 June 2005; Interview with UK academic, 17 June 2005). However, the initial suggestion for an ESDP takeover was rejected by the member states, and the actual takeover was delayed on account of unresolved issues between NATO and the EU with regard to the Berlin plus agreements.

The debate over a potential EU takeover of the NATO mission first arose publicly out of the continuing need to fill the impending security vacuum left by the end of Operation Essential Harvest (see also International

Crisis Group, 2001c). On 5 September, EUSR François Léotard proposed to send a 1500-strong multinational EU force to keep the peace after the end of the NATO mission, a proposal he claimed had been discussed with the British, French and German governments, and that was said to have the backing of the French government (*Financial Times*, 6 September 2001). At the informal meeting of EU foreign ministers at Genval near Brussels, Javier Solana was to ask colleagues to agree on what tasks any new force in FYROM should perform before deciding on which organization would be best equipped to undertake it. However, a number of member states – including Britain and Germany – considered an ESDP operation too early in light of the unresolved institutional issues over EU–NATO cooperation.

At least one member state, then, had come to look for a more robust military role in FYROM in an effort to give credibility to the emerging ESDP. The operation in FYROM was as much, if not more, about its symbolic character for the EU rather than about the nature of the mission (Interview with EU official, 21 June 2005). At the Laeken summit in December 2001 the Belgian EU Presidency declared ESDP operational and capable of conducting some crisis management operations, and both the Spanish EU Presidency in the first half of 2002 as well as President Chirac urged the EU to take over the mission in FYROM (International Crisis Group, 2002). At the European Council in Barcelona on 15–16 March the EU pledged to take over from NATO, declaring the 'EU's availability to take responsibility, following elections in FYROM and at the request of its government, for an operation to follow that currently undertaken by NATO in FYROM, on the understanding that the permanent arrangement on EU–NATO cooperation ("Berlin Plus") would be in place by then' (cited in NATO Notes, 27 March 2002: 1). With regard to Operation Amber Fox, the operation following Essential Harvest, Secretary of State Colin Powell hinted that the US would not object if the EU wanted to take over responsibility in the Balkans. From the part of the US, then, there seemed to be little objection in principle for the EU to take over a security function in FYROM, including under the ESDP label (Interview with US official, 20 October 2005). Member states reservations by that time appeared to have been resolved in favour of an ESDP mission provided the 'Berlin Plus' agreement were in place.

But the dispute between Greece and Turkey over EU access to NATO assets prevented the formulation of a timetable for EU troops to assume the mission. After the EU–NATO declaration on the 'Berlin-plus' agreement on 16 December 2002 that gave the EU access to NATO assets for crisis management (NATO, 2 December 2004), EU foreign ministers formally approved the first EU military mission in FYROM. Operation Concordia was launched on 31 March 2003 with Admiral Rainer Feist, the Deputy SACEUR, as Operation Commander. Its operational tasks were to 'contribute to a stable, secure environment to allow the [Macedonian] government to implement the Ohrid Framework Agreement' (Council of the European Union, 27 January 2003). EU liaison officers were working alongside their NATO colleagues in the NATO command structure, both at the strategic level in an EU cell at SHAPE in Mons, Belgium, and at regional level at AFSOUTH in Naples, Italy. In the field, in Skopje, the Force Commander French Major-General Maral and his staff were working closely with the NATO Senior Military Representative. It was the first EU operation to draw on the 'Berlin-plus' arrangement and involved 350 lightly armed military personnel. Initially expected to last six months, its mandate was extended at the GAERC council on 21 July until 15 December 2003, after which a police operation – Operation Proxima – succeeded Concordia to help FYROM authorities develop their police forces. Whereas member state policies and preferences in the case of FYROM leaned towards the application of CFSP and eventually also ESDP instruments, this was not the case in a second crisis that erupted in the second half of 2001: the terrorist attacks on 11 September and the subsequent war in Afghanistan.

Afghanistan and EU foreign policy

The significance of the war in Afghanistan in the first instance lies in the fight against terrorism following the attacks on 11 September, as well as in the changing nature of international coalitions: the US, rather than calling on NATO for support in its fight against the Taliban through Operation Enduring Freedom (OEF), instead relied on ad-hoc coalitions of the willing, thereby calling into question the role and purpose of military alliances in the post-11 September era (see Lieven, 2001). Military operations in Afghanistan initially were conducted in the framework of two separate operations. Operation Enduring Freedom (OEF) centred on the fight against terrorism whereas the initial role of ISAF was to assist the Afghan Transitional Authority (ATA) prior to the country's 2004 elections in providing a safe and secure environment within Kabul and its surrounding areas.

In the context of the EU and its emerging CFSP/ESDP, responses to the attacks of 11 September brought with it the apparent renationalization of foreign policy (see Hill, 2004), as individual EU member states – Britain, France and Germany at the forefront – sought to contribute to the US-led war on terror both to Operation Enduring Freedom (OEF) and the International Security Assistance Force (ISAF) and to demonstrate their solidarity with the US. This in turn provoked resentment not only for compromising EU unity but also for engaging in what may be termed mini-lateralism: discussing contributions in closed meetings, often ahead of EU summits – thereby sidelining smaller EU member states, including Belgium, which held the EU presidency during the second half of 2001. To be sure, the overriding instinct and determining factor of international policy responses to Afghanistan was solidarity with the US and the recognition that this was a case of self-defence and that the US as a result would determine much of the military policy towards Afghanistan. However, for EU member states, the war in Afghanistan nevertheless posed the problem of what sort of a political role the EU CFSP could and should play in the reconstruction efforts, to what extent – if at all – EU member states were ready to subsume their military and political actions under an EU label, and what sort of role the EU should assume in the crisis management and reconstruction efforts in Afghanistan. The emerging contradictions between national contributions and the simultaneous search for a political role for the EU in response to the crisis thus make the war in Afghanistan a pertinent case study of member states' preferences on the role of the EU CFSP in crisis management. The rejection of suggestions for a possible 'EU force' as part of ISAF in particular illustrated the divergent views on the part of EU member states as to the EU CFSP/ESDP's global and military reach and ambitions. More broadly, it illustrates the tension between transatlantic and European commitments in reaction to a systemic shock.

The war in Afghanistan also raises issues of reconstruction, state building and the provision of humanitarian aid to a war-torn country. The events of 11 September brought Afghanistan, one of the poorest countries in the world, once more to the fore of world attention. Located at the crossroads of Central Asia, Afghanistan's strategic position has long made it a target for invasion by regional as well as great powers. During the Cold War the Soviet Union invaded in 1979 and was driven out by the Mujahidin in 1989 (Roy, 2004). The US, until the Soviet withdrawal, funded the Afghan war efforts and maintained strategic linkages with Afghan mujahidin who came to occupy the power vacuum left behind. Soon after the fall of the Soviet-backed government in Kabul in 1992, the various Mujahidin religious, tribal and linguistic factions began a devastating civil war. The Taliban ('religious students'), under the direction of Mullah Muhammad Omar, began their ascent to power around Kandahar in 1994, took control of Kabul in 1996 and soon controlled most of the country, bringing about order through the institution of a very strict interpretation of Sharia, or Islamic law (Roy, 2004). Human rights abuses, particularly of ethnic and religious minorities and women were widespread. Under the Taliban, Afghanistan also became a haven for terrorist groups, in particular al-Qaeda. Prior to the fall of the Taliban regime, Afghanistan was one of the world's worst humanitarian emergencies: a quarter-century of civil war had left an estimated one million people dead and over six million people displaced, many as refugees in neighbouring Pakistan and Iran (UNHCR 2005). The country was one of the most heavily mined in the world, and per capita GDP was on par with Somalia and Eritrea, estimated at $140 – $180 (European Commission, 2003). The development task alone, therefore, was and remains a significant challenge.

The reconstruction of Afghanistan has been placed under UN auspices in order to coordinate economic and political measures on the part of the various international actors involved in the reconstruction of the country. The peacekeeping operation, also sanctioned by UNSC Resolutions, was eventually placed under overall NATO command. NATO became formally involved in February 2003, when Germany and the Netherlands assumed ISAF command and sought NATO support for the planning and execution of the operation. European activities are thus spread across three dimensions and include security, political and economic contributions. The EU and its member states have been active in all three, but with various degrees of coordination and not always under an EU label. The EU did not assume a role in the military aspect of crisis management through ISAF – this task fell to individual nations including EU member states, and later to NATO as the institutional framework – but it did carve out a significant political and economic role with regard to Afghanistan, both in terms of the financial contributions to the country's reconstruction as well as a political profile (and influence) for the EU in Afghanistan and worldwide through the office of the EU Special Representative (EUSR) Klaus-Peter Klaiber and later Francesc Vendrell. The emphasis on a profile for the EU in the reconstruction of Afghanistan suggests considerations that would support the Europeanization hypothesis, despite the overwhelming influence of the US on the policies towards Afghanistan.

OEF and the war on terror

After the attacks on 11 September, the US took steps to oust the Taliban from power. However, rather than calling on NATO for military contributions – NATO had, for the first time in its history invoked article 5 of the NATO treaty on 12 September 2001 – the US instead decided to form coalitions of the willing for OEF, accepting military contributions from Britain and, to a lesser extent, France and Germany, under overall US command. While military contributions on the part of the US' allies are not surprising given the magnitude of the event and the US' right to self-defence, they nevertheless appear to contradict engrained national positions in two of the three member states analysed: anti-Americanism on the part of France, and remnants of post-World War II pacifism on the part of Germany.

EU policy responses towards 11 September and the war in Afghanistan have made use both of Community and CFSP instruments. The initial response to the attacks of 11 September was immediate – and common, as the EU and its member states declared solidarity with the US and established an Action Plan for the fight against terrorism at the Extraordinary European Council in Brussels on 21 September (Council of the European Union, 21 September 2001). Beyond questions of solidarity, particularly with regard to contributions to the US-led military operation as well as a peace keeping force for reconstruction, contradictions between national commitments and the EU soon became apparent, as individual leaders offered national contributions to the US war effort, eclipsing not only the country holding the EU Presidency, Belgium, but other member states as well. This was true in particular for Britain and France. Tony Blair earned some resentment for his active cooperation with the US as well as his calling of a strategy meeting in London between Britain, France and Germany. Jacques Chirac was also criticized for calling a tri-lateral meeting prior to the EU summit at Ghent to discuss the national contributions to the war in Afghanistan.

Military operations against the Taliban under Operation Enduring Freedom (OEF) began on 7 October 2001. UK Forces participated in OEF from the start through Operation Veritas, which had as its goal the capture of Osama bin Laden and other al-Qaeda leaders, the prevention of further attacks by al-Qaeda, the end of Afghanistan's harbouring of terrorists, their training camps and infrastructure, and the removal of Mullah Omar and the Taliban Regime (BBC News, 16 April 2002). In contrast, France had 2,000 military personnel in the region as of early November 2001. In addition to the support for the ground operations in Afghanistan, France took part in the maritime patrol. A French task force composed of soldiers from the 21st Marine Infantry Regiment was deployed on 17 November 2001 to survey the modalities of operations aimed at repairing the airfield at Mazar-e Sharif (US Department of Defence, 14 June 2002). Germany began participating in OEF on 27 November 2001 by dispatching three Transall transport aircraft in order to assist the US Air Force in its operations in Afghanistan. A few days later, reconnaissance commandos flew to Bahrain to prepare for naval deployment. In addition, up to 100 troops from the Special Commando Forces (KSK), a unit specialized in covert operations, made short-term missions in Afghanistan (US Department of Defence, 14 June 2002). There were also plans for future cooperation with the German Navy that included the allocation of areas of deployment of the US, French and German Navies to patrol waters between the Arabian Peninsula and the east African coast. With regard to OEF, the individual national contributions were regarded as expressions of solidarity with the US and contributions to the war on terror. Although these contributions were not contentious in terms of EU unity or decision-making, the closed meetings between the UK, France and Germany ahead of the Ghent summit in November 2001 to coordinate military contributions to the war on terror raised concerns over a directorate in EU decision-making and appeared to further damage EU unity.

The reconstruction of Afghanistan

The UN assumed a central role in the reconstruction and the creation of an interim government in Afghanistan. In December 2001, at the Bonn Conference on the future of Afghanistan, Afghan factions, assisted by the UN, agreed on a transitional process leading to elections for a 'broad-based, gender-sensitive, multi-ethnic and fully representative government' (United Nations, 7 December 2001). The Afghan Interim Authority (AIA) under the leadership of Hamid Karzai was established for a six-month period. An Emergency Loya Jirga met in June 2002 and elected Karzai as the Chief of State and Chairman of the Afghan Transitional Authority, which governed the country until elections could be held. After a nationwide Loya Jirga in 2002, Karzai was elected interim President.

As for the EU Council, and reflecting EU/EC Cooperation objectives, the 2001 and 2002 General Affairs and External Relations Council (GAERC) agreed to the following overall objectives for the EU/EC in Afghanistan: to promote the Bonn Agreement; restore stability to the country; provide support for civil, social and military structures; promote democracy and human rights; give special attention to the inclusion of women; reinforce the fight against illegal drugs and terrorism; and promote cooperation with neighbouring countries. The EU played an important role in post-conflict reconstruction and the release of economic aid. Since the fall of the Taliban the Commission has set its support in the context of the provisions made in the 2001 Bonn Agreement. At the Tokyo Conference in January 2002 the EC pledged about €1 billion over five years. About €207 million were spent in 2002 on recovery and reconstruction, plus €73 million from ECHO. €400 million were earmarked for 2003–04, with continuing humanitarian assistance from ECHO, up to €55 million in 2003. The first year in particular, given the huge scale of the reconstruction task faced by the country and the need for strong political commitment and leadership, led to the creation of the Afghan Reconstruction Steering Group (with the co-chairs US, EU, Japan and Saudi Arabia) to provide strategic direction. The Commission made effective use of its conflict prevention instrument, by drawing €4.93 million from the Rapid Reaction Mechanism (RRM) for use in Afghanistan following the Bonn Conference in 2001 in order to help legitimize the political transition; and the EC also moved swiftly to open a representative office in Kabul in February 2002 (International Crisis Group, 2005).

With respect to the political aspects of the reconstruction of Afghanistan, on Germany's suggestion EU foreign ministers agreed in their meeting in Brussels to appoint a special envoy for Afghanistan to coordinate humanitarian aid and the political efforts to contribute to rebuilding the country (CNN.com, 19 November 2001). Klaus-Peter Klaiber, former assistant secretary-general of NATO was appointed EU Special Representative at the 10 December 2001 foreign minister meeting. His initial mandate was due to expire on 10 June, but was extended to 30 June at the Council Meeting on 27 May 2002 (Council of the European Union, 27 May 2002). The foreign ministers welcomed the signing of the inter-Afghan agreement in Bonn on 5 December, and stated that they were prepared to consider a contribution by the EU member states in furtherance of UNSC Resolutions, including the establishment of an international security force. The EU also re-emphasized its commitment to play a key role in the international effort to rebuild the Afghan society and economy. Klaiber's appointment was to 'help the EU speak with one voice again', despite the shift to bilateralism in the wake of September 11 (*Financial Times*, 15 December 2001; see also Klaiber, 2002).

Klaiber proved pivotal in coordinating efforts of the member states through meetings, for example, with French Foreign Minister Védrine on 7 January 2002 to discuss reconstruction. He also often spoke on behalf of ISAF; for instance he suggested that it might be necessary to broaden the mandated area of ISAF to include areas outside Kabul (Agence France Press, 10 January 2002), and lobbied among several EU capitals for an extension of the ISAF mandate beyond June 2002 and in an extended geographic focus, in light of the reluctance on the part of most European countries to commit to a longer-term operation in Afghanistan. Klaiber stated that the EU should follow through politically, not just limit itself to its financial contributions and travelled to neighbouring countries, visiting Pakistan in April to meet with senior Pakistani ministers and officials to assess the post-Taliban situation and its impact on the Afghan refugees living there. Klaiber also distanced himself from US statements that Iran was working to destabilize Afghanistan and expressed reservations about President Karzai, who in his view travelled too much rather than concentrating on work inside the country itself. In contrast to FYROM, Solana's role in Afghanistan was not as pronounced (Interview with former German official, 9 February 2006), although he did visit Kabul at the end of May 2002 to consult local leaders before the opening of Afghanistan's emergency Loya Jirga, as the EU ministers had agreed on 15 April at the meeting in Luxembourg. Francesc Vendrell, a 62-year old Spanish diplomat who had served as the UN Secretary General Kofi Annan's special representative for Afghanistan from February 2000 to the beginning of 2002, was subsequently appointed EUSR after the expiration of Klaiber's mandate.

ISAF and its institutional anchoring

Like OEF, ISAF, the peacekeeping force assembled under the framework of UNSC Resolution 1378 and Lakhdar Brahimi, the UN's Secretary-General's Special Representative, was a coalition of the willing that initially did not include US forces. ISAF worked closely with the United Nations and the Afghan interim government and had three principal tasks: to aid the interim government in developing national security structures; to assist the country's reconstruction; and to assist in developing and training future Afghan security forces. Rules of engagement were to be closely linked to the terms of the military-technical agreement between the British commander, Major-General John McColl, and the interim government in Afghanistan on 31 December 2001. Under the agreement, the ISAF had 'complete and unimpeded freedom of movement throughout the territory and airspace of Afghanistan' (UK Ministry of Defence, 2001). Apart from the UK, a number of countries were expected to become lead nations of ISAF, including France and Germany. While the UK made a significant contribution to ISAF as the first lead nation, Germany made a substantive commitment to Afghanistan with 3,900 troops, which marked another major step in the country's willingness to send troops abroad in peace-keeping operations.

With respect to ISAF, several issues in particular proved contentious: the geographic extension of the mandate beyond Kabul, the temporal extension of the mandate altogether, and the strengthening of numbers. There was also a debate over US command over ISAF, and the mixing of the peace-keeping and counter-terrorism operations. While Britain was in principle in favour of a single US command for both OEF and ISAF, Germany rejected this idea partly out concern over attaining domestic consent for the sending of Bundeswehr troops to an offensive military operation. Differences in the command structures of the coalition forces limited the role of Paris as well: Chirac insisted on a multilateral command structure for ISAF, but France found itself sidelined by the US. ISAF and OEF thus remained separate – until 2006, when the missions became more closely coordinated and the respective command structures merged with the deputy Commander of ISAF, Lieutenant-General Karl Eikenberry, continuing to lead the OEF mission.

Discussions of assembling a multinational peace-keeping force had progressed by the time the EU heads of state met in Laeken. Disagreement broke out at the EU Summit when Belgian Foreign Minister Louis Michel in a press conference on 14 December 2001 termed the contributions to ISAF of the individual EU member states as an EU force, prompting speculation by the media that an 'EU army' was to be sent to Afghanistan. Member states, Britain at the forefront, stated that 'there was no question of the EU being able to deploy a defence force it doesn't have in Afghanistan' (*Financial Times*, 15 December 2001). On 14 December, at the EU Council in Laeken, EU leaders agreed that member states would take part in ISAF, even if the EU was not putting together its own force for Afghanistan. While Belgian Foreign Minister Louis Michel welcomed this step as being 'of capital importance for European security and defence policy' and 'an extremely significant precedent', British foreign minister Jack Straw stressed that the EU states were still examining what forces they could offer to the international force. Solana, meanwhile, stated that ISAF would face 'a task more difficult than other peacekeeping missions in the past' (BBC News, 14 December 2001). The Presidency Conclusions on the European Council meeting in Laeken stated that 'the participation of the Member States of the Union in that international force will provide a strong signal of their resolve to better assume their crisis-management responsibilities and hence help stabilize Afghanistan' (Council of the European Union, 14/15 December 2001).

Initially at least, NATO did not play a role in OEF and ISAF, suggesting that the US after the events of 11 September viewed NATO as a political forum rather than a military alliance: the US called on individual nations, not on NATO, for support against the war against the Taliban. Given the invocation of Article 5, NATO involvement was first raised in November 2001, but blocked by several NATO countries, including France. Germany, on the other hand, was in favour of NATO assuming

ISAF command whereas France was not eager to see a 'NATO flag in Kabul' (NATO Notes, 19 December, 2002). This points towards difference with respect to the role of NATO among member states and towards the explanatory potential of the alliance politics approach for policy decision taken by at least one member state (France). On 16 April 2003 the North Atlantic Council decided to approve the deployment of NATO troops to Afghanistan to work under the ISAF mandate and on 11 August 2003, NATO assumed the lead of the International Security Assistance Force in a Transfer of Authority Ceremony in Kabul, Afghanistan (NATO Notes, October 2003).

Plus ça change? European crisis management in Lebanon and DRC

Seven years after the creation of ESDP and three years after the launch of the first military ESDP operation in FYROM, the policy's institutional framework had evolved considerably – as had the number of ESDP missions (even if the majority of these missions were civilian rather than military crisis management operations). Although the fall-out over the war in Iraq in 2003 revealed a significant rift among member states and painfully demonstrated the ineffectiveness of the EU where member states publicly disagree, it also led to the formulation and the adoption of the European Security Strategy (ESS). Although not synonymous with the emergence of a European strategic culture or convergence around foreign policy goals, the ESS did serve to provide cohesion and a strategic roadmap (Biscop, 2007). The development of military and civilian crisis management instruments, and the gradual emergence of the concept of security sector reform (SSR) as a policy priority, in conjunction with the experience of individual member states as part of ISAF in Afghanistan, highlighted the need for a comprehensive approach and civil–military coordination. The EU is the only international security actor that has civilian and military tools at its disposal, and is therefore at least in principle in an advantageous position when it comes to post-conflict reconstruction. The expanding toolbox of the EU, and the increasing role played by its foreign policy institutions, particularly the Political and Security Committee (PSC), which increasingly serves as a locus of consensus-finding and of socialization (Meyer, 2006: 112–37), helps explain why the EU was playing a more active role in the Middle East; and why member states accepted and supported the EU as an important platform for political negotiations and decision-making in the crisis in Lebanon. The manner in which ESDP was brought into the conversation but never considered a serious option for a peacekeeping force in Lebanon, however, reveals both the evolution of member states' attitudes towards the use and geographic reach of ESDP as well as the limitations that continue to act on decisions towards the utilization of ESDP instruments.

Sub-Saharan Africa, by contrast, did not have the same geo-political urgency as the crisis in Lebanon did. The region had nevertheless become one of the priority areas for EU including ESDP involvement. By 2006 the Democratic Republic of Congo (DRC) had hosted a number of ESDP missions with the first one, Operation Artemis, taking place in 2003 shortly after the launch of Concordia in FYROM. DRC, and sub-Saharan Africa more generally, had also been identified by the French in particular as a theatre for ESDP especially as far as military crisis management was concerned, explaining French lead in initiating the two military operations, Artemis and EUFOR RD Congo. While the deployment of an ESDP operation was not contested politically, decisions over national involvements reveal the difficulties of selling ESDP and military operations to domestic constituencies; and member states' pressure on one another to commit forces to this particular operation. Taken together, the two cases demonstrate that the constraints acting on, and challenges facing ESDP have evolved starkly since the policy's beginning. Whereas in 2001 transatlantic relations had overshadowed much of the decision-making, 2006 saw member states concerned over EU–UN coordination in DRC and the task at hand – for which ESDP was still not considered capable – in Lebanon. Geographical constraints, and US preferences overshadowing policy decisions to the point that EU contributions could not be coordinated, or be recognized as such, were no longer an issue: the EU gaining visibility and regional influence, on the other hand, was.

Lebanon and EU foreign policy

The 2006 Lebanon War was significant for EU foreign policy for a number of reasons. First, although EU Middle East policy has been constricted by diverging views in the individual capitals, by 2006 the EU and its member states had succeeded in carving out an accepted – and increasing – role for CFSP diplomatic activities. These include the EU 3 format in negotiations with Iran; Solana's political efforts in the Middle East Peace Process; and the EU being party to, along with the UN, the US and Russia, the Middle East Quartet. Two small ESDP operations had also been launched in the Middle East in 2005: a EU Border Assistance Mission at the Rafah crossing post (EU BAM Rafah) and a police training mission in the Palestinian Territories (EUPOL COPPS). In addition, both CFSP and ESDP policies are embedded in a broader regional approach through the European Neighbourhood Policy (ENP). Despite diverging views on the Arab-Israeli peace process, and despite the 2003 Iraq crisis, by 2006 the EU had succeeded in putting together a potentially coherent and mutually reinforcing set of policies. A unified response to the crisis was therefore of high salience for member states. Against this background, national reactions towards the war in Lebanon as well as the question over putting together – and participating in – a stabilization force in Lebanon as well as its institutional anchoring is highly topical. As in Afghanistan in 2001, the idea of an ESDP format was briefly floated during the crisis in Lebanon but abandoned in favour of an enhanced UNIFIL force. Despite the fact that this force was made up of European forces, it did not carry a EU-label.

However, unlike the two crises in 2001, transatlantic considerations were not influential in European decision-making when it came to the question over giving UNIFIL an EU label, or when it came to making troop contributions. Instead, the decision not to launch an ESDP operation were due to a level of discomfort of member states wishing to avoid 'getting their finger into the mangle' (Interview with British official, 19 November 2007) when it came to ESDP in the Middle East. Although EUBAM Rafah and EUPOL COPPS were in place and termed successful, there was still a level of nervousness about the Middle East – despite the fact that not just CFSP but also ESDP was then considered an appropriate tool in the Middle East as well, something that had not been the case in 2001–03. Importantly, however, these considerations were less shaped by US reservations towards ESDP and transatlantic tensions among (and within) member states. The Bush administration from the outset had adopted a more relaxed stance on ESDP than the Clinton administration; and although the US overshadowed much of the political decision-making in the case of Lebanon, when it came to considerations over deploying ESDP, transatlantic considerations were not a factor in the same way they had been in FYROM and Afghanistan. NATO had ruled itself out as it would not have been perceived as a neutral actor in enforcing a ceasefire; and ESDP was not seriously considered also because UNIFIL was already in place. Whereas member state reactions can be termed Europeanized in the sense that consensus and pressure to contribute to UNIFIL was forged in the PSC, this did not extent to deploying forces under a EU label.

Political responses to the crisis: getting to a ceasefire

The war in Lebanon was a 34-day military conflict in Lebanon and northern Israel involving Hezbollah paramilitary forces and the Israeli military that continued until a United Nations-brokered ceasefire went into effect on 14 August 2006. The conflict formally ended on 8 September 2006 when Israel lifted its naval blockade of Lebanon. The conflict began when Hezbollah militants fired rockets at Israeli border towns as a diversion for an anti-tank missile attack on two armoured Humvees patrolling the Israeli side of the border fence. Of the seven Israeli soldiers in the two jeeps, two were wounded, three were killed, and two were seized and taken to Lebanon. Five more were killed in a failed Israeli rescue attempt. Israel responded with massive air strikes and artillery fire on targets in Lebanon and a ground invasion of southern Lebanon. Hezbollah then launched more rockets into northern Israel and engaged the Israel Defence Forces (IDF) in guerrilla warfare. More than a thousand people were killed during the conflict, most of them Lebanese civilians. The war also severely damaged Lebanese infrastructure; and displaced 974,184 Lebanese and 300,000–500,000 Israelis, although most, if not all, were able to return to their homes. After the ceasefire, some parts of Southern Lebanon remained uninhabitable due to unexploded cluster bombs. The humanitarian aspect of the war, therefore, was severe.

Upon the outbreak of the crisis, both the EU and the UN announced emergency diplomatic trips to the Middle East; and a statement issued by the Finnish EU Presidency called Israel's use of force disproportionate and its air and sea blockade of Lebanon unjustifiable (*Guardian*, 14 July 2006). There was consensus among member states that the EU would make a contribution to de-escalating the conflict; and all member states welcomed an active role of the EU that, it was agreed, should be closely linked with the UN, and the Middle East Quartet where the EU was represented through Solana and Ferrero-Waldner (Interview with member state official, 17 December 2007). The close link between the EU and UN was also evident from Kofi Annan's attendance of the emergency meeting of European Union foreign ministers on 25 August when member states pledged military commitments to UNIFIL.

However, individual member states differed in the severity of their responses: whereas Britain along with the US, operating under the assumption that international intervention would do little unless the two parties were ready to stop the fighting, refrained from condemning Israel's actions, French foreign minister Philippe Douste-Blazy termed Israel's actions a disproportionate act of war that could plunge Lebanon back into a state of conflict. President Chirac took an even stronger stance, calling Israel's offensive 'aberrant' and demanding immediate negotiations towards a ceasefire; and sent the prime minister and foreign minister to Beirut to meet with officials and express support for

Lebanon (*International Herald Tribune*, 19 July 2006). There was also outright disagreement with the US in the framework of the G8 summit in St Petersburg, Russia, not just on whether or not Israel force was 'excessive' but also over whether or not the G8 was calling for a ceasefire (*International Herald Tribune*, 17 July 2006): whereas France stated that the G8 was calling for a ceasefire, the US flatly contradicted this statement. Germany was in support of the US view (Interview with member state official, 17 December 2006), with Merkel stating that the captured Israeli soldiers must be returned unharmed and attacks on Israel must stop as a precondition for ending Israeli military action (*International Herald Tribune*, 17 June 2006).

France also directly challenged the US' approach to the crisis by pushing for action by the UNSC by circulating proposals that could form the basis of a UNSC resolution – a call that was not received favourably by the US, which responded with 'a mixture of nervousness and irritation' (cited in the *Guardian*, 20 July 2006). For its part, the US was accused of deliberately delaying diplomatic action so as to give Israel time to inflict maximum damage on Hezbollah – a charge that was denied (*Guardian*, 20 July 2006). The US blocked calls for a ceasefire and through its ambassador to the UN John Bolton responded to the French proposal saying that 'the notion that you just declare a ceasefire and act as if that's going to solve the problem I think is simplistic' (cited in the *Guardian*, 20 July 2006) – and generally expressed doubt as to the possibility of Israel negotiating a ceasefire with a terrorist group (Bolton, 2007).

Thus, despite Solana's diplomatic visit to the region on 16–18 July, diverging member state positions on the question of whether or not to demand an immediate ceasefire at the G8 summit in St Petersburg, gave the appearance of EU disunity (*Guardian*, 18 July 2006) and eclipsed Solana's efforts – although the coordination of tasks and efforts on the part of member states support the Europeanization hypothesis. On 17 July EU foreign ministers issued a statement calling on both Israel and Hezbollah to cease their attacks, but avoided calling for an outright ceasefire. During the Foreign Minister meeting there was consensus that European security interests were at stake – although, as stated above, the difficulty was to develop concrete options for an active EU policy in the management of the crisis; and the Council Secretariat/Robert Cooper suggested to use the Gymnich meeting in September to make a concerted effort to think of the EU's role in the Middle East (Interview with member state official, 17 December 2007).

Conversely (and ironically), despite the high profile of individual member states rather than that of the EU platform alone, it was clear for member states, given the urgency of the crisis, that the EU would have to play a role (Interview with member state official, Brussels 17 December 2007) – even if, given that member states were divided over the political question of a ceasefire, the EU could not play a decisive or highly visible political role. Differences continued during the Rome crisis conference on 25/26 July 2006 where officials of Western governments, Russia and Arab states, including Lebanon, met to discuss the crisis: France pushed for an immediate ceasefire whereas Britain and the US continued to oppose any call for an immediate halt to the fighting (*Irish Times*, 1 August 2006).

On the question of a ceasefire, then, the positions of the US and Britain, but also Germany, were lined up against that of France and a number of smaller EU countries. And, given that the crisis was negotiated during high profile meetings such as the G8 summit, the Rome crisis conference and in the framework of the UN Security Council, member states rather than EU officials took centre stage both where national positions and national visibility were concerned. This applied to Britain and France in particular – France took the lead in negotiations in the UN Security Council, both on account of its historic role in Lebanon and because it held the presidency of the Security Council at the time of the crisis, whereas Blair and Bush continued the pattern of close transatlantic cooperation that had been apparent in Afghanistan five years prior. Still, as the next section demonstrates, on the question of putting together the peacekeeping force, and of generating the political will to contribute militarily, the EU and in particular the PSC played a crucial role in building collective will among EU member states to make a common contribution to UNIFIL (Interview with member state official, Brussels 17 December 2007). This suggests that Europeanization pressures were at work in a conflict where there existed entrenched national positions and preferences.

To UNIFIL or not to UNIFIL: explaining the absence of an ESDP operation

Whereas member states differed on their positions vis-à-vis Israeli military operations, they were quick to call – and agree on – the deployment of a peace-keeping force in Lebanon. Israel early on called for an international force to fill the security vacuum following Israel's withdrawal from southern Lebanon, although it made no specifications as to what sort of force this was going to be – except for stating that 'the core of the group should be European' (Interview with member state official, 17 December 2007). The UN, for its part, agreed with the need for an international force although not a muscular one as envisaged by Israel (Bolton, 2007: 394), although it was clear that any force would require a ceasefire. The preference of the US was not leaning towards the UN, with Rice stating that she wanted a non-US force to fill the security vacuum in Lebanon (Bolton, 2007: 396). Most member states, however, favoured at most a 'enhanced UNIFIL' without enforcement authority rather than a force which would disarm Hezbollah and fill the security vacuum, as the US would have preferred (Bolton, 2007: 398). The French position, by contrast, was that the conflict must be ended in a two-step approach: a peace-keeping force ought to be assembled once a ceasefire had been agreed on.

EU foreign ministers expressed support for the initiative to send a peace-keeping force to Lebanon on 17 July, which was announced by Tony Blair and Kofi Annan in St Petersburg. Blair stated that 'the blunt reality is that this violence is not going to stop unless we create the conditions for the ceasefire ... the only way is if we have a deployment of international forces that can stop bombardment coming into Israel' (cited in *International Herald Tribute*, 17 July 2006). Solana briefed ministers in Brussels and urged participation in a peace-keeping force if the UN were to approve it: 'it is important that member states are ready to consider participating in this force. I am confident they are ready to take part if required. But at the moment this is just an idea' (quoted in the *Irish Times*, 18 July 2006). UN officials speculated about a possible EU leadership role in the proposed force even if Israel could resist the idea of an EU-led force (*Irish Times*, 18 July 2006) – and Finnish foreign minister Erkki Tuomoija stated that 'it could be that the European Union or the United Nations might have a peacekeeping role' (*International Herald Tribune*, 18 July 2006). While Solana and the member states were clear on the fact that a military force must be under a UN flag and must not be a coalition of the willing, the matter of an ESDP label as a political question remained a 'no go area' due to the high-end Petersberg task, the region it was to act in and the size of the operation.

It was clear from the outset that any international force would operate under a UN (or possibly EU) flag as NATO is not seen as neutral in the region but rather as representing American interests (Interview with member state official, December 2007; *New York Times*, 25 July 2006). Israel reacted with scepticism to the force, citing the UN record at the border and military realities on the ground, stating that it was too early to contemplate international intervention, and reiterating that the primary Israeli goal was to 'neutralize Hezbollah' (*International Herald Tribune*, 17 July 2006). Still, support for an international military force was building quickly, with the US and Britain opting out of military contribution from the outset; France on the other hand expressed willingness to take the lead and Germany signalled interest in participating under certain conditions. There was, of course, the question of whose soldiers would be on the ground, with one senior European official reported as saying that 'of course everyone will volunteer to be in charge of the logistics in Cyprus' (*New York Times*, 25 July 2006) – indicating that actual force commitments were not automatically forthcoming. This raised concern over lacking political will among member states; at the same time, Brussels was closely involved in the decision-making and consensus-forging. Solana on 25 July stated that 'it is not an easy force to deploy but we have been working since Wednesday to try to construct a concept that would make it possible to deploy under the umbrella of the UN Security Council' (*Irish Times*, 25 July 2006). Plans were further consolidated at a crisis conference in Rome on 26 July, although a peace deal or the formation of such a force was not in sight (*Financial Times*, 26 July 2006).

Force generation among EU member states encountered problems when France, widely expected to lead the force and to make a sizeable contribution, offered only two hundred soldiers (Gowan, 2007), justified its reluctance with the ambivalent mandate of UNIFIL II and demanded strong rules of engagement before fulfilling its promises (Dembinski, 2007). Italy jumped into the breach by offering to contribute 3,000 troops, as well as assuming the operational command of the force. Faced with intra-European pressure, France increased its troop commitments to 2,000 and exerted operational control over UNIFIL. Italy was asked to succeed France in commanding the force as of February 2007. Spain also promised a battalion of 1,000 to 1,200 troops, with Belgium, Finland and Poland offering to contribute 300, 250 and 500 soldiers, respectively (*New York Times*, 26 August 2006). The PSC served as a key locus for member states to coordinate and pressure one another to increase contributions, demonstrating the influence of a EU-level institutional platform in pressuring member states to adapt their contributions and political attitudes to the troop requirements. Importantly, however, this influence extends to a coordinating role of member state positions rather than an influential role for the EU institutional level: at the 27 July meeting, representatives of the Council Secretariat suggested that the Council Secretariat could act as coordinating body of military contributions to humanitarian relief effort, a suggestion that was not taken up by the member states who did not perceive value added in such a move (Interview with member state official, 17 December 2007). At the same meeting, member states expressed willingness to commit troops to an enhanced UNIFIL force – and at the PSC meeting of 23 August Italy, France and Spain requested substantial contributions, and Britain a fast decision for the 25 August Extraordinary European Council meeting. That Council meeting was seen as an opportunity to emphasize the contribution of EU member states as well as support the political will of the EU as a whole, to work towards a resolution of this conflict. Without the coordination process it was unlikely that the member states would have arrived at this position (Interview with member state official, 17 December 2007).

On 25 August, the day of the Extraordinary European Council meeting, member states – France, Italy and Spain – pledged significant troop numbers to UNIFIL and the Council Conclusions stated that 'the significant overall contribution of the Member States to UNIFIL demonstrates that the European Union is living up to its responsibilities. The Council welcomes Member States' intentions to commit a substantial number of troops to be deployed in Lebanon [...] this gives a leadership role for the Union in UNIFIL' (Council of the European Union, 25 August 2006). And indeed, about half of the 15,000 strong force is made up of EU members – even if the force was not an EU force 'on account of a certain nervousness on the part of member states when it came to ESDP and the Middle East' and because UNIFIL 'was already there and it made more sense to keep the UN framework' (Interview with member state official, 17 December 2007), reporting on UNIFIL emphasized that the crisis showed 'the substance of a common European foreign and defence policy, including the use of force abroad' (*The Economist*, 24 August 2006).

On 11 August 2006, the United Nations Security Council unanimously approved UN Resolution 1701 in an effort to end the hostilities. The resolution, which was approved by both Lebanese and Israeli governments in the following days, called for disarmament of Hezbollah, for withdrawal of Israel from Lebanon, and for the deployment of Lebanese soldiers and an enlarged UNIFIL force in southern Lebanon. UNIFIL had been created by the Security Council in 1978 to confirm Israeli withdrawal from Lebanon, restore international peace and security and assist the Lebanese Government in restoring its effective authority in the area. Under its enhanced mandate, UNIFIL was to monitor the cessation of hostilities; accompany and support the Lebanese armed forces as they deploy throughout the south of Lebanon; and extend its assistance to help ensure humanitarian access to civilian populations and the voluntary and safe return of displaced persons (United Nations, 2008). The Lebanese army began deploying in southern

Lebanon on 17 August 2006 and Israel lifted the blockade on 8 September 2006.

When it comes to member state military contributions, just as in the case of Afghanistan five years earlier, member states differed over how to portray the role of the EU and the member states: whereas France favoured emphasizing the EU as a whole and its willingness to assume responsibility, Britain but also Germany maintained that contributions to the operations took place in a UN framework to which member states made contributions (Interview with member state official, December 2007). While it was in all member states' interest for the EU to progress as a security actor, France was alone in trying to portray the EU as an international actor in crisis management. However, in a clear departure from crises past, member states focused on the role of the PSC and the EU platform in general to generate political will on the part of the member states. Another evolution was that Solana played a central role in garnering member state and international support for an EU role – and that this role was acknowledged by the UN, and that this created a degree of trust in the EU and its ability. This improvement in confidence and acknowledged role of the EU in generating political will is also interesting with respect to the role of the US in the Middle East. The Annapolis Conference had shown that the Middle East is still a prestige object in foreign policy, and deemed important as far as the substance of the policy is concerned. The emergence of 'radical Islam' in addition to strong ties with Israel have not lessened but shifted the interest of the US. This shows that the EU evolved in terms of its space for action even in a policy field where there continues to be a strong US interest and presence. Even though this did not end up an ESDP force, member states felt that, would it be necessary to act more forcefully and under an EU label, the political will to do so is now greater than it was six years ago (Interview, member state official, December 2007).

DRC and EU foreign policy

By 2006 DRC – and sub-Saharan Africa more generally – had become a priority area not just for ESDP but also for EU foreign policy. The African Great Lakes region (Burundi, DRC, Kenya, Rwanda, Tanzania and Uganda) had been troubled by civil wars, inter-state conflict and problematic democratic transitions; DRC in particular has been defined by political instability and two destructive wars. The war of 1996–97 led to the removal of President Mobutu and brought Laurent Kabila to power. The war of 1998–2003 pitted Kabila against former backers Rwanda and Uganda, and developed into what became known as the

'First African War' – causing an estimated 3.3 million casualties between 1998 and 2002 (*Observer*, 2004). The 1999 Lusaka Accord, a ceasefire agreement, evolved into a political and military stalemate. Following the assassination of Laurent Kabila in 2001, the Pretoria agreement signed in December 2002 engaged the DRC in a transition process that was to unify the national territory, establish a national army and basic security, and prepare national, democratic elections. The United Nations Mission in the Democratic Republic of the Congo (MONUC) was established in 1999 to facilitate the implementation of the Lusaka Accord and the subsequent transition process. Troop strength in light of increasing violence was augmented from 5,000 troops in 2003 to its current size of 17,000 military personnel (MONUC, 2008). MONUC thus developed into the largest and most expensive mission in the UN Department of Peace Keeping Operations (DPKO) with a budget exceeding one billion dollars. MONUC is mainly based in the east of the country, where the situation is the most volatile.

Creating a common foreign policy towards DRC has been a challenge for the EU. No foreign policy existed prior to the appointment of a EUSR for the Great Lakes region, Aldo Ajello, in 1996 (Grevi, 2007), mainly because EU member states differed over their approach towards the crises in the region, which made coordinating positions difficult. Whereas France and Belgium maintained a close interest in DRC, they also differed from other key countries such as the UK in their strategy to bring stability to the East of the country, where Rwanda and Uganda waged a proxy war. With respect to development and humanitarian cooperation, the then-EC had suspended cooperation with DRC in 1992 as a consequence of the high degree of corruption and the lack of progress in the democratization process. Cooperation was restarted in 2002 under the Cotonou Agreement; since then, the EU and its member states have turned into the most important donor to DRC. The elaboration and adoption of the Joint Africa–EU strategy in December 2007 means that European security policies have become increasingly embedded in a broader European political and economic framework of cooperation. Individual member states, including Britain and France, adopting Africa as a priority area means that political engagement now involves both a broader European in addition to national policy frameworks, and that these frameworks are, at least in principle, mutually reinforcing.

Besides their military and financial commitments through the UN, therefore, EU member states as well as the EU are independent actors in the transition process in DRC. Since 2003, international support for political aspects of the transition process has been led by the International

Committee to Assist the Transition (CIAT), where the EU is also represented through the Presidency and the Commission. From the start, the Congolese peace process witnessed several crises, including deteriorating security in Ituri in 2003, which led to the ESDP Operation Artemis, which was initiated and for the most part also staffed by, France. Although limited in scope, Artemis was important as it not only demonstrated that the EU was investing in the support of the transition process and that the EU could deploy military troops 4,000 miles away from Brussels – it also saved the UN's credibility in the peace process because it allowed MONUC breathing space to reinforce its presence on the ground. It has since been argued that the experience of Operation Artemis not only simulated the battle-group concept but also influenced thinking about military ESDP missions more broadly – and especially the role of ESDP missions deployed in hybrid frameworks alongside forces in other organizations (Gowan, 2007). Aside from Operation Artemis, by 2006 the EU had also launched two civilian crisis management operations: EUPOL Kinshasa provides advice and assistance for the training of police, whereas EUSEC RD Congo provides assistance and advice to Congolese authorities on security sector reform.

As far as the ESDP operation EUFOR RD Congo was concerned, this was about EU–UN cooperation and implementing 'effective multilateralism' more so than a debate over the appropriateness of an ESDP operation in this particular geographic region. After all, the 2003 Operation Artemis had established the EU as a military actor in DRC. This shows that the debate and political concerns to do with deploying ESDP operations had evolved considerably since the policy's early days in the Balkans. Both ESDP operations, Artemis and EUFOR RD Congo, were conducted in support of MONUC. This illustrates once more that the debate over European crisis management conducted in an ESDP framework had now shifted away from launching missions itself to interaction and coordination with the UN.

Launching EUFOR RD Congo

EUFOR RD Congo was an autonomous military operation that took place as a response to a UN request in December 2005, when the UN invited the EU to consider the possibility of deploying a military force to DRC to assist MONUC during the election process in summer 2006. EUFOR RD Congo was to be a deterrent force, serving as a backup for MONUC. The request, formulated by under Secretary-General Guehenno was not surprising given that the EU but also its member states have been actively involved in the support of the transition process in the Great Lakes region, and given that the EU had launched ESDP Operation Artemis in 2003. In light of the background of previous EU and ESDP engagements in DRC, EUFOR RD Congo was considered a logical prolongation of EU commitments both by the EU and the UN. Still, internal debates took place within individual member states about the benefit of such an operation, the rationale for it, but also over which member states would contribute to the force. This suggests that the case of EUFOR RD Congo is not as straightforward a case of Europeanized crisis management as would be assumed, given the density of EU foreign and security policy activities in DRC. The question over who would lead the mission arose because France argued that it had already taken the lead of Artemis; London pointed to its engagement in Afghanistan and Iraq; and Germany faced domestic pressure not to intervene in Africa. There was also concern in Berlin over being 'instrumentalized by Paris, which was pushing Germany into Africa' (cited in Gegout, 2007: 7) – although Germany did agree to take leadership of the mission in the end. From the perspective of Paris, it was Berlin's turn to lead a mission, given that Artemis had been French-led and Althea British-led. Once Berlin agreed to lead the mission, France emphasized that the mission was an example of European unity (see Gegout, 2007).

Following the UN's request, the EU Council approved an option paper in March 2006 expressing possible EU support to MONUC and decided to launch the military planning process. The Council also took note of the disposition of an Operations Headquarters (OHQ) in Potsdam for the planning and command of the operation. A few days later, the Finnish EU presidency confirmed the principles of the EU military support to MONUC. On 25 April 2006, the UN Security Council adopted unanimously Resolution 1671 that authorized the EU to deploy forces in DRC to support MONUC during the election process. EUFOR RD Congo was deployed under Chapter VII and was charged with the following tasks: 'to support MONUC to stabilize a situation, in case MONUC faces serious difficulties in fulfilling its mandate [. . .], to contribute to the protection of civilians under imminent threat of physical violence in the areas of its deployment [. . .], to contribute to airport protection in Kinshasa, to ensure the security and freedom of movement of the personnel as well as the protection of the installations of EUFOR RD Congo, to execute operations of limited character in order to extract individuals in danger' (United Nations Security Council, 2006).

Two days later, on 27 April 2006, the EU Council adopted the Joint Action, which forms the legal basis of the operation. Lieutenant-General Karlheinz Viereck (Germany) was appointed EU Operation Commander, with the EU Operational Headquarter to be located at the Armed Forces Operations Command in Potsdam, Germany. Major-General Christian Damay (France) was appointed EU Force Commander (FCdr), to be stationed in the Force Headquarters (FHQ) in Kinshasa, DR Congo (Council of the European Union, 27 April 2006). The Joint Action underlined that the PSC, under the responsibility of the Council of the EU, would exercise political control and strategic direction of EUFOR RD Congo. Solana, assisted by the EU Special Representative and in close cooperation with the EU Presidency, was to act as 'primary point of contact' with the UN, the authorities of DRC, neighbouring countries and other relevant actors. On 23 May the PSC approved the Operation Plan and the Rules of Engagement, which were further discussed and approved by the Council of Ministers on 29 May. The EU Operation Commander was to cooperate, in close coordination with the HR/SG, with the DKPO and MONUC. These arrangements had been finalized by an exchange of letters between Javier Solana and the UN Secretary-General Kofi Annan at the end of July 2006 (see Major, 2008).

Following German parliamentary approval for troop deployment on 12 June 2006, the EU Council adopted the decision to launch the operation. Accordingly, EUFOR RD Congo included the deployment of an advance element to Kinshasa of *c.* 450–500 military personnel and the availability of a battalion size 'on-call' force over the horizon outside the country, in Gabon, ready to be quickly deployed upon decision by the EU. The biggest contributors were France (1,090 troops) and Germany (780). The rapid reaction force within EUFOR was supplied by Spain (130), while a Polish military police company was in charge of protecting the EUFOR headquarters and base at N'Dolo airport. Special forces provided by France, Sweden and Portugal further strengthened EUFOR's capabilities. French and German forces, by contrast, had more conventional duties including patrols, contacts with the civilian population, and support tasks.

As for its geographical scope, EUFOR RD Congo focused on Kinshasa, but was allowed to intervene, if needed, in the whole area of DRC. However, there were different terms of geographical scope for the different units within EUFOR as the mandate agreed by the German Parliament limited the deployment of German troops to the area of Kinshasa. EUFOR RD Congo was deployed for a period of 4 months, from 30 July–30 November 2006, starting with the first round of the presidential and parliamentary elections. Overall, including pre deployment and withdrawal phases, EUFOR was present in DRC for about 6 months – and remained in the country until mid-December, and therefore slightly after the mandate (see Major, 2008). The presidential and parliament elections in DR Congo took place simultaneously. The most promising candidates were outgoing president Joseph Kabila, son of murdered former president Kabila, and vice-president Jean Pierre Bemba. As the first round of the presidential elections on 30 July 2006 did not see one candidate reaching the necessary 50 per cent of the votes to win, a second round took place 29 October 2006. As a result, the Congolese Supreme Court of Justice declared Joseph Kabila president of DRC with 58,05 per cent of the votes and rejected the complaint filed by Bemba. Kabila was invested president on 6 December 2006.

With the exception of some limited actions mainly for presence missions, EUFOR's activities concentrated in Kinshasa. Led in close cooperation with MONUC as well as EUPOL Kinshasa, these activities aimed to assure the visibility and credibility of EUFOR in order to dissuade potential attacks on the electoral process and to reassure the population. Overall, the operation went smoothly and did not face serious military conflict. Two incidents nevertheless required EUFOR to take action: in August, after the announcement of the results of the first elections round, and in October around the second round of the elections. The incidents with the greatest potential for destabilization occurred 20–2 August 2006. On 21 and 22 August, following the demand from MONUC, EUFOR intervened in cooperation with MONUC, when violent confrontations followed the announcement of the results of the first round of the presidential elections. The main intervention took place when vice-president and presidential candidate's Jean Pierre Bemba's HQ came under attack from elements of the Presidential guards, usually assigned to president Kabila while Bemba was receiving members of CIAT, including the ambassadors of the five permanent members of the UN Security Council. The concerted intervention of two companies of MONUC and one from EUFOR managed to separate the conflict parties and brought the CIAT representatives to safety. By intervening timely and cooperating efficiently with MONUC, EUFOR was able to demonstrate its force, but also its neutrality, both of which had been questioned by the local population beforehand, with demonstrations against EUFOR taking place (*Die Welt*, 2006). Overall, the intervention of EUFOR alongside MONUC forces was considered decisive for containing the violence. The objective of EUFOR RD Congo – securing the election process in Kinshasa – has been reached. Moreover, EUFOR did not suffer casualties. Except for the events of 20–2 August 2006, it has not been involved in serious military exchange.

During the operation EUFOR was considered a success by both the EU and the military. According to Solana, EUFOR RD Congo was 'a success, both in the way it has been conducted and in its contribution to the overall conclusion of the transition in DRC' (United Nations Security Council, 2007). During the August incidents, the only major incident that often serves as criteria for assessment, EUFOR was able to transform into a military deterrent force. It demonstrated rapid deployment capacity, including the reinforcements brought in swiftly from Gabon on a number of occasions. Overall, EUFOR, in close cooperation with MONUC, was thus decisive in limiting the number of incidents and in containing the potential spread of violence at particularly sensitive moments in the election process. Other international observers were generally more cautious about the success of EUFOR RD Congo. The International Crisis Group (2006: 4) in particular claimed that 'neither the MONUC nor EU troops in Kinshasa acted quickly enough to prevent the August violence from escalating'. Moreover, while recognizing that EUFOR fulfilled its mandate in terms of assuring the smooth running of the elections, they pointed out that EUFOR would not have been able to affront bigger military challenges and criticized that the limited mandate also affected the deterrent character of the mission. These comments echo criticism voiced prior to the operation of EUFOR RD Congo not being much more than 'a cosmetic operation' (Haine and Giegerich, 2006) rather than one designed to make a difference as far as root causes of the conflict were concerned (Gegout, 2007).

The question of maintaining the force, even on a smaller scale, was raised several times by the members of several fact-finding missions to Kinshasa, including the European Parliament. The question was particularly relevant given outbreaks of violence in the capital during the month of November and growing tensions between President Joseph Kabila and his main rival Jean-Pierre Bemba. France and Belgium in particular would have preferred to extend the operation. Although European authorities in the field agreed that the timing of the withdrawal process was unfortunate, Germany supported a departure in time with the four-months mandate and each unit withdrew at its own pace. The last to leave were the French at the end of December 2006 and the beginning of January 2007. This again shows that the willingness to engage in the region beyond the narrow confines of the original EUFOR RD Congo mandate on the part of member states was rather slim.

From 'European' to 'Europeanized' crisis management?

Contrasting the experiences in 2001 with those in 2006 reveals important developments in CFSP and ESDP that point towards increasing

'Europeanized' – in the sense of missions carrying a EU label – crisis management. The geographic scope of ESDP had expanded beyond the Balkans and sub-Saharan Africa to include the Middle East, Asia and the Caucasus; and European foreign and security institutions, most of all the Political and Security Committee (PSC) had become increasingly important. These institutions, together with a growing ESDP agenda that increasingly focused on EU–UN cooperation in the pursuit of 'effective multilateralism' reflects increasing pressure on member states' participation and active consent to ESDP operations. Showing an EU flag in crisis management beyond missions that had been planned ahead – such as EUFOR RD Congo or Operation CONCORDIA in FYROM – remain contested, however. As a result, European contributions in Lebanon as well as in Afghanistan did not carry an EU label, with one key difference between the operations in Afghanistan and Lebanon being that in the case of Lebanon, EU member states shaped the agenda to a much larger extent than they had in the case of Afghanistan.

3
Britain: Balancing European and Transatlantic Commitments

Introduction: Britain and European foreign and security policy

On account of strong transatlantic ties as well as a historically ambivalent relationship to Europe, Britain was the most sceptical – but also, given the size and strength of its military, an essential – member state when it came to the creation of a EU security and defence policy. The Premiership of Tony Blair, and his relenting on the question of an EU defence policy outside NATO structures, therefore not only rang in a sea-change in British foreign policy but also made possible the creation and eventual deployment of military crisis management tools under ESDP. Scepticism on substantial parts of the British policy establishment as well as public opinion on the prospect of an 'EU army' and a concurrent weakening of NATO, however, meant that ESDP was not communicated to the British public (Howorth, 2005). The preparation of the first ESDP operation was closely aligned with the US and NATO in order to ensure close transatlantic relations. And, the British position with respect to the evolving utility of ESDP in military crisis management remained careful – and pragmatic even in the absence of strong transatlantic objections to ESDP. Whereas London valued ESDP as a civilian and military crisis management instrument as part of a comprehensive approach to crisis management and SSR, after the events of St Malo, London did not push for a greater involvement or a greater scope for military crisis management.

2001: FYROM and Afghanistan

British decisions towards the crisis in FYROM, particularly those concerning the political negotiation of the crisis, show some evidence of

Europeanization. The UK actively supported the negotiation efforts of Javier Solana and thus the establishment of the EU CFSP as a political actor in the negotiation of a regional crisis. With respect to the involvement of NATO, however, British policy decisions were determined by alliance politics because the appropriate military tools were located in NATO and on account of the trust enjoyed by NATO in FYROM among both parties to the conflict. As for the ESDP takeover of the NATO operation, evidence of Europeanization is weak. While there was no objection in principle to an eventual ESDP takeover of the NATO operation, decisions over the operation's timing were determined by alliance politics considerations. These included US reactions towards ESDP and relations with the incoming Bush administration in addition to delays in the conclusion of the Berlin Plus agreements resulting from Turkish reservations about EU use of NATO assets. Domestic politics played a role as well, less so on account of the June 2001 elections but because of negative public opinion of the EU and ESDP in particular that were in direct conflict with Blair's professed goals of giving the UK leadership in Europe and of pushing for a stronger and more united EU foreign policy and policy capabilities.

In Afghanistan, Britain's foreign policy decisions were motivated above all by the UK's close ties with the US. Tony Blair in particular sought to not only demonstrate solidarity with the US but also to use his influence to shape US policy in Afghanistan towards making use of multilateral institutions and to coordinate the contributions of other EU member states. This use of the EU platform was met with criticism from other member states, including the then EU Presidency, Belgium. While the first point (transatlantic ties) demonstrates the validity of the alliance politics framework, the second (attempts to shape an EU response and to influence other EU member states using the EU platform) point towards some evidence of Europeanization understood as policy projection, even if, importantly, this did not result in a coordinated EU military action either as part of OEF or ISAF. When it came to the political and economic reconstruction of Afghanistan, the UK supported the EU pillar in the country's reconstruction as well as the appointment of a EUSR in Afghanistan. But, significant bilateral developmental cooperation with Afghanistan as well as the central coordinating role played by the UN also suggests that in the eyes of London, the EU was one of a number, and not necessarily the most important, political institution to tackle the reconstruction of Afghanistan. This demonstrates that national rather than European commitments were of high salience.

FYROM and the support for the EU CFSP in the political negotiations

Upon the outbreak of the crisis in March 2001, the UK was concerned first and foremost with applying the main lesson learnt from Kosovo: to act rapidly to prevent the outbreak of full-scale violence that could destabilize the Balkan region. This is illustrated by a statement of the Select Committee on Foreign Affairs in the House of Commons, which read that:

> Macedonia has been a model in the region of a multiethnic and democratic government, which has not so far been the subject of widespread ethnic violence. If Macedonia should disintegrate into another Kosovo, Bosnia or Croatia, it would be a massive reverse for the United Nations, the EU and NATO. We recommend that the British government take the most urgent steps to galvanize the international community into giving both the UN and NATO a clear remit to bring the situation in Macedonia under control and to counter Albanian extremist violence against Macedonia. (House of Commons, 27 March 2001: 2)

With respect to the Foreign Office, Foreign Secretary Robin Cook pledged full support for the Macedonian government, insisting that there was no prospect of the redrawing of borders towards a greater Albania (Press Association, 20 March 2001), and urged both ethnic Albanian opposition parties to attend the signing of Macedonia's Stabilization and Association Agreement with the EU (*Financial Times*, 6 April 2001). Importantly, the UK embassy in Skopje played a key role in the initial management of the crisis as it was the main diplomatic mission among the EU member states in FYROM. Sweden, which held the EU presidency in the first half of 2001, did not maintain diplomatic representation in FYROM and the British embassy assumed its role (Piana, 2002). Then-UK ambassador Mark Dickinson thus took on a key position by encouraging negotiations and setting up meetings with Macedonian officials for Solana. On a very practical level, then, the UK embassy supported Solana's role in the negotiation of the crisis starting in mid-March, when Solana first visited Skopje (Interview with UK official, 29 June 2006): a demonstration that the UK supported the proactive role taken by Javier Solana (and Chris Patten) in the crisis.

With respect to the broader geopolitical picture, there was agreement among the UK government that a united stance on the part of the international community was important, including having Russia on board (Interview with UK official, 29 June 2006). This included meetings with the Contact Group in order to coordinate the broader response as well as common statements with the US. The EU and the US agreed to coordinate their efforts to promote a political solution to the crisis, as Bush confirmed at the US–EU Gothenburg summit (Europe Report, 16 June 2001). The role of Prime Minister Blair in the negotiation of this crisis was not as active or visible as it was during the Kosovo war. However, bilateral coordination between Prime Minister Blair and President Bush show that US involvement in regional security impacted British policy choices with respect to the handling of the crisis in FYROM. The UK also used its position as a permanent member of the UN Security Council, together with France, to submit a resolution on the crisis asking the international community to pledge support for FYROM and for strengthening the current mandate of NATO forces stationed in Kosovo (Agence France Presse, 20 March 2001). Despite the key role played by the British government in addressing the crisis, there were concerns within the UK government that London was not doing enough to stop the violence: as the crisis intensified in mid-June, Prime Minister Blair made efforts to coordinate policy action bilaterally with French President Chirac and US President George Bush after shadow foreign secretary Francis Maude said that Britain must be 'far more active in helping suppress those forces still willing to use violence to achieve their ends' in FYROM and Kosovo (Press Association, 29 June 2001).

The broad goals in the crisis in FYROM – preventing the outbreak of large-scale violence and a speedy resolution of the crisis – were thus shared among the different branches of government. This was irrespective of changes in personnel following the June 2001 election when Robin Cook was replaced by Jack Straw as Foreign Secretary. To underline the continuity of the Foreign Office's preference with respect to FYROM following the June elections, Jack Straw's visit to Skopje following the General Affairs Council in Luxembourg on 25 June, was for the purpose of underlining 'along with other European leaders [. . .] the Government's commitment to the search for political stability' (Downing Street Press Briefing, 25 June 2001).

Europeanization vs. alliance politics

The UK supported Javier Solana and the CFSP in the political negotiations of the crisis and assumed a lead role in this area due to its privileged position on the ground. This confirms the Europeanization hypothesis in so far as the salience of the European agenda is concerned. British actions in support of the EU CFSP in the political solution of the crisis in FYROM show that the British goal of a 'more effective joint EU voice and capability' under the Blair premiership took shape (Riddell, 2005: 376) and reinforce Blair's stated aim of a more capable European foreign and security policy (Blair, 21 November 2001) with Britain as a leader.

The key role played by the UK ambassador in the early part of the crisis equally indicates national projection: through the subsequent appointment of Mark Dickinson as special representative to FYROM, the UK increased its profile in the management of the crisis in the European arena. This underlines that Europeanization understood as a policy preference and national projection both apply and are not easily separable empirically. A success for the EU CFSP and Javier Solana as well as a peaceful outcome of the peace negotiations meant a success both for the EU as well as the UK – and confirms the (instrumental) notion that 'Britain continues to pursue the "politics of scale", collaborating at the EU level for the sake of greater effectiveness in the pursuit of shared and common international goals' (Smith 2006: 169). Nevertheless, the support for the EU CFSP as an institutional venue and British efforts at the establishment of its credibility run counter to arguments of the avoidance of a full commitment to European cooperation (Wallace 2005: 57), even if the tensions in British foreign policy as apply to Britain's traditional attachment to NATO and the evolving CFSP and ESDP (Hill, 1996: 85) can be clearly observed in the handover to ESDP as well as in London's policy towards the war in Afghanistan.

There is also some evidence of alliance politics in the negotiation of the crisis – that of preference given to NATO for utilitarian reasons. NATO was considered an appropriate resource for reasons of prior involvement in the region, and because NATO was the preferred option for the host country, FYROM, where NATO enjoyed a high level of trust among the political elite as well as the Albanian guerrillas (Interview with EU official, 21 June 2005). By contrast, the EU CFSP had yet to establish itself as a trusted negotiator and there were practical concerns that made the presence of NATO indispensable, both in the political and military part of the negotiation of the crisis. Any EU effort, and potential military operation undertaken under ESDP had to succeed – and the biggest concern on the part of the British Foreign Office was thus over buying time to resolve the crisis (Interview with UK official, 29 June 2006) rather than the introduction of new policy instruments. This supports the conclusion that the emphasis on a NATO presence arose out of utilitarian considerations rather than out of a fundamental transatlantic preference.

Participation in NATO Operation Essential Harvest

With respect to the UK's participation in and support for the NATO Operations in FYROM there was broad consensus among the different branches of the British government that NATO should assume a security function in post-crisis FYROM and that the UK should actively participate in this operation. Blair was keen for the UK to take a military lead in this operation, emphasizing that 'the history of our engagement in the Balkans had taught us that it was better to make preparations sooner and to stabilize the situation rather than wait and let the situation deteriorate. That was why British troops were in Macedonia. It was a precisely defined operation. Our aim was to help achieve a political settlement there' (Government Press Briefing, 28 August 2001).

In the eyes of London NATO involvement was not to extend to military commitments during the crisis but should involve only the post-settlement stage; London initially had no plans to reinforce its 5,500 strong KFOR contingent in support of stability in the region, which partly reflected domestic concerns over British military commitments elsewhere, such as Sierra Leone (Press Association, 20 March 2001). However, the UK supported NATO as a central actor in the negotiations and as a guarantor of the peace after the signing of the Ohrid Agreement, which suggests an overall priority given to the involvement of NATO in FYROM.

Military commitments in FYROM also reinforced London's claim to be the lead nation in security discussions and to set an example for the rest of Europe (*Financial Times*, 18 August 2001). Upon the launch of Operation Essential Harvest, General Barney White-Spunner commanded the pre-deployment force of Operation Essential Harvest and Britain provided the headquarters and up to 1,800 troops of the 3,500 strong Operation Essential Harvest, although the command of the operation was given to Danish General Lange (NATO, 17 August 2001). The deployment also played to British strengths – of providing the initial deployments – and Britain was also one of the few NATO countries able to supply an operational headquarters (*Financial Times*, 18 August 2001).

But the initial restriction of the operation to 90 days and Whitehall's determination to have a clear exit strategy for British troops (*Guardian*, 18 August 2001) did not turn out to be realistic, even if the UK did not aim to maintain its lead status among NATO and EU members in this particular NATO operation due to commitments elsewhere. Although the UK took a lead role among NATO member states in the initial stages of the management of the crisis and the preparation and participation in the NATO operations, there were some domestic concerns over the UK's growing military commitments elsewhere – an issue that became increasingly urgent after the attacks of 11 September and the UK's growing military commitments in the war on terror.

Europeanization vs. alliance politics

With respect to NATO and its engagements in the Balkans in general and FYROM in particular, the continued engagement of the US in the region – both as part of NATO and to add political weight unilaterally – was deemed of vital importance across the spectrum of UK foreign policy actors. This demonstrates the explanatory potential of the alliance politics framework. The importance of keeping the US involved in European security concerns, particularly as they relate to the Balkans was of particular concern as the US was reluctant to commit troops to FYROM to begin with (*Financial Times*, 14 June 2001; Interview with EU official, 11 September 2006). The Select Committee on Foreign Affairs in the House of Commons accordingly noted that 'a greater danger for the Balkan states would lie in US political disengagement from the region, followed by a military withdrawal' (House of Commons, 18 December 2001: 18). While it was acknowledged that there was little prospect of such a disengagement in the short term the Committee went on to warn that

> the eyes of the United States are presently turned elsewhere, and history serves as a reminder of the folly of relaxing vigilance over the Balkans. We recommend that [...] the Government act to avoid any loss of momentum for reconstruction in the Balkans, by working for the continued full involvement and active participation of the United States in the Balkans. (House of Commons, 18 December 2001: 18)

In addition to the goal of keeping the US involved in European affairs, there also remained a clear transatlantic preference on the part of the British policy establishment: although the early 1990s 'saw the acceptance in the British defence establishment that they were becoming part of an EU defence structure [...] this was not seen in exclusive terms, and priority was still given in many respects to NATO as the keystone of Britain's contribution to collective defence in such places as the former Yugoslavia' (Smith, 2006: 168). For Blair in particular

> what we want is a situation where NATO is the basis and cornerstone of our defence, where by preference NATO where it wants to be engaged, in other words where the Americans want to come in on an operation, NATO is going to be the body that we use [...] And I think if we approached it in that way we preserve the strength of the

Transatlantic Alliance but we also give ourselves the option, where we want to, to make sure that Europe has its own capability. (Blair, 17 October 2003)

British participation in Operation Essential Harvest reflects the essence of this statement – despite considerations that point towards Europeanization in the decision to have the EU CFSP and eventually also ESDP to assume a political and military role, NATO remained a focal point in British policy-making.

The ESDP takeover from NATO

Although there was disagreement over the timing of the operation as well as over its effect on transatlantic relations within the British government, there were no fundamental objections on the part of the Foreign Office to the creation or application of ESDP instruments (Interview with UK official, 29 June 2006) – but there were differences among individual branches of British government. While the Foreign Office was in principle in favour of an ESDP operation, the Ministry of Defence regarded an early handover as hazardous (*Financial Times*, 4 March 2002). Together with Blair's shifting policy priorities with respect to NATO as well as Europe and Britain's global role after 11 September, moreover, this meant that decisions over the timing of the ESDP handover from NATO were contested within the British government. Concerns over timing for the UK arose both from ESDP not having been declared formally operational and from the absence of a formal agreement of NATO over the use of assets for an ESDP operation. With respect to declaring ESDP operational in 2001 (without having capabilities to carry out the full spectrum of Petersberg tasks), the 'UK tried hard to persuade its EU partners that premature statements were not only meaningless but potentially dangerous' (Howorth, 2003–04: 179). Blair in turn stated that 'once the EU–NATO links are in place, I am keen to see an ESDP operation in Macedonia, to show that Europe can play its part in bringing security and stability to this part of the continent' (Blair, 25 November 2002).

This affirms the argument that British concerns were over appropriate capabilities and principles, and that the British approach to ESDP was essentially one of caution. It also demonstrates that the takeover of ESDP was not objected to in principle: rather, 'the UK was determined that the first EU military operation should be a success; it was concerned therefore that all the right "bricks" should be in place before it was launched' (Interview with former UK official, 23 September 2006). The conclusion of the Berlin Plus agreement over the use of NATO assets came to be the UK's prerequisite for the first ESDP military operation in FYROM (*Financial Times*, 30 October 2002), even if the mission itself was small and devoid of substantive risk.

Europeanization vs. alliance politics

Despite hesitations over the timing of the first ESDP mission, the British policy stance with respect to an ESDP operation supports the Europeanization hypothesis. It does so with respect to a number of indicators, although these were not shared among all branches of the UK government.

The salience of the European agenda in the case of the first ESDP operation is illustrated by the fact that interest in using ESDP instruments arose early on during the crisis, despite practical hesitations in light of the fact that an ESDP mission would have to succeed both on account of the situation in FYROM as well as the success of the emerging policy (Interview with UK official, 29 June 2006). And, although the delay of the Berlin Plus agreement meant that ESDP could not be applied in FYROM after the Seville European Council, repeated efforts made particularly on the part of British diplomats to resolve the differences with Turkey (Howorth, 2006) in order to conclude the Berlin Plus agreements demonstrates that the UK was not only keen on arriving at a formal delineation of tasks between NATO and ESDP, but by extension also to be able to employ the military instruments located in ESDP in FYROM.

The indicator of policy adaptation, and of Britain giving up on traditionally-held policy objectives is demonstrated by the fact that the UK, once the Berlin Plus agreements had been concluded, gave up objections against the deployment of an ESDP mission. A foreign policy official from another member state put it more directly: 'well, after St Malo, they had to agree to an ESDP mission' (Interview with French official, 27 April 2006). Adaptation pressures from the EU-level are also evident from a leaked documents that show a split in opinion between the Ministry of Defence and the Foreign Office: whereas the Ministry of Defence argued that ESDP was not ready to undertake such a mission and endanger the lives of British troops, the office of Foreign Secretary Straw wrote on 17 January that 'if we do look like becoming isolated we would be better to accept an EU mission and shape it to our specifications. We would also need to consider whether the UK should contribute some forces to take part in this, first, ESDP mission. The political case for doing so would be strong' (cited in the *Guardian*, 4 March 2002).

In addition to adaptation pressures, preference among elites came to lean towards ESDP. This is illustrated by Foreign Secretary Straw's statement at the Select Committee on Foreign Affairs where he stated that 'Essential Harvest and the work that followed [...] had to be put together on a bilateral/multilateral basis, in a rather ad-hoc manner. The ESDP, with the very active support of NATO, would provide a better focus for all of this, and a better means of decision making. It also ensures that the burden of providing these forces did not always fall to two or three countries' – an indicator of the salience of the EU agenda, even if Straw simultaneously issued a word of caution in saying that despite Europe having to shoulder a greater burden in regional/Balkan security as a result of 11 September and the likely evolution of the role of forces under the ESDP, 'one of the reasons why the language of Laeken is likely to be careful is that we do not want to run before we have learned to walk in terms of the practical sides of the ESDP' (Straw, House of Commons, 5 December 2001: 23).

The timing of the ESDP handover in large part reflected British concerns over a negotiated agreement over the relationship between NATO and ESDP. As a result, one indicator of alliance politics, that of preference given to NATO out of transatlantic preference – and the necessity for a prior formalized agreement with NATO as part of this transatlantic preference – can be observed. With respect to NATO and ESDP, the European Union Committee stated unequivocally, that:

> there may be a temptation, if the political need for an operation arises, to conduct an EU-led mission for symbolic purposes before the EU is ready to do so. What is imperative is that the EU must not lead an operation before it has achieved the full range of capabilities necessary to conduct it or can rely on the assistance of NATO. (House of Lords, 29 January 2002: 86)

The decision-making processes in the actual handover from NATO to ESDP shows that objections to an ESDP operation arose not as a question of principle but as a question of timing and prior arrangements with the US. Considerations of US preference and the role of Britain in moderating between Europe and the US became increasingly important on account of the events of 11 September and caused a shift in Blair's policy priorities as a result – as is evident from British policies towards the war in Afghanistan, the subject of the next section.

Afghanistan: OEF and the war on terror

Prime Minister Blair occupies a central role in the formulation of British foreign policy in the war in Afghanistan – in large part on account of what has been referred to as a presidential style of decision-making (see Foley 2000, 2002, 2004). The conceptual literature on the role of the Prime Minister in British government, in particular the core executive model (see Heffernan, 2003) takes issue with the portrayal of a presidential approach while at the same time emphasizing the growing role of the individual leader. This literature speaks of 'prime ministerial dominance' (Heffernan, 2003: 350) or emphasizes 'the structurally advantageous position' of the prime minister in government (Smith, 1999: 77). Blair had sought to increase his influence in foreign policy prior to the events of 11 September and, following the attacks, appointed a personal representative for Afghanistan, a position held until December 2001 by Paul Bergne. Robert Cooper, the former Director of Asia in the Foreign Office assumed the post until mid-2002. The fact that Blair held only two meetings of his cabinet between 11 September and the first strikes as part of OEF on 7 October, neither of which contained debate (Kampfner, 2003: 129), reinforces the impression of Blair's strong hold over the formulation of foreign policy.

The close personal connection between Bush and Blair was a second important factor in shaping Blair's policy responses to the terrorist attacks and the war in Afghanistan. Foreign Secretary Straw consequently stated that the policy was 'set by President Bush and our Prime Minister in terms of the overall objectives of this military action' (Straw, House of Commons, 20 November 2001a). This also shows that the role and influence of the Foreign Office was less instrumental in determining policy outcomes even if the formulation of policy was developed with the support of the Foreign Office (Interview with EU official, 11 September 2006).

Prior to the attacks of 11 September, Blair's determination to play the traditional role of bridge between the US and the EU had been made difficult by the advent of the Bush administration in 2001, and European disagreement and discomfort at the policies of the incoming US administration (Whitman, 2004: 443). After the attacks of 11 September, the first instinct on the part of Blair was that the US should not feel isolated. In a conversation with Bush on 12 September, the two agreed to support from NATO and the UN for a legal and political basis for a military response. Blair thus supported the US while at the same time coordinating EU actions, as well as regional diplomacy with Afghanistan's neighbouring states: Blair called on Pakistan's leader on 18 September, for instance, and it was announced that Straw would visit Iran (see House of Commons, 12 June 2002a). In addition to the transatlantic priorities in British foreign policy, to members of the Foreign Office but also the Prime Minister the attacks of 11 September represented an opportunity to 'fix' Afghanistan, as the stabilization of the country had been a concern for the UK prior to the attacks on the United States (Interview with EU official, 11 September 2006). Through Britain's military participation in the war on terror and the close links with the US Blair was able to wield influence in the EU-15 (*Spectator*, 27 October 2001), although later events surrounding the Iraq war and Blair's unwavering support for the war in Iraq and US policies threw off the fine balance and accounted for a loss of influence in Europe and the collapse of the 'transatlantic bridge' (Wallace and Oliver, 2005; Riddell, 2003).

A European response was of importance to Blair, including agreeing on a common European line that included supporting the military campaign as long as it was restricted to Afghanistan; a collectively agreed upon 'post-Taliban scenario' with a lead role for the UN in post-war Afghanistan; and a settlement of the Israel–Palestine conflict. But, the 'Downing Street Dinner' also gave the impression that London had become the centre of European policy-making, and that Blair 'made virtually no concessions to Brussels along the lines of stepping aside to let Solana, Prodi or Verhofstadt present a truly common EU stance to Washington. Blair showed little sympathy for EU leaders of small states who complained of being cut out of decisions taken in mini-summits of the "big three" ' (Peterson, 2002: 7).

Domestically, Blair by and large had support for the military action in Afghanistan: a report issued by the Select Committee on Foreign Affairs in June 2002 explicitly approved Blair's decision to support the US and to take a lead role in coordinating allies' military contributions (House of Commons, 12 June 2002a). Still, cracks appeared with some MPs voicing concerns about the nature and frequency of the bombing campaign – some Labour MPs expressed concerns over the length of the bombing while the Liberal Democrat front bench was divided between foreign affairs spokesman Menzies Campbell who backed the government's approach and Jenny Tonge, shadowing international development, who joined the call by aid agencies to pause military actions (*The Times*, 18 October). Differences between Blair and other MPs also arose with respect to the geographic expansion of the war against terrorism to include countries beyond Afghanistan (Kampfner, 2003: 102), foreshadowing the domestic and international divisions over Iraq.

Europeanization vs. alliance politics

Blair sought to shape EU policy in response to the attacks on 11 September in line with his commitment to act as a bridge between the US and Europe. A number of initiatives and policy positions were subsequently taken by the UK that support the Europeanization hypothesis. This did not only apply to the Prime Minister, however: the Committee on Foreign Affairs noted that the immediate response to the 11 September attacks 'was impressive, but progress became bogged down in the following months [. . .] nonetheless, the habits of intergovernmental cooperation created through the EU proved valuable in this crisis' (House of Commons, 12 June 2002a: 59). This in turn supports the argument that the EU was regarded as a useful platform. But, as in France and Germany, the EU CFSP was not the only platform considered and the three states, rather than predominately acting through the institution, acted 'in concert with EU institutions, as opposed to working at cross purposes' (Peterson, 2002: 9).

Attempts at projecting national policy preferences on to the EU were evident from a number of actions. At the 8 October General Affairs Council, Britain took the lead in organizing military contributions and welcomed pledges from France, Italy, Germany and Spain. And, Britain, together with the countries named above insisted on the phrasing that the EU was 'in total solidarity' with the US, and on spelling out the post-Taliban future of Afghanistan in the EU document (*Independent*, 18 October 2001). The suggestion and use of the EU to coordinate action suggests that the CFSP constituted an institutional platform through which to increase national clout. But the strict adherence to US solidarity also indicates that the European framework was also used to strengthen the UK's position vis-à-vis both its European allies as well as the US, rather than develop a joint response out of a reflective European preference. The first instinct was to turn to the US.

At the Laeken summit, Britain forced the EU to drop a drafted warning to the US not to extend its self-declared war on terrorism beyond Afghanistan, which had stated that 'approval of the international community must be sought prior to any geographical extension of those operations' (Agence France Presse, 15 December 2001). This is again an indication that the EU policy platform served to reinforce the UK position vis-à-vis the US rather than the EU acting as an adaptation influence or EU unity representing a normative goal.

The alliance politics framework provides a strong explanatory model for British decisions taken with regards to OEF and the war on terror. However, this does not refer solely to NATO as an institution: on the question of the role of NATO, or military alliances in general after 11 September, US Secretary of Defence Rumsfeld famously stated that 'the coalition must not define the mission' (Rumsfeld, 23 September 2001) indicating that the role of NATO in the war on terror was going to be negligent. And the fact that the US declined NATO and NATO Secretary-General George Robertson's offer of help raised the bar for NATO to prove that it was not redundant in the post-11 September world (Toje, 2003). Alliance politics in this case, therefore, refers to UK relations with the US and other participating allies in addition to that of the use and attitudes towards NATO as an institutional framework. The fact that NATO was not used did not render it unimportant in the view of the UK military establishment, however. Rather, 'in many ways NATO acts as a glue in military terms. The fact that we are used to working together, have common procedures, common doctrine, we know a lot of the people involved personally, means that even if we are operating [. . .] without NATO, NATO still acts as a very powerful binding mechanism to enable us to operate more effectively' (Major-General Milton, House of Commons, Committee on Defence, 7 November 2001: 24).

Several aspects of UK politics point towards alliance politics. British support for the invocation of NATO Article V demonstrates the recognition that the US in the first instance at least had the right to retaliate against the attacks on its territory and that NATO was the appropriate institution for legitimizing such decisions. This demonstrates that the initial reaction from the UK government was not just solidarity with the US, but also to revert to NATO as a multilateral forum for a political and military response to the attacks. This is illustrated by the fact that Defence Minister Hoon was sent to NATO immediately following the attacks on 11 September (Kampfner 2003: 115), which demonstrates the centrality of NATO in policy considerations. More than just supporting the invocation of Article V, however, Britain played an 'active role' in promoting the NATO decision to invoke Article V, and 'pushed forward the deployment of joint NATO assets' and the decision that 'NATO AWACS were sent to patrol US airspace on 9 October in an operation code names "Eagle Assist"' (House of Commons, 12 June 2002a: 48). The decision to invoke Article V and the investment on the part of Blair and Straw were also positively noted and supported in the House of Commons (House of Commons, 12 June 2002a), supporting the conclusion that this policy priority was shared among other branches of the government as well.

Blair's alignment with the US in order to influence US political decisions also is a strong indicator of alliance politics. The first consideration on the part of the UK was to cooperate and show solidarity with the US although this was not necessarily in direct competition with European commitments or institutions: with regards to Britain's role in OEF and the broader war on terror close cooperation on military and intelligence matters with Washington complemented rather than competed with closer links with EU institutions on other matters (*The Times*, 19 October 2001). A report issued by the Select Committee on Foreign Affairs on British–US Relations noted that 'the UK's prompt actions immediately after the events of 11 September were regarded by the Americans not only as significant symbolic acts of solidarity, but also as very concrete expressions of the special relationship. The very spontaneity of the reaction illustrated perfectly the instinctive nature of the relationship' (House of Commons, 12 June 2002a: 31). Moreover, the strong transatlantic orientation in British foreign policy in this case shows that alliance politics was the primary political concern of the UK government in response to the attacks of 11 September, and that other policy aims were subordinated to that objective.

The reconstruction of Afghanistan

The UK did not occupy a leadership position in Afghanistan's reconstruction to the same extent that it did in the coordination of military contributions for ISAF and OEF. This was because the task of reconstruction was placed in the hands of the UN, involved more than one national and institutional actor,[1] and because coherence and support for the UN effort represented a policy objective for the UK. In addition, the involvement of a number of actors in the reconstruction effort as well as the fact that another EU member state, Germany, hosted the Bonn Conference, meant that visibility for the UK was correspondingly lower. The European agenda did not have a substantive profile in UK policy coordination although Britain did support the appointment of an EUSR and therefore a political role for the EU in the reconstruction of Afghanistan. In addition, the UK took a national lead in the area of drug eradication, further raising its national profile in one aspect of Afghanistan's reconstruction and coordinating on a bilateral basis with the country taking the lead in police reform, Germany.

With respect to the reconstruction of Afghanistan, the relevant branches of government active in this policy field were the Foreign Office as well as the Department for International Development (DFID) headed by Clare Short, the UK Secretary of State for International Development (1997–2003), particularly in the area of providing humanitarian assistance to Afghanistan. No. 10 was also active and involved (Interview with EU official, 11 September 2006), with Blair sending an observation delegation to the Bonn talks. With respect to Blair's preferences on the war and the reconstruction of Afghanistan, Blair preferred to finish the war quickly and was dubious about Brahimi's 'light footprint' approach and 'would have preferred someone like Paddy Ashdown' who was more forceful (Interview with EU official, 11 September 2006). A report by the International Development Committee noted that 'Lakhdar Brahimi's request for a "light footprint" approach is connected to a recognition by the international community of the importance of Afghan involvement in setting policy and spending priorities' (House of Commons, 14 2003: 37). This demonstrates that the international constraints acting on the Prime Minister in the reconstruction of Afghanistan did not permit the same personal leadership style – or impact on policy decisions – as did the decisions on OEF and the war in Afghanistan.

The provision of humanitarian aid and the future shape of the Afghan interim administration were the two primary poles of international support for the reconstruction of Afghanistan, and the British government did not play an active but rather a supportive role in negotiating the post-Taliban interim administration for Afghanistan under UN auspices. But the UK was the first donor country to pledge assistance, even prior to the UN inter-agency donor alert and thus took the lead in the international aid effort in Afghanistan. DFID set aside £1 million to support the UN Secretary-General's Special Representative Lakdhar Brahimi and the Integrated Mission Task Force (IMTF) to consult the Afghan Diaspora (Short, House of Commons, 20 November 2001b).

The UK government did however establish an observer delegation to the Bonn negotiations led by Robert Cooper; and Blair sent Paul Bergne as his personal envoy to support the UN's lead role who in turn tried to move Northern Alliance members towards accepting concessions to form a post-Taliban government (House of Commons, 12 June 2002b). Foreign Minister Straw played an active role through 'a series of conversations' with Abdullah Abdullah, the Foreign Minister of the Northern Alliance, as well as the Russian and Iranian foreign ministers to ensure that members of delegations other than those of the Northern Alliance would be accommodated within the constitution (House of Commons, 12 June 2002a). Stephen Evans, finally, acted as the British Government's representative in Kabul, making contact with other members of the Northern Alliance 'to help meet the objective [...] of producing a broad-based multi-ethnic government' (Straw, House of Commons, 20 November 2001a: 6). His efforts were not integrated with those of UN Special Representative Brahimi on behalf of the UN and his tasks were thus more hands-on than that of the observer delegation to the Bonn talks: 'although it is important that UN Ambassadors like Mr Brahimi should have our full support, which they do [...] this was also provide them with a perspective from a bilateral relationship with one of the great parties involved in the military coalition which he may not get for himself' (Straw, House of Commons, 20 November 2001: 6). The UK, therefore, was keen to exert at least some influence on the UN decision-making process.

Europeanization vs. alliance politics

Given the UN lead in the reconstruction effort, neither the Europeanization or the alliance politics models convincingly explain British policy decisions in this case. Informal meetings of EU Development Ministers including Clare Short took place on 10 October and 8 November, and the UK contributed 19 per cent of the overall EU humanitarian aid commitment of €44 million in 2001 (House of Commons, 23 November 2001). At the same time, DFID was equally in contact with other governments through the Afghanistan support group of major donors, including the USA, Japan and European member states (House of Commons, 23 November 2001) – and, DFID saw the role of the EC in the release of funds to 'support infrastructure repair, de-mining, and local policing; humanitarian aid delivery; and administrative support to interim government' (DFID, 13 November 2001) rather than a useful political platform in the reconstruction of Afghanistan. While the EU constituted a useful platform to hold meetings on the release of foreign aid, and a mechanism and resource for the delivery of humanitarian aid and to lay the foundation of long-term reconstruction of Afghanistan, this did not involve CFSP instruments but referred to the first pillar and thus resources of the European Commission.

The UK did, however, support the German policy initiative to appoint a EU Special Representative both as a response to another member states' policy initiative and out of some value attached to giving the EU a political profile in the reconstruction of Afghanistan. This points towards evidence of policy adaptation, as London did agree to another member state's policy initiative even if there was no apparent UK preference in favour of such an appointment.

While the evidence of Europeanization is weak, neither is the alliance politics framework suited to explain British policy choices. To be sure, there were differences between the US and European member states in the question of Afghanistan's reconstruction that included the policy towards warlords (United States Institute for Peace, 2003) or the need for nation-building and to fight drugs where member states had pointed out to the US that there was a need to look at this sooner (Interview with Commission official, 26 July 2006). However, in light of the UN having taken the lead in coordinating reconstruction efforts, transatlantic relations were not used to initiate or harmonize policies towards the reconstruction of Afghanistan.

Participation in ISAF

British participation and military lead in ISAF show a continuation of the basic impulses and policy preferences that shaped British responses towards the attacks on 11 September and UK participation in OEF. They were, essentially, close coordination with the US, and a British leadership role in the construction of ISAF within the EU as well as with non-EU contributing forces. A coalition of the willing rather than a proper NATO (or EU, for that matter) force, the military planning under UK lead took place in close cooperation with the US.

As in the decision surrounding participation in OEF, Blair continued to have a strong preference on the formation and role of the UK in ISAF and maintained a high and public profile with respect to ISAF and Afghanistan both by agreeing to troop deployments and coordinating international (in particular European) contributions, but also through high profile visits to British troops in Afghanistan in the context of a mission to Bangladesh, India and Pakistan to defuse regional tensions (Agence France Presse, 8 January 2002). However, there were reservations on lengthy British military involvement in Afghanistan: in his evidence to the House of Commons, special envoy Bergne stressed that British forces should be succeeded as rapidly as possible by a multinational force given the history of Britain's relations with Afghanistan (House of Commons, 12 June 2002b).

Although some seventeen other countries also declared their willingness to participate in ISAF, Britain was very much in the lead. This was important to Blair as it demonstrated his willingness to show off the peace-keeping role of the military, even after 11 September (Kampfner 2003: 146). The British lead also resulted from the fact that the UK and Germany were the two European countries with the strongest level of interest and engagement in Afghanistan (Interview with EU official, 11 September 2006). To guard against accusations of overstretch – and out of consideration of Britain's history of military engagement in Afghanistan and the resulting legacy (House of Commons, 12 June 2002a) – it was agreed that leadership of the force would be handed over to Turkey the following April. The negotiations and deliberations on the construction of ISAF took place on a bilateral basis and in the UN Security Council. The EU, while not the locus of policy-making, was at least kept informed of policy developments (Interview with EU official, 11 September 2006).

With respect to ISAF and the reconstruction of Afghanistan, there were differences between the US and UK as well as within the UK government on the political and military decisions with respect to ISAF and its role in Afghanistan's peacekeeping and reconstruction. For instance, Clare Short complained that the US were not taking the aid situation seriously enough, and the Foreign Office and US State Department wanted to extend ISAF's remit beyond Kabul but were overruled by the Pentagon and Ministry of Defence, whereas Blair did not see this as essential, although desirable (Kampfner 2003: 146). Robert Cooper also tried to persuade the US to agree to a geographic extension of the mandate, and to think about involving NATO. On the question of an extension to the mandate beyond Kabul, the key for the UK was whether or not the US would back ISAF in case of crisis – with no affirmative response from the US, however, the UK did not proceed with this initiative (Interview with EU official, 11 September 2006). Domestically, there were some concerns and reservations over the need to establish Afghan consent to the British presence, the danger of 'mission creep' and the need for US support for the stabilization of the mission. Blair responded to these concerns that it was vital that Britain bolstered the political agreement for Afghanistan and that it was 'the country best placed to lead that force' (*Irish Times*, 20 December 2001), which illustrates that domestic reservations over the size and strength of ISAF did not impact policy decision-making.

The promise of 'limited deployment' of British troops under a three-month ISAF lead raised confusion and concerns domestically that the UK could get drawn into a more lengthy deployment. The opposition in particular wanted assurance that British troops would not be left in Afghanistan beyond their 90-day tour of duty, but with Turkey seeking assurances over the cost and guarantees from the US that their troops would be evacuated if unrest broke out in Kabul the change in lead nation status took an extra 90 days to take place (*Turkish Daily News*, 26 February 2002). With respect to the number of British troops deployed as part of ISAF, on 19 December 2001 Defence Secretary Geoff Hoon announced the dispatch of up to 1,500 British soldiers, the bulk of them paratroopers, to Kabul, with an advance party of 200 Marine commandoes flying in immediately to head the International Security Assistance Force (ISAF).

Europeanization vs. alliance politics

There is little evidence of Europeanization when it comes to British contributions to ISAF. Rather, the outright rejection of the 'EU force' indicates instead that the EU platform was not of salience in this particular policy area but rather considered inappropriate to begin with, and that the EU CFSP or ESDP did not represent a means through which to project any national preferences. On the contrary, the strong reaction on the part of the government as well as the domestic opposition suggests that in the case of ISAF, the idea of a coordinated 'EU force' invoked a direct threat to NATO and the UK's transatlantic credentials.

The issue of an 'EU force' flared up at the Laeken Summit in December 2001 when Belgian Foreign Minister Michel, in the view of the British press at least, presented 'the force as some sort of embryonic army' and SG/HR Solana stated that the force would be 'basically an EU force led by one country of the EU' (*The Times*, 15 December 2001). British ministers and spokesmen rebuffed these statements, with Jack Straw saying that 'there's no question of the EU having a defence force, still less being able to deploy one it doesn't have in Afghanistan', whereas Peter Hain, Foreign Office Minister, stated that the 'EU rapid reaction force is not even walking yet, let alone running and able to run an operation like that'. Downing Street issued a statement saying that ISAF was 'an UN-mandated international force which will have EU members. It will also have a range of other countries. Quite clearly it is not an EU force' (*The Times*, 15 December 2001).

The question of an EU-force was therefore also a topic of political tension and debate domestically. Charges of a political fix arose in early 2002, when Defence Secretary Geoffrey Hoon distanced himself from the Canadian charges that the EU had deliberately limited ISAF to European units (United Press International, 10 January 2002). British Conservative Party defence spokesman Bernard Jenkins repeated and expanded on these accusations saying that they were an embryonic Euro-army in all but name (*The Times*, 9 January 2002). This shows that a significant part of the policy elite were concerned not just over the prospect of an 'EU-ization' of ISAF but opposed to ESDP in general – and confirms the strong transatlantic orientation of much of British foreign policy.

There is considerable evidence of alliance politics, and several policy decisions taken by the UK support this conclusion. Britain stated early on that it would only agree to lead ISAF if the force came under overall US command, with MOD sources cited as saying that it would be impractical and risky to run two operations, the peace-keeping and the offensive missions, separately (*The Times*, 15 December 2001). This shows that from a military planning standpoint, the UK – the MOD in particular – was leaning towards an alliance politics framework for ISAF. More fundamentally, the 'special relationship' and the strong value placed on the UK's close ties to the US as a result determined much of the UK's policy response in this case. In conjunction with the UK lead in coordinating

European contributions to OEF, a transatlantic emphasis in the construction of ISAF was a logical corollary to the UK's goal that the US should not feel isolated following the attack of 11 September, but that influence on US policies was best achieved through partnership rather than competition.

2006: Lebanon and DRC

Although British views on the utility and purpose of ESDP had evolved considerably since the policy's early days in FYROM, decision-making in Lebanon and DRC shows limited evidence of Europeanization when it comes to the application of CFSP and ESDP instruments. Essentially, the UK's position on ESDP had developed to the extent that London was happy to lend political support to ESDP operations, including military missions in sub-Saharan Africa. Investment in ESDP did not extend, however, to the contribution of resources to EUFOR RD Congo. Politically as well, British policies continued to be determined by transatlantic ties, specifically in areas where British military forces were deployed, including Iraq and Afghanistan, or where there was a strong interest on the part of the US.

Unsurprisingly, therefore, during the war in Lebanon decision-making with respect to getting to a ceasefire was determined by the alignment of views with the US rather than by efforts to arrive at a European position. While British officials were clear on the fact that the EU would have to play a visible role in the resolution of the crisis, this did not translate into political action in the response to the crisis beyond support for Javier Solana and a place for the EU in the Middle East Quartet. Three years after the intra-European but also domestic divisions over Iraq, London continued to align its position with that of the US to the detriment of public support for government actions. When it came to putting together an enhanced UNIFIL force, Britain supported the mission politically, including persuading the US and Israel of the utility of such a force, but left the overall initiative to France. With respect to a potential ESDP operation, the UK remained careful not to create more complexity in military operations or political decision-making and this ruled out ESDP as an option. This shows that, rather than an underlying instinctive preference for a European format in crisis management or force generation, the UK continued to adopt a pragmatic and instrumental approach to EU institutions that had marked decision-making in 2001–03 as well. But, the acknowledgment of the utility of the PSC as a format for coordinating position does point towards Europeanization.

members of the Foreign Office maintained that there was no substantial disagreement between the two branches of government on the need for a sustainable ceasefire, nor that there were mixed messages. Rather, in the view of the Foreign Office, this was joined-up government with neither the Prime Minister nor the Foreign Office leading or eclipsing the other in decision-making (House of Commons, 2006–07; Interview with senior British official, 17 December 2007).

The position of the government on the ceasefire was not shared across the political spectrum. There were strong public protests against Blair's refusal to call for an immediate ceasefire, and for not attempting to influence the US position in the crisis, which John Williams, former FCO chief spokesman, called 'a terrible failure for president Bush's championing of Middle East democracy' (Guardian Unlimited, 1 August 2006). Williams argued in favour of Blair using his influence on the US to seek support for a EU-3 mission to Israel and Palestine to hold a conference that would force the parties to sit down and negotiate a peace agreement (Guardian Unlimited, 1 August 2006). A 35,000 petition that was backed by various aid agencies and the Muslim Council of Britain, was handed to Downing Street demanding a call for an immediate ceasefire in the region. Public opposition to UK official policy, and the UK's close coordination with the US was significant because there were accusations that the US was deliberately obstructing calls for an immediate ceasefire to give Israel a chance to defeat Hezbollah – to which John Bolton was reported to have responded 'what's wrong with that?' (House of Commons, 13 August 2007: 46). While officials denied being in collusion with the US to support the continuation of hostilities, it was suggested that the UK was aware of efforts to obstruct the diplomatic process, although no definite verdict was reached in the UK Parliament (House of Commons, 13 August 2007). As for the UK Parliament, the House of Commons Select Committee on Foreign Affairs was also critical of the decision not to call for an immediate ceasefire, and to not work on a dual approach of calling for the cessation of hostilities while working on a Security Council Resolution at the same time, and concluded that 'the Government's decision . . . has done significant damage to the UK's reputation in much of the world' (House of Commons, 13 August 2007).

Europeanization vs. alliance politics

Given London's overarching policy goal of achieving a sustainable ceasefire, which was in line with US preferences, evidence of Europeanization is rather limited. To be sure, there was concern on the part of the Foreign Office that there would be a European common position and the recognition that Europe would have a role to play in ending the conflict (Interview with senior British official, 17 December 2007). At the same time, it was clear to the Foreign Office that any political solution would depend on the US, and that it was not possible for the EU to act on its own. This means that, although there was some salience of the European agenda, this was subordinated to transatlantic considerations. The US had adopted a position early on that had a bearing on how the crisis evolved; and it was 'no secret' that the US was an important player in the conflict (Interview with senior British official, 17 December 2007). A EU format for negotiating the crisis similar to the EU-3 formula was, therefore, not of interest. Instead, diplomatic action was to take place at the UN Security Council, as France, who assumed a lead in the negotiation and later on in UNIFIL, wanted room to manoeuvre. There was, therefore, no appetite for a more Europeanized crisis response. And, for British officials, the first reaction in response to the crisis was to arrive at a ceasefire; and the UK wanted one that would stick – priorities, therefore, were not about what Europe could do, but how the crisis could be stopped.

Keeping the US on board both as far as policies towards a ceasefire, and arriving at a UNSC resolution were concerned, were important considerations – alliance politics, therefore, has some explanatory value in this case. This pertains specifically to the indicator of minding US preferences, and of acknowledging US interests in this particular region that had to be taken into consideration. Given that US and UK preferences with respect to a ceasefire overlapped, the indicator of transatlantic preference also applies – even if it was clear that, on account of the partial position of the US towards Israel, the US would not be perceived as a neutral actor in the region. As a result, a European lead in the peace keeping operation was regarded as necessary.

Creating UNIFIL

As for the question of a peace-keeping force, the UK was in favour of the EU having a role to play, although this did not necessarily mean ESDP but rather EU member states. Given military commitments in Iraq and Afghanistan, however, a British contribution to the peace-keeping force was not intended. To London it was clear that Paris would have to undertake a lead role, and it appeared more sensible to reinforce UNIFIL. Other models, including NATO and ESDP were under consideration as well – however, these were not decisive or contested subjects as the priority was to arrive at a Security Council resolution to strengthen UNIFIL. But, given Israeli criticism of the existing UNIFIL mission, Israel and the

US needed persuading of that option. Adding an ESDP dimension would have complicated that particular task, although it would have been convincing to Israel. Beyond agreeing to an enhanced UNIFIL force, given in particular the French lead, London stood at the sidelines as it did not contribute troops.

Europeanization vs. alliance politics

Although the political responses to the war in Lebanon were overwhelmingly determined by transatlantic ties there is some evidence of Europeanization when it comes to creating UNIFIL. This applies specifically to the indicator of salience of the European agenda, as the EU platform was seen as an appropriate institution in terms of decision-making. The development of EU institutions since ESDP was declared operational meant that the EU, in this case the Political and Security Committee (PSC), was regarded as a valuable platform to coordinate the military contributions of individual member states. Raising the European profile during intra-European discussions over contributions to UNIFIL by means of increased discussions in the PSC in the British view added value without complexity (Interview with British official, 19 November 2007) – a sentiment that expresses the continued pragmatic attitude towards ESDP on the part of the British policy establishment.

Although the UK was convinced that there is a role for the EU in the Middle East, in practical terms the UK regarded the EU's potential contribution in this geographic area in the area of civilian crisis management. While there is, then, no geographic limitation to ESDP activities, there is a balance between military and civilian mission, with military operations remaining contested in transatlantic relations. Accordingly, a British official stated that 'it is inconceivable that the EU would launch a military operation without US political support – the UK would fight to prevent that from happening' (Interview with senior British official, 17 December 2007), a statement that reflects an ongoing discussion over the balance as to what role ESDP and NATO can play in military crisis management terms.

While the evidence of Europeanization is thus rather limited, neither do transatlantic considerations fully explain policy decisions and preferences in this case – rather than paying heed to US preferences, the UK helped to politically persuade the US as well as Israel of the need for an enhanced UNIFIL force under European lead rather than a NATO or ESDP mission, which would have either been regarded as pro-Western in the case of NATO; or added too much military and political complexity in the case of ESDP.

DRC: launching EUFOR RD Congo

In DRC, as in UNIFIL, Britain was not willing to contribute forces due to military overstretch. And, although London was in agreement on the purpose of the mission, the lead was left to France due to the strong French interest and policy entrepreneurship in this case. Although the UK held the EU Presidency when the request for an ESDP mission materialized from the UN, London was not able to play a role in the informal EU decision-making process given that informal decision-making channels, to the surprise of other EU member states, were bypassed altogether. Partly as a result, and also in light of Franco-German leadership in this matter, there was little enthusiasm on the part of the UK to participate in the mission even if there was no political objection towards the mission's objective or increased EU–UN cooperation in crisis management. In addition, the ESDP operation in DRC was not an easy sell domestically, and given the overstretch of British armed forces preferences was for others to undertake that mission.

Lack of military contributions do not mean, however, that the UK was opposed to stronger commitments in sub-Saharan Africa, or to French initiatives towards the region, or towards greater EU–UN cooperation in military crisis management – after all, at St Malo in 1998 Britain and France had also decided on cooperation with respect to their individual policies towards Africa – and were especially concerned with the crisis in the Great Lakes region. At the 2003 Toucquet Summit Chirac and Blair adopted a broad view of policies towards Africa, and stressed the importance of addressing both political and economic matters and to strengthen Africa's peacekeeping capability (see Gegout, 2005).

Military overstretch in addition to substantial bilateral relations between the UK and sub-Saharan Africa meant that there was little interest on the part of London to participate in the mission even if it was happy to lend political support. The UK provided two personnel – one in the Operation Head Quarters (OHQ) in Potsdam and one in the Force Head Quarters (FHQ) in Kinshasa. Beyond the small contributions to EUFOR, however, Britain continues to participate in the EU Security Sector Reform mission EUSEC RD Congo.

In the eyes of London, when pursuing British relations with sub-Saharan Africa, bilateral or UN activities continue to be regarded as quicker and more effective. While the institution of the EUSR is perceived as good for diplomatic backup and information gathering, with EUSR Ajello held in high regard, political coordination with the EU, therefore, is not necessarily seen as effective (Interview with member state official, 19 December 2007). As a result, the EU represents a secondary political platform to pursue British interests in sub-Saharan Africa – and British policy choices with respect to the EU continue to be made by pragmatic rather than doctrinal reasons.

Europeanization

While Britain did not participate significantly – either in political or military terms – to EUFOR RD Congo, its consent to the launch of the mission provides evidence of Europeanization mainly in terms of adaptation pressures acting on the UK. The two indicators of Europeanization applicable to this particular decision are the salience of the EU agenda, and of agreeing to another member states' initiative in order to allow the progress of further EU policies.

The salience of the EU agenda is evident from the fact that greater EU–UN cooperation in crisis management, and a broad approach to security governance are viewed positively by the UK. The British position on EUFOR RD Congo as well as ESDP also underlines that the UK's view on ESDP utilities increasingly focuses on the civilian crisis management and broad-spectrum aspects of the policy. Under its EU Presidency the UK launched a Concept for Security Sector Reform (SSR) that 'will underpin work the EU is undertaking in, for example, the Democratic Republic of Congo to help improve security institutions, where the EU can bring military, police, judicial and economic expertise together with access to finances' (House of Commons, 14 June 2006). Rather than moves towards strengthening the EU's military profile, then, for Britain military crisis management instruments are explicitly framed as part of a broader SSR approach.

While the EU agenda was of salience, however, reliance on just EU foreign policy instruments was not regarded as being in the best interests of the UK. An Explanatory Memorandum at the end of the UK Presidency thus stated that 'ESDP has now come of age' and that 'the key challenge is no longer one of institution building, but is now one of ensuring an effective EU response ... to make ESDP more active, more capable and more coherent, including through better cooperation and coordination with other international organizations and non-EU states' (House of Commons, 14 June 2006). British officials in the Foreign Office are more direct – in their view, although the view on ESDP had changed and 'ESDP is now viewed in more pragmatic terms than during 2001–03, priority during a crisis is to put something on the ground – and the EU is seen as too unwieldy' (Interview with British official, 19 December 2007). This means that, although the EU platform has increased in salience, Britain is clear on the necessity to pursue a pragmatic policy to further national interests, and that this is often done more effectively through bilateral – or UN – channels.

With respect to adaptation, Britain consented to the mission although 'that the UK would have initiated this particular operation is doubtful' (Interview with British official, 19 November 2007). This means that, although adaptation pressures acted on the UK to consent to this particular mission, adapting to a member states' initiative came at low political cost – there were no transatlantic differences at play and the mission was not contested; and the UK did not contribute financially or militarily to his particular mission. Overall, then, while evidence of Europeanization in this particular case exists, it did not come at great political cost – or was otherwise politically contested, the way it had been in FYROM, for instance – to the UK.

Priorities informing crisis decision-making in 2006, then, do not support conclusions over a significant shift in the degree of Europeanization in British foreign policy. However, it is possible to observe a gradual adjustment in the view of the overall utility of ESDP: while the official British view remains that ESDP is a useful tool if the US and NATO cannot or does not want to be involved – also with respect to transatlantic burden-sharing – there has been an increasing realization that the EU, and ESDP, can make a difference also with a view to its ability to deploy a broad spectrum of instruments in a post-conflict theatre (Interview, member state official, 19 December 2007).

Conclusion

The UK has made strides in support for ESDP despite Blair's renewed focus on transatlantic relations following the events of 11 September. As ESDP came of age the UK was also able to shape the agenda towards a greater emphasis on a comprehensive approach and on Security Sector Reform (SSR). Although there is instinctive opposition or mistrust towards ESDP on the part of the public and parts of the policy establishment, ESDP is still seen as a pragmatic choice on a case-by-case basis – unlike France, a country with a clear overall ESDP agenda. Although the UK has not advocated the use of ESDP instruments in crises, it increasingly lends political support. However, bilateral and national preferences are not subsumed under the EU – or the UN for that matter – which was evident from the policy in Afghanistan. Maintaining a national profile in international politics – rather than a continued reflexive multilateralism evident in German foreign policy – is one key similarity with France, the country analysed in the next chapter.

4
France: Exporting National Preferences

Introduction: France and European foreign and security policy

France is the country with the strongest, and most defined, agenda for ESDP: unlike the UK, with its substantial shift in position, Paris remained constant in its support for ESDP as a means to project national influence and pursue French national interests in establishing an autonomous European security institution beside NATO. As a result, the export of national preferences onto the EU can be clearly observed in FYROM and DRC – as can the limits of Europeanization in Afghanistan and Lebanon. The UN, or national contributions weighed more heavily as political platforms in the case of Lebanon and Afghanistan, respectively, as they allowed for greater national influence and the shaping of policy decisions. As a consequence Europeanization is strongest in ESDP's current geographical scope in the Balkans and sub-Saharan Africa, rather than in geopolitically more contested areas. Unlike Britain, France has tended to pursue its European agenda in tandem with Germany as a means to strengthen its political position and its influence in the European setting.

2001: FYROM and Afghanistan

France took a lead role in shaping the EU crisis management response in FYROM and attempted to carve out a stronger role for the EU CFSP, including ESDP. This applies both to the management of the crisis as well as the post-crisis period, where France initiated a discussion of the ESDP takeover of the NATO operation. What was later to become Operation Concordia had symbolic value both for the application of EU crisis management tools as well as for member states vested in the development of the EU ESDP and its application, particularly in the Western Balkans. Although the initial suggestion for an ESDP mission had to be abandoned because of opposition from other member states to any initiative outside the NATO framework in the absence of a formal agreement over EU access to NATO assets, it provided the impetus for a broader discussion and eventual realization of the ESDP takeover from NATO. The Europeanization model offers a convincing explanatory framework for French decision-making in the case of FYROM.

However, this does not apply in the case of the war in Afghanistan. French reactions to the attacks on 11 September were marked by a set of interrelated themes: military participation in the war in Afghanistan as a show both of solidarity with the US but also as an assertion of national influence and personal prestige on the part of President Chirac; a central role assigned to the UN and a fundamentally multilateral conception of the appropriate response to the fight against terrorism, the war and reconstruction of Afghanistan; and domestic concerns over the impact of the war in Afghanistan in light of the size of the French Muslim population. The nature of the conflict, the privileged position of the UN as a multilateral forum to sanction the use of military force and to coordinate the reconstruction of the country, and the primacy of US preferences in what was perceived as a legitimate case of self-defence against a terrorist attack meant that the EU CFSP and ESDP did not hold as privileged a position in French political considerations as it did in the case of FYROM. There was no appetite for pushing for an EU label in what was, essentially, a transatlantic moment and a conflict where a European approach was regarded as of little added value.

FYROM and the support for the EU CFSP in the political negotiations

French involvement in the crisis in FYROM is best understood in light of previous engagements in the Balkans from the early 1990s, and in terms of the significance of EU crisis management instruments located in CFSP and ESDP in FYROM, as well as for the future course of developments of EU crisis management in the Balkans and beyond.

France from the beginning of the crisis supported a strong role for the EU, and initially emphasized the commitment for the territorial integrity of FYROM. Given the central role played by the US in the previous conflicts in the Balkans, coordination with the US was regarded as important on the part of Paris. President Chirac thus pursued political initiatives in the framework of the Contact Group, and initiated a meeting in Paris on 11 April to discuss the general situation in the Balkans.

Key members of the French government sought to play a lead role in European efforts in the negotiation of the crisis. France did so in particular through the Franco-German relationship, through which a number of policy initiatives were generated. This is consistent with the argument that France has consistently 'pursued the idea of Europe as a political as well as an economic force by means of a special relationship with Germany' (Blunden, 2000: 19).

The crisis in FYROM and how to respond to it was on the agenda in bilateral meetings during the French-German Herxheim summit on 20 March 2001. At the suggestion of Chirac, both countries also suggested that it would be a positive step to have the Macedonian President address the European Council on the situation in FYROM, a suggestion that was subsequently taken up by the Swedish EU Presidency. At the press conference following the European Council, Chirac emphasized that 'we [the Council], notably France, have encouraged the Macedonian authorities to deepen their political dialogue and their inter-ethnic cooperation, meaning their effort at better integration of the Albanian-speaking community in Macedonia' (Chirac, 24 March 2001). In addition to demonstrating the salience of the EU agenda in French foreign policy, this statement also serves to underline national influence on the formulation of European policies.

Paris also sought to increase its own national standing within the EU through the appointment of a EUSR. Foreign Minister Védrine and the Director of Strategic Affairs at the time, Gerard Araud, were keen on appointing a French national as EU Special Representative in order to increase French influence on EU policies (Interview with French official, 8 September 2006) – an idea that also originated in discussions between France and Germany. The emphasis on the appointment of a French national shows that strengthening the voice of the EU in the negotiation phase was a priority, and that French influence in the EU negotiations was important.

But, France also sought to play a key role in the crisis through the Contact Group and to retain US and Russian involvement in the crisis. Importantly there is no evidence of domestic differences between the Elysée and the Quai d'Orsay as to the nature and the means to pursue French interests in the crisis. This confirms the cohesion of the French policy (and intellectual) elites – and the concentration of power and influence at the centre, the Presidency and the Quai d'Orsay in particular (see Niblett, 2001; Blunden, 2000).

Europeanization vs. alliance politics

French foreign policy decisions with respect to the support for the EU CFSP in the political negotiations exhibit evidence of Europeanization. The EU was regarded as a platform to enhance French influence, and the EU agenda in this crisis was of high salience. French policy decisions and the underlying motivations behind them therefore support indicators of Europeanization that point towards adaptation and projection. First, the salience of the EU agenda was high in this case and policy elites favoured the application of CFSP instruments; second, the EU was used as a platform in an attempt to increase national influence; third, and related, the EU was used as a cover to initiate policies on the domestic or international level. Paris did pursue national policy preferences – to maintain a high French profile in the management of the crisis – through initiating policy through the EU CFSP.

As for the salience of the EU agenda, an official in the Quai d'Orsay stated that 'France is implicated in the EU CFSP where national action is subsumed in a European framework. Since Dayton, EU policy action in the Balkans is an illustration of what the EU should do and how it should use its instruments, civil and military tools, first and second pillar instruments' (Interview with French official, 12 August 2005). This implies a general salience of the EU agenda in French politics towards the Western Balkan region to begin with; and conditioned French responses to the crisis itself.

The salience of the EU agenda is also evident from a statement made by François Léotard looking back on his appointment where he said that 'Europe's leadership (in the negotiation of the crisis) is uncontested' (Assemblée Nationale, 23 October 2001). More generally the view on the crisis in FYROM, applied to both the political negotiations as well as military crisis management was that 'the EU must be ready, Europe must be an actor, when possible it must act. It's the French European method: to push the agenda, and if we can show that the EU is an actor we should show that the EU can do it alone' (Interview with French official, 8 July 2005).

With respect to the second indicator of Europeanization, the use of the EU platform in an attempt to increase national influence is evident from the appointment of a French national as EU Special Representative, particularly from the lobbying for the appointment of a French national who served as Minister of Defence during the 1990s. Based on his past experience and stature he was sure to be able to use the EU platform to increase French visibility and influence in EU foreign policy and to pursue national as well as European efforts and policy ideas.

By appointing a high profile French national to work alongside Javier Solana, France was able to actively shape EU negotiations in this case. This is also confirmed by a member state official who stated that 'Léotard had a strong personality, and frequently did manage to eclipse Solana' (Interview with member state official, September 2005). This suggests that Léotard did not strictly adhere to his mandate of acting 'under the authority of the High Representative' (Council of the European Union, 29 June 2001). Lastly, the fact that 'given the urgency of the situation, and exceptionally, most administrative expenditure of the Special Representative shall be covered by France' (Council of the European Union, 29 June 2001) suggest that Léotard's, similar to that of Klaus-Peter Klaiber in the case of Afghanistan, was at least as much a national as a European appointment.

There is little evidence of policy adaptation, however: France did not adhere to common policy objectives over other considerations and preferences. Paris also did not explicitly equate national with European preferences with respect to the case of FYROM, although members of the French policy elite have on other occasions made general comments on the effect of Europe on national foreign policy (see Hoffman, 2001). The use of parallel platforms of negotiations and the aim of retaining national influence mean that the pressure to adapt to any EU policy was low, as France was quite influential in shaping policies both at the European level and in the framework of the Contact Group.

France was also keen on involving and cooperating with the US in the crisis in order to ensure a peaceful outcome. French foreign policy thus also exhibits some evidence of alliance politics, in particular the aim of keeping the US involved in European security. This is evident from visits to the US where the crisis in FYROM and American commitment to the Balkans more generally was discussed, and from the initiation of meetings of the Contact Group as forum of negotiations. Rather than a fundamental transatlantic preference, however, the underlying motivation for cooperation and for involving the US best fits the indicator of utilitarian reasons for involving the US.

During Hubert Védrine's visit to Washington on 26 March 2001, the first after the new administration had taken office, Védrine warned the US against removing troops from the region, and from disengaging from the Balkans. In press statements following his meeting with Colin Powell, Védrine accordingly stated that 'we are keen to cooperate much and as well as we can in a whole series of areas' including FYROM, and 'we want to work together to find the solution to these problems, point by point, crisis by crisis [...]. We wish to do so in a spirit of friendship, frankness and very open, intense and dynamic cooperation' (Védrine, 26 March 2001). Unlike the UK or Germany, where cooperation with the US tended to be phrased in terms of a general transatlantic preference with an emphasis on the centrality of US-German/British relations, Védrine's phrasing neither indicates blanket support for the US nor a fundamental transatlantic preference for resolving regional security issues.

Participation in NATO Operation Essential Harvest

This section shows that French foreign policy with respect to the involvement in NATO Operation Essential Harvest – as with respect to the political negotiations – was keen to build on its previous investment in FYROM and the Western Balkans more generally. In contrast to Britain and Germany, France is not a member of the NATO Central Military Command although President Chirac had normalized its relations with the alliance and had begun to reintegrate into the military structure of the Alliance in order to allow for French participation in combined operations in Bosnia under NATO command (Lansford, 2002: 128). This illustrates the difficult position of France vis-à-vis NATO and indicates utilitarian rather than fundamental preferences in the choice for NATO as well as French preferences for an early (and autonomous) ESDP takeover.

The Franco-German relationship proved a key platform for negotiating the terms of French (and German) engagement in the NATO Operations. At the summit in Freiburg on 12 June, Chirac's suggestion for military cooperation with German units within NATO was confirmed by Schröder and put in place by the foreign and defence ministers of the two countries on 5 July. Both countries cooperated in NATO Operation Essential Harvest – two German, two French and one Spanish companies were placed under overall French command (NATO, 16 December 2002).

Chirac's input in decision-making on the international and NATO level built on previous French involvement through NATO, where France had been active in FYROM prior to the onset of the crisis due to its commitment in KFOR. A French general, Marcel Valentin, had lead the extraction force XFOR in FYROM in 1999 that was charged with protection over the first deployments of KFOR in Kosovo. General Valentin was later given the command over KFOR, the first time a French general had been placed at the head of the entire KFOR mission rather than a particular sector (Interview with policy analyst, 10 June 2005). Chirac accordingly highlighted French contributions and the situation in FYROM in his address to the NATO North Atlantic Council meeting where he stated that with regard to the Balkans, and as a French general prepares to take over command of the KFOR, I would like to mention the dangers of the crisis affecting Macedonia [. . .]. We must state clearly that we will not accept a new outbreak of violence [. . .] we must not preclude any form of actions needed to thwart such developments. (Chirac, 13 June 2001)

This shows that the priority of Chirac was to highlight France's national commitments within NATO rather than moves to work outside the NATO framework. While there is no evidence of a fundamental disagreement over the use of NATO instruments as opposed to those located in the EU ESDP, Chirac took pains to point out European cooperation within the NATO operation and to emphasize French national contributions – reinforcing the conclusion of France maintaining its *rang* and international status through the use of multilateral institutions (Treacher, 2003).

Europeanization vs. alliance politics

As is to be expected, there is little evidence of the Europeanization framework as policy decisions concerning French military commitments involved NATO, not the EU. However, French officials frequently framed the NATO operation as a 'European action' and as a demonstration that Europe could act, even if an operation under the EU label had not yet materialized. This reflects a general and fundamental preference towards an EU approach, which included the application of ESDP instruments and points towards Europeanization. But, as in the case of Germany, French policy makers were keen to point out the 'European nature' of the troop deployment, which suggested a European preference. Alain Richard stated that 'the operations in Macedonia are the first ones carried out and practically led exclusively by Europeans within the Alliance [. . .] which shows us that Europe is both politically and militarily ready to act' (Richard, 2 October 2001).

A number of indicators of alliance politics are applicable with respect to the NATO operation. First, France had an interest in keeping the US involved in European security – in particular because the incoming Bush administration had made it clear that it did not favour continued US deployment in the Balkans. This affirms the first indicator of alliance politics, where states align with NATO and the US to keep the US involved in European security. Second, and partly as a result, there were utilitarian considerations at play as well. NATO, based on its military possibilities and by virtue of already being in the area, was considered the more appropriate political and military institution with respect to Operation Essential Harvest.

With respect to the NATO operation, the empirical evidence supports the alliance politics model: France considered NATO the appropriate forum for the launch of Operation Essential Harvest, and contributed sizeably to the mission. Although some members of the French government were keen to label this effort as proof of European capabilities and cooperation, these forces were under NATO command. It also confirms the assessment of an interviewee who stated that 'France is more pragmatic towards NATO than it is given credit for. We will not stand in the way if NATO is the smarter solution' (Interview with policy analyst, 10 June 2005).

The ESDP takeover from NATO

The suggestion for an ESDP takeover from NATO first arose from a proposal by EUSR Léotard. Although the EU Special Representative does not serve in a national capacity but is to act on behalf of the EU, Léotard's proposal for an EU force to take over from NATO in particular was said to have the backing of the French government. This indicates that the motivations behind the proposal reflected France's position on the issue of an EU takeover of the NATO mission in FYROM, and towards ESDP in general. Key participants in the governmental process supported an early handover from NATO to ESDP, and did not regard prior institutional arrangements between NATO and the EU as a prerequisite for the application of instruments located in ESDP. The consensus of the different branches of government on this issue also indicates that policy elites favoured the application of ESDP instruments.

Léotard's proposal arose out of the security vacuum left by Operation Essential Harvest: a conflict that was to break out after a NATO operation expired would likely be more dramatic than the one just behind. His proposal stated that if the member states are in agreement, and NATO gives its logistical support, it should be possible to deploy a European force of between 1,500 and 2,000 troops to protect the EU and OSCE observers (*Financial Times*, 6 September 2001). Léotard's proposal stemmed from a consideration that was affirmed by a French official interviewed that 'from a military point of view, in the view of France, it was not necessary to use NATO but possible to put together an ad-hoc European-led group similar to Operation Alba in 1997' (Interview with French official 20 June 2005).

The stated preference among French elites was to gain European auton-omy from NATO in the case of FYROM. One French official interviewed stated 'we thought at the beginning that it would be possible to do it without NATO because it was a very small operation. But it was, let's say, a political requirement from the British and other members' (Inter-view with French official, 20 June 2005). This statement was echoed by a member of the French Ministry of Defence: 'do not overestimate that the EU wasn't ready, Europeans were able to do the job' (Interview with French official, 11 July 2005).

Germany and France discussed Léotard's proposal for an EU force on 5 September, but Foreign Minister Fischer did not endorse the plan but pre-ferred an international force backed by a UN mandate (*Financial Times*, 6 September 2001). Germany's position, although in principle in favour of a gradually expanding role for the EU CFSP and ESDP in the Balkans, depended to a great extent on the position of the US and on clearly defined arrangements between NATO and the EU. This position indi-cated to French officials that the timing for an ESDP takeover from NATO was premature, and that the takeover required further negotiations.

Védrine therefore rejected the proposal of an EU force, stating that 'if the new European security and defence arrangements were organized enough for this mission, it would be a good idea. But because it isn't quite ready yet, I think it is more sensible, easier and more practical to act in a NATO framework' (Agence France Presse, 8 September 2001).

Europeanization vs. alliance politics

French actions and policy decisions confirm a number of indicators of the Europeanization hypothesis. The salience of the European agenda was high. This is demonstrated by France initiating the process through the initial suggestion in September 2001, and by the importance attached to the application of instruments located in the EU CFSP and ESDP. In fact, with respect to FYROM, the French position was to switch as much as possible over from NATO to EU, 'because we have a policy in the Balkans, the EU is active in the Balkans, so the rationale was to take over – we decided to have ESDP and should be ready for an operation in the Balkans' (Interview with French official, 20 June 2005). French interest in an ESDP mission subsequently arose because at the time there was a trend towards a step-by-step increase of EU activities in the Balkans, plus a gradual disengagement of the US (Interview with French official, 29 June 2005).

Consequently, looking back on his appointment, Léotard expressed disappointment at not deploying the weapons collections mission under a European label (*Frankfurter Allgemeine Zeitung*, 25 October 2001). This demonstrates that the preferences of the Foreign Ministry and the EUSR leaned towards the utilization of ESDP instruments. Neither of them considered institutional arrangements between the EU and NATO a prerequisite for launching an EU Operation, although the Foreign Ministry had to relent on this question on account of British and German (as well as other member states') opposition.

The consensus among the different branches of government on this issue also indicates that policy elites favoured the application of ESDP instruments and thereby confirms the existence of norms and preferences that point towards Europeanization. The homogenous public opinion on this issue is confirmed by the statement of an outside observer: from the point of view of Paris, 'NATO was in Kosovo, France supported this because it was necessary, but really this was seen as scandalous – it's an old reflex; France is not pragmatic like the US or the UK, but orthodox' (Interview with member state official, August 2005).

In its acquiescence to the Berlin Plus agreement, French policy decisions also reflected the relaxation of traditional positions to accommodate the progress of EU projects, in this case the first ESDP mission. In the face of British and German objections to ad-hoc arrangements between the EU and NATO, France compromised on its initial preference to push for European autonomy and for making NATO less relevant – in the view of one official 'it had always been clear that it was really about these two issues' (Interview with former German official, 8 February 2006).

Given the overwhelming evidence of Europeanization in this particular policy area, it is perhaps not surprising that there is little evidence in French decision-making that would point towards alliance politics. In addition to the general absence of a fundamental transatlantic preference on the part of France, NATO at least initially was not considered of utilitarian value in this case. The military operation was small enough for the EU member states to manage its execution on their own. And, Leotard's resignation to Solana on 10 September signalled the existence of disagreements on further steps in FYROM after NATO completed Operation Essential Harvest, with a news agency citing French sources as noting that 'NATO's leadership preserves full political control over pursuing the West's policy in the Balkans' (ITAR-TASS News Agency, 10 September 2001).

The preferences of individual policy makers involved in this decision as well as their stated and underlying preferences thus demonstrate that the EU ESDP was considered the appropriate political and military instrument for addressing the security vacuum resulting from the end of NATO

Operation Essential Harvest. The fact that this consideration had its roots in the symbolism attached to an EU-label and the overall, often stated preferences of developing the EU into a foreign and security policy actor, underlines the fundamental preference of French policy makers with respect to the application of instruments located in the EU CFSP/ESDP. Evidence of alliance politics is present only insofar as NATO was considered the appropriate institutional framework for utilitarian reasons after the initial suggestion of an ESDP operation had been rejected.

The suggestion and subsequent debate over an EU rather than a NATO mission for FYROM reveals different national perceptions and preferences on ESDP. Whereas Britain insists on ESDP being as close as possible to NATO, for France this should be done only when necessary – 'and in the case of FYROM it did not seem to be necessary' (Interview with French official, 20 June 2005). The resulting French position was that the EU must be a security actor. Therefore, France pushed the agenda to show that the EU could do so and is an actor beyond the political aspect of crisis management. And, the risk of failure of an ESDP operation was low, given the small size of the mission and the conclusion of the Ohrid Peace Agreement and relatively successful implementation.

In conclusion, France did use the EU CFSP in the crisis in FYROM as a platform to further its agenda for a larger role for the EU that would include military operations, and to shape EU policies towards FYROM. The aim was also to capitalize on the St Malo process and to hurry along the process towards launching an ESDP operation. Thus, there was a clear and early choice for Europe, including a military dimension, with a broader regional view and the EU's role in the region, that affirms the applicability of the Europeanization concept to explain French policy choices.

Afghanistan: OEF and the war on terror

French contributions to OEF were motivated first and foremost by considerations of solidarity with the US. The alliance politics framework, understood as the recognition of the US' right to self-defence in light of the terrorist attacks as well as the need for a transatlantic stance against international terrorism that included a military component, offers a strong explanation for French policies in this case. However, the alliance politics framework does not account for the strong multilateral impulse in French foreign policy which accorded a central role for the legal sanctioning of the intervention, as well as measures against international terrorism more broadly, to the United Nations. Participation in OEF and the war on terror also provided a key opportunity for President Chirac to increase his personal profile vis-à-vis the centre-left government under Prime Minister Jospin in light of the impending elections in 2002. Domestic electoral concerns thus played a role in the presentation if not the formulation of these policies for the President, especially where military participation in OEF was concerned.

President Chirac was the first head of state to visit Washington on 18 September where he declared French solidarity and offered military contributions to a US-led war against terrorism in Afghanistan. The emphasis on military assistance without 'a blank cheque' and the condition of France being consulted in advance about the objectives of military action (Gordon and Suzan, 2002) signalled that France was unwilling to go along with a geographic expansion of military operations. Significant military participation in OEF was, however, not in question (Chirac, 7 October 2001). France played a major role in the air campaign and contributed substantially to OEF. France put 22 combat aircraft at the disposal at the US, and was the only other country besides the US to operate combat aircraft in Afghanistan, carrying out bombing missions as part of 'Operation Anaconda'. France also made available the Charles de Gaulle carrier battle group (US Department of Defense, 14 June 2002). France also, together with Britain, provided special forces – but made clear in meetings with Blair that a wider war against terrorism involving Iraq and Egypt would be difficult to maintain in light of France's historic links in the Middle East and North Africa (*Observer*, 23 September 2001), hinting early on French opposition to US plans to widen the scope of military attacks to Iraq. Accordingly, a statement by the Ministry of Foreign Affairs on the question of US attacks on other countries said that 'if the US asks for a strike elsewhere, we will have to retain our authority to consider it' (Ministry of Foreign Affairs, 9 October 2001).

While opinions on the appropriate response to the attacks, voiced as military participation in OEF sanctioned by a UN Security Council Resolution, was broadly shared among members of the French government, there were nuances in the positions and preferences of the key government figures. Foreign Minister Hubert Védrine in particular drew attention to concerns over US multilateralism à la carte and the potential geographic expansion of the military strikes to include Iraq, whereas president Chirac initially highlighted French solidarity with the US and military contributions to the US-led war on terror.

The Jospin government, lastly, was more critical of the US and military operations and highlighted the societal implications of the war on terror on the French Muslim population. Jospin stated that while France would not 'shirk its responsibilities' it would reserve the right to make 'a free judgment about French participation in a military engagement' (Gordon and Suzan, 2002: 1). This also shows that while Jospin's socialist government broadly supported military operations in response to the terrorist attacks, it was more nuanced with respect to solidarity with the US. The French government was careful not to frame the conflict as a clash of civilizations (Assemblée Nationale, 3 October 2001).

In addition to military measures, the solidarity with the US was also expressed on a public level, with the French newspaper *Le Monde* declaring in response to the attacks of 11 September that 'we are all American' (*Le Monde*, 13 September 2001), and Chirac affirming that 'France has placed itself at the side of the American people. Out of friendship, out of solidarity. But also because we know that all democracies are in danger when one of them is struck in the heart like this' (Chirac, Paris, 16 November 2001). Védrine stated that the French government approved of the American reaction not only out of solidarity but because of the shared political objectives 'to cut the terrorist network of Bin Laden' (Védrine, Assemblée Nationale, 9 October 2001). Although foreign minister Védrine later criticized the US for a post-11 September 'simplistic attitude' following Bush's state of the Union address on 29 January 2002 (*International Herald Tribune*, 7 February 2002), the initial preference on the part of the French government was solidarity with the US, visibility for French military contributions, and a public profile for President Chirac.

In addition to the military contributions to the war on terror and relations with the US, France also pursued policies through the UN, which was a vital platform for Paris to formulate multilateral policies towards OEF and the war in Afghanistan. The UNSC resolution 1368 sanctioning OEF and the toppling of the Taliban regime was a joint initiative of France and the UK (Chirac, 16 November 2001), that was initiated by Chirac in response to the attacks on 11 September as France held the rotating presidency in the UN Security Council that month (*New York Times*, 8 September 2002). This reflected the preference for a multilateral approach on the part of France and the search for a political solution to the fight against terrorism.

Europeanization vs. alliance politics

The primary impulse for French policy makers was that of solidarity with the US and the importance of a multilateral approach to the conflict. The UN constituted the most important multilateral forum to sanction military action against Afghanistan as well as political actions in the reconstruction of Afghanistan. Considerations of the EU CFSP were subordinated to these fundamental impulses.

The use of the EU as a political platform resulted in charges of increasing Chirac's personal profile but did not result in a policy proposal, and did nothing to further the appearance of EU unity: rather, the Ghent summit 'was a disaster, with the Union appearing both marginalized and crippled by internal bickering. After the summit, the UK, France and Germany all insisted that the Taliban government had to be toppled, thus effectively disowning a common EU declaration advising that the West should not impose a government on Afghanistan' (Peterson, 2002: 6). The Belgian EU Presidency was disappointed at the meeting and critical of President Chirac who, 'presumably for electoral reasons' had publicized the separate meeting – and in fact, since the attacks of 11 September and statements and US visits by Chirac, his popularity had increased, while that of his rival, Lionel Jospin, had fallen (BBC Monitoring Europe, 19 October 2001). Chirac, attending Blair's Downing Street Dinner in early November 2001, similarly gave the impression of EU disunity, although Peterson (2002: 6) notes that 'what matters most about the meeting was its original purpose – to agree the essential points of a common European line ahead of Chirac's visit to Washington – and its success in agreeing such a line'. This demonstrates that Chirac aimed to speak for Europe, but also that formulating a European position was of importance for the President. Nevertheless, this did not result in policies adopted under the EU CFSP.

As in the case of FYROM, the Franco-German relationship as a means to initiating policy proposals was a second platform for formulating French policy responses within the EU CFSP. France together with Germany brought an action plan to the Foreign Minister's meeting in Luxemburg on 8 October with the aim to define a EU position and to initiate an common political strategy for the EU. The final statement subsequently read that 'the military action being taken is one part of a wider multilateral strategy in which the European Union is committed to playing its part. This involves a comprehensive assault on the organisations and financing structures that underpin terrorism' (General Affairs Council, 8 October 2001).

This shows that the EU platform was used to submit proposals previously formulated with Germany, highlighting the role of bilateral relations with another member state. With respect to the underlying motivations these moves do serve as evidence of two indicators of Europeanization: that of the salience for the European agenda, where the application of EU CFSP instruments is deemed important on the part of policy decision makers; and of policy projection, where the EU is used to transport and thereby reinforce, national policy preferences onto the EU platform.

However, the fact that EU action towards the war on terror did not go beyond statements of solidarity with the US and the conceptualization of a larger multilateral strategy in the war on terrorism through judicial means that were taken up by the Spanish EU presidency in the first half of 2002 shows that, while the EU CFSP constituted an institutional platform through which to reinforce French national preferences, the EU was not considered the central political platform to formulate political responses.

Alliance politics considerations, expressed as solidarity with the US and the recognition that this was essentially a US-led war, offer a more convincing explanatory framework for French policy actions as they concern participation in OEF. The professed solidarity with the United States supports one indicator of alliance politics: that of states aligning with the US out of a transatlantic preference and solidarity with the US, which was reinforced by the invocation of Article V. It also made the military contribution to OEF uncontested. Thus, a member of the Foreign Ministry was cited in the press as stating 'it's a case of legitimate self-defence, the Americans call the shots here' (*Irish Times*, 6 March 2002). US preference towards requesting assistance from individual NATO allies supports the alliance politics indicator of states adhering to US preferences, even if the US did not choose to involve NATO as a whole in the military operation.

The reconstruction of Afghanistan

With regard to the reconstruction of Afghanistan, the political approach taken – an overall UN umbrella to organize the reconstruction with a political role for the EU to raise its political and economic profile in Afghanistan – was uncontested among the branches of the French government. On 1 October the government through Foreign Minister Védrine presented a plan on the humanitarian and political aspects of reconstruction of Afghanistan that contributed to the international effort in these matters and helped orient and define the work of the UN as set out later in UNSC Resolution 1378 (Assemblée Nationale, 21 November 2001), which was also highlighted by the President (Chirac, 6 November 2001). At the 8 October foreign minister meeting in Luxembourg, France pushed a detailed option that involved setting up an 'interim structure' under the UN to tackle the most urgent consequences of the crisis, after which a transitional administration representing all

Afghan factions should be set up. According to this plan, the EU would help with the reconstruction programme, coordinated by a group set up under the UN and bringing together all the countries bordering Afghanistan (Press Association, 8 October 2001). The UN thus had a central role in French conceptions of a political solution for Afghanistan's reconstruction, although the European Commission was considered to play a central role in the reconstruction of the country.

The EU also represented an important platform to push for and propose political actions for the EU CFSP, again through the formulation of policy proposals through the Franco-German relationship. At the EU summit, France and Germany proposed that Afghanistan's former king become a national figurehead and called for UN role in the reshaping of Afghanistan (CNN.com, 17 October 2001). Chirac agreed with Lakhdar Brahimi, the UN Special Representative that 'absolute priority must be given to putting in place a political solution and to take into account the humanitarian drama that risks unfolding if we do not do all that is necessary to prepare all that is essential' (Chirac, 8 November 2001). Chirac also stated that the resolution prepared by France and the UK that was to be voted on 15/16 November was important not because it would solve everything, but because it 'will confirm the authority of the United Nations to put in place a political solution to the Afghan problem' (Chirac, 8 November 2001). This call for a UN role was repeated by Prime Minister Jospin, who urged quick action by the UN for a peaceful transition in Afghanistan following the fall of the Taliban (Agence France Presse, 13 November 2001). Subsequently, France fully supported the Bonn process and the political state-building process that this necessitated and that the international community, France included, would support.

Europeanization vs. alliance politics

For France, the EU CFSP represented an important and relevant platform through which to give the EU a voice in Afghanistan and through which to highlight the EU's efforts in the country's reconstruction. This included both economic and political efforts and thus the application of instruments located in pillar 1 and pillar 2 were concerned. As in the case of OEF and ISAF, however, the involvement of the UN held a central place in French political considerations under which EU involvement was subsumed. This means that the Europeanization hypothesis only accounts for parts of French political considerations.

France supported the German proposal on the appointment of a EUSR, and did highlight the substantial financial contributions of the

EU Commission. Together with early proposals on action plans for Afghanistan that were brought to the Foreign Minister meeting and European Council following the attacks on 11 September, this also suggests a salience of the EU agenda reflecting a French preference in favour of a strong political profile for the EU. Unlike Germany, where the EU platform constituted an important institutional venue through which to 'upload' German policy preferences and to increase Germany's clout, however, uploading specific policy preferences, or ensuring a strong national influence on the formulation of EU politics was not as important a consideration for France.

As a permanent member of the UN Security Council, France had more latitude to influence the UN's response and as a result also the global approach to the conflict and the country's reconstruction. As both terrorism and the reconstruction of Afghanistan were regarded as global rather than as regional challenges that to a significant extent involved non-European powers (unlike FYROM, which essentially represented a regional crisis), the UN was the natural forum for resolving questions of the reconstruction of Afghanistan. There was no conflict between the UN and the EU agenda in this case – the primacy of the UN was not contested. The fact that not all economic and political assistance was subsumed under an EU label but was publicly highlighted and explicitly framed as national contributions to the reconstruction of Afghanistan does not support the Europeanization approach, and there is no evidence of national preferences being compromised or adapted in favour or in light of EU adaptation pressures.

With respect to the reconstruction of Afghanistan, the division of labour and burden-sharing between the US and other industrial countries was that the US had borne responsibility for providing security and expected others to take the lead in the economic reconstruction of Afghanistan (Balaj, 2002: 44). This meant that the EU, but most importantly the UN, was afforded a significant place in national decision-making where the reconstruction of Afghanistan was concerned than was the case in the military operations OEF and ISAF. While the resulting political initiatives partially support the Europeanization hypothesis in terms of the salience of EU political and economic instruments, it means that the alliance politics framework has no explanatory value in this case.

French participation in ISAF

Alliance politics considerations, understood both as French-US relations and bilateral relations with other NATO members, go a long way in explaining French policy decisions when it comes to ISAF and its institutional anchoring. The question of an 'EU force', while attractive for policy makers in principle, particularly as a way to 'sell' ISAF politically as an EU action, did not result in policy actions in reality or even in concrete policy proposals to that effect.

Compared to French participation in OEF, military contributions to ISAF were comparatively small, as Paris agreed to a force of 550: headquarters staff, battalion HQ, infantry company and others (United Press International, 10 January 2002). Having secured a UNSC Resolution for setting up ISAF, French support for the construction of the force itself was not in question. However, among allies there were diverging positions on the question of the institutional anchoring of ISAF, its geographic scope and the role of NATO in overall ISAF command.

On the question of an EU force, this was discussed informally, and there were some differences between the Foreign Ministry and the Ministry of Defence: 'whereas the military favoured an EU format for practical reasons, the Quai d'Orsay from a political standpoint leaned towards NATO' – albeit cautiously due to 'the geographic reach of the mission and the signal it would send towards the Muslim world to have NATO operating in Afghanistan' (Interview with policy analyst, 10 June 2005). In contrast to the crisis in FYROM, where two branches of government, the foreign ministry and the ministry of defence, were in agreement that an EU force was expedient and appropriate but compromised the idea on account of the preferences of Britain and Germany, there did exist differences of opinion within the French government on this question. But, importantly, for the foreign ministry the war in Afghanistan was not regarded as a European conflict where the EU could make a difference politically through an EU force (Interview with policy analyst, 10 June 2005). The aim of coordination with the preferences of the US and other allies as well as the nature of the conflict itself meant that an EU format was not considered practical in this case and the foreign ministry prevailed in the question of institutional format for ISAF.

France also took the position that ISAF should not expand beyond Kabul, signalling differences with the UN as well as EUSR Klaiber on the nature of the mandate as well as the geographical scope of ISAF, as both Brahimi and Klaiber were in favour of an expansion beyond Kabul. As part of ISAF, France was in charge of securing the main road from Kabul to the airfield in Bagram (*Neue Zürcher Zeitung*, 2 March 2002) and agreed that its 500-strong detachment in ISAF would stay beyond the planned end of the mission on 30 April. France, ahead of the presidential election in April and weary of increasing troop commitments, rejected calls for an expanded presence with Chirac stating that he was 'not convinced that [expansion of ISAF] is the right solution' (Human Rights Watch, 2002: 47).

On the question of the construction of ISAF, then, there existed some differences in preferences among branches of the French government. However, Chirac did make efforts to 'sell' ISAF as well as the contribution of Eurocorps in leading ISAF as a proof of *l'Europe de la défense*, suggesting a preference on the part of the President for Europe to show face in the military peace-keeping operation as well.

Europeanization vs. alliance politics

With respect to the construction of ISAF as well as the question of its institutional anchoring, there is little evidence of Europeanization. The EU ESDP did not constitute a platform to launch policies or to export national preferences or influence. Neither is there evidence of policy adaptation, as there was a low salience of the CFSP/ESDP agenda. Similarly, Paris did not compromise on national policy preferences or positions to accommodate the progress of EU policies in this case.

The swift dismissal of the suggestion of an 'EU force' was mainly on account of the fact that the ESDP had not sufficiently evolved in its capabilities for France to consider the application of EU instruments in peace-keeping in Afghanistan. Unlike the case of FYROM, there was no 'added value' for an EU label in the construction of ISAF (Interview with French official, 28 June 2005), in particular given the sensitive nature of the operation and concerns that a NATO – or the EU label, for that matter – for ISAF would invoke concerns over a 'clash of civilizations', and a battle between the West and Islam (Interview with policy analyst, 10 June 2005). While discussions of an EU force and efforts to portray this multinational force as a European effort demonstrate the salience of the ESDP agenda in French foreign policy in general, they do not confirm any additional indicators of Europeanization, such as adaptation pressures acting on French policy makers, or of the EU CFSP and ESDP representing a vehicle to increase national influence.

In addition to the 'value added' of an ESDP operation or a coordinated 'EU-force', officials in the Foreign Ministry were clear that ESDP and the EU would not have been ready to assume an operation in Afghanistan. According to one official:

and it was before Macedonia, so it was not possible to have an EU operation, and I guess that we would not have been ready for that. It was more logical to begin with the Balkans. I remember also that when we decided to launch Artemis some, even the Germans, were not ready to do it. (Interview with French official, 20 June 2005)[1]

This demonstrates that for France ESDP was not perceived as an appropriate tool to undertake a peace-keeping mission in Afghanistan, and this for a variety of reasons: the fact that ESDP had not sufficiently evolved, reluctance on the part of other EU member states, and the centrality of the US in this case. And, in the long run, the situation in Afghanistan remained volatile: 'violence is still going on, the political process is too fragile, and it is not a job the EU can do on its own' (Interview with French official, 11 July 2005).

French political decisions with regard to participation in ISAF as well as ISAF's institutional anchoring show evidence of Europeanization only insofar as the popular portrayal of the multinational force as a 'European' if not under an actual EU label demonstrate a preference on the part of the government to show that the EU was capable of acting. Even if it was not considered practical operationally to conduct ISAF in an EU format, it was nevertheless expedient for Chirac to label this if not an EU force then at least as a European endeavour. At a joint press conference at the European Council of Laeken, Chirac conflated the national and the European contributions to ISAF by stating that

> as you are aware, they [the countries of the European Union] have announced their willingness to participate in an international force that will be deployed in Kabul, Afghanistan, under the mandate of the UN and made up essentially, and also in totality, in any case in terms of the actual numbers, of European soldiers. They act as national contributions, to be sure, but they act as a clear sign of the place taken by the EU on the international scene. (Chirac, 15 December 2001)

Pressed on the issue of the Belgian statements that national contributions contributed a multinational European force, Chirac retracted part of the statement and indicated that this, despite the 'spectacular result' of the ESDP since the declaration at St Malo, would have been a premature move, stating that 'Yes, effectively one could have quickly made a uniform for Mr Solana, a General's uniform, and place him at the head of our troops over there. But things did not work out that way' (Chirac, 15 December 2001), and that ISAF constituted a multinational force under UN authority, and contributions of the member states did not constitute the European army – to that are probably the British, the Germans, the French' (Chirac, 15 December 2001). Still, the efforts to portray European contributions to ISAF as signalling the EU's ambitious role in the world constitute evidence of the salience of the European agenda in French attempts to sell member states' contributions to ISAF as a European effort, as statements by President Chirac reveal.

In contrast, the alliance politics framework partially accounts for French decision-making in this case, despite initial French objections to the use of NATO instruments. French decisions confirm two indicators of alliance politics: preferring NATO for utilitarian purposes, and accommodating the preferences of the other alliance members. France initially was in agreement with having ISAF be a multinational force under UN leadership with partial NATO involvement. ISAF from the beginning relied on some NATO operational capabilities, but there was reluctance on the part of France to operate under a NATO label so as not to evoke suspicions that this was a clash of civilizations, or a Western effort in a Muslim country (Interview with policy analyst, 10 June 2005). France also held that the out-of-area nature of the Afghanistan mission exceeded NATO's legal and institutional framework and was therefore not in favour of giving NATO overall command over ISAF. A combination of utilitarian reasons of NATO's operational capabilities as well as the preference of the US and other alliance members, help explain French decision-making in this case and the relenting of a previously held position with regards to NATO involvement in Afghanistan. Commentators also made the link between France's relenting on the question of NATO command in Afghanistan and the political fall-out with the Bush administration over the war in Iraq (*San Francisco Chronicle*, 16 April 2003; *The Economist*, 1 May 2003).

France reluctantly accepted a wider NATO role after blocking initial attempts by NATO to play a greater role in Afghanistan, where Germany and the Netherlands were taking over joint command at the beginning of 2003 (*Financial Times*, 10 February 2003). NATO expanding its role to take control of ISAF ran counter to the French conception of NATO's core mission of defending its members rather than a geographical extension of NATO's mandate, in addition to concerns that a NATO commitment would place a greater burden on French troops (*San Diego Union-Tribune*, 27 February 2003). Chirac later reflected on the changing circumstances of NATO and was cited as stating that 'you have to be realistic in a changing world. We have updated our vision, which once held that NATO had geographic limits. The idea of a regional NATO no longer exists, as the alliance's involvement in Afghanistan demonstrates' (*Washington Post*, 4 February 2004).

Chirac also suggested that Eurocorps take command over ISAF ahead of the NATO summit in Prague. And, upon the takeover of ISAF command of NATO and the assumption of lead nation by Eurocorps under the command of a French General, Chirac labelled the assumption of Eurocorps command under NATO a proof of *l'Europe de la defense*, showing that this was not only compatible but also necessary for a military organization like NATO (Chirac, 28 June 2004). This statement also indicated the importance of a 'European' label for domestic purposes and reinforced France's contentious relationship with NATO, and constituted another case of the constant '*französische Nadelstiche*' – French needle marks – (Interview with German official, 1 September 2005) against NATO. This confirms France's ambiguity towards NATO and its place in the global and European security architecture and the way in which French contributions were 'sold' domestically and internationally.

As in the case of OEF, the Europeanization approach constitutes a weak explanatory framework for French decision-making. However, initial French objections to NATO command of ISAF indicates that alliance politics does not offer a full explanation for French policy preferences, either. Importantly, however, neither approach accounts for the central role of the UN in French political considerations.

2006: Lebanon and DRC

The period between 2001 and 2006 did not witness a significant shift in French preferences with respect to ESDP but rather a continuation of trends evident from the policy's early days. France continued to advance the EU agenda, which included ESDP operations in the Balkans and sub-Saharan Africa, and the strengthening of EU–UN cooperation in crisis management. Paris not only initiated discussions over the takeover from NATO in FYROM, but also pushed for the launch of Operation Artemis in DRC – the first autonomous ESDP military operation outside Europe in June 2003 where France acted as framework nation and provided the bulk of personnel (see Gnesotto, 2004). Operation Artemis, and considerable bilateral involvement in sub-Saharan Africa reflect French interests in the region. Support for increased EU–UN cooperation in military crisis management, as well as 'Europeanizing' French interests in sub-Saharan Africa by means of launching EUFOR RD Congo in 2006, therefore, are a continuation of long-standing trends in French EU and African policy, and built on French initiatives in the UN Security Council to send a peace-keeping force to the DRC beginning in 1998 (French Foreign Ministry, 2008). However, the EU agenda did not touch on crises or issue areas with strong national interests, or issues where a French lead through the UN was more effective in maintaining French influence, as the case of Lebanon demonstrates.

The war in Lebanon touched on close French historical ties within the region – also informed by a large Lebanese diaspora and close personal relations between President Chirac and former Lebanese Prime Minister Rafiq Hariri – and built on French involvement both in the original UNIFIL as well as the French position as a permanent member of the UN Security Council. Accordingly, French foreign policy emphasized the privileged position of the UN and opposition to the US approach towards the war in Lebanon. While the EU did not constitute a platform onto which to export national preferences, France did seek to lead the EU in terms of political decision-making when it came to calling for a ceasefire in order to reinforce French preferences. Brussels-based institutions also exerted some adaptation pressures on France to commit extra troops and to lead an enhanced UNIFIL – this shows that Europeanization dynamics changed somewhat in that pressures went beyond policy projection and included adaptation pressures as well.

The war in Lebanon: political responses

French responses to the crisis differed significantly from those of Britain and Germany. France, due to its historical links with Lebanon and its generally friendly relations with the Arab world, had a differently weighted interest in the crisis from Britain and Germany. President Chirac subsequently reflected on France's privileged position in the region by stating that 'we have certain traditional, historical knowledge of the region. We probably benefit from a certain trust on the part of the Lebanese in the broadest sense of the term, and also from their environment, in the Arab world' (*Le Monde*, 27 July 2006). President Chirac not only had a key personal interest in Lebanon; a second motivating factor was also Chirac's goal to improve low approval ratings and to end his political career with a political success, given his impending departure from office in May 2007 (BBC News, 8 August 2006). Given its position as a permanent member of the UN Security Council, France played a key role in the diplomatic efforts to achieve a political settlement. The fact that Paris, together with Washington, co-sponsored the UN Security Council Resolution demonstrates the privileged role played by France in bringing an end to the war.

However, France's political position on the crisis was in direct opposition to that of the US in its call for an immediate ceasefire in order to arrive at a political solution. In addition to the question of an immediate ceasefire, Paris also differed from the US on the purpose of an international force – whereas Washington had argued for an international force to disarm Hezbollah, Chirac stated that 'I do not believe that an international force, in the case where no political commitment could be obtained, would have the capacity or the mandate to disarm Hezbollah. It is up to the Lebanese authorities to do so' (*Le Monde*, 27 July 2006).

There was key agreement on the necessary steps in the political solution of the crisis between the President, the Prime Minister and the Foreign Minister, with President Chirac setting much of the direction of French foreign policy in this case. Chirac's position was echoed by Prime Minister De Villepin, who repeated the French position on needed steps towards ending the conflict as 'immediate cessation of the hostilities in order to get a sustainable ceasefire [...], a political agreement between all the parties [and] deployment of a UN-mandated international force'. De Villepin also stressed that 'yesterday France presented a draft resolution to the Security Council designed to take account of all the factors involved in the conflict [...] We are obviously ready to work together with all our partners, and particularly the Americans, the five permanent members of the Security Council, our European partners and the Arab countries, to reach an agreement as fast as possible (French Foreign Ministry, 31 July 2006). The emphasis on working with Arab countries again reflects closer ties to the Arab world than in the other two countries analysed, as well as a greater regional concern.

In addition to directing diplomatic efforts through the UN and, to a lesser extent the EU, France also engaged in bilateral diplomacy particularly in the run-up to the 26 July international meeting in Rome that was to discuss both humanitarian measures as well as a political settlement to the crisis following a ceasefire (French Foreign Ministry, 11 September 2006). Intensive French-Lebanese diplomacy took place during the negotiations towards a ceasefire. Foreign Minister Philippe Douste-Blazy subsequently travelled to Beirut frequently for meetings with Lebanese officials, later also to clarify the objectives of the draft resolution France submitted to the UN Security Council (French Foreign Ministry, 31 July 2006b). It was clear for French policy-makers that the UN framework was central to the conflict solution, with Foreign Minister Philippe Douste-Blazy stating that 'for France, the United Nations is the natural and necessary framework for defining the conditions for ending the crisis' (French Foreign Ministry, 26 July 2006).

Paris used both the EU platform to try to unite member states behind its position, and used its privileged position as permanent member of the UN Security Council to shape international and European policy towards the conflict (BBC News, 8 August 2006). Within the EU, France furthermore led European protests at Israel's 'disproportionate' military response. While shaping a European line in support of French policies, France's European lead in Lebanon diplomacy also helped to improve relations with the United States: given the lingering resentment over the fall-out over the war in Iraq, this was a not inconsiderable consideration (BBC News, 8 August 2006). The importance Paris attached to raising the profile of French diplomacy was also illustrated by the way Foreign Minister Philippe Douste-Blazy described the 1 August agreement by EU foreign ministers to call for an immediate cessation of hostilities 'an important victory for French diplomacy' (cited in BBC News, 8 August 2006).

Europeanization vs. alliance politics

The French position differed considerably from that of the US, both with a view on the need for an immediate ceasefire in order to arrive at a political resolution as well as the purpose and institutional make up of a peace-keeping force. There is, therefore, no evidence of alliance politics in French responses to the war in Lebanon. As for Europeanization, although the EU did not constitute the most important institutional platform in the resolution of the crisis, uniting EU member states around the French position and to thus reinforce Paris' stature was of value, which points towards evidence of Europeanization understood as projection. However, there is no evidence of adaptation pressures acting on Paris.

With a view to the fundamental difference in position Chirac answered a question on the US argument that the time has come for a 'new Middle East' by stating that 'one thing is certain; we cannot change a region by force [. . .]. There have been developments [in the region] and something that worries me enormously, the hardening of relations between Islam worldwide and the West [. . .] all that this brings with it in terms of fostering the development of terrorism, (*Le Monde*, 27 July 2006). Together with the French emphasis on its relations with the Arab world and reluctance to back the US and its close ties to Israel, this statement also reinforces the broader concern over the West's relations with the Arab world that was already evident in reactions to the war in Afghanistan – a consideration largely absent in US political decision-making. Fundamentally, as US and French preferences diverged, none of the indicators of alliance politics conceptualized in Chapter 1 apply to this case. Rather, due to differences in approach, and means to assert national influence in a region of considerable interest to France through the UN, alignment with the US and US policy preferences was not an option – nor were there utilitarian incentives or motivations to keep the US involved that would have led France to back the US position. But concerns over improving relations with the United States given the fall-out over the war in Iraq do point towards alliance politics considerations. If not keeping the US involved in European security, then at least assuring a good working transatlantic relationship, constituted a French policy preference.

With respect to Europeanization, although the EU platform did not have the same significance as the UN institutional framework, there is some evidence to support Europeanization, understood as policy projection. France, in its attempt both to pursue its own line on the Lebanese conflict separately from the US and for French diplomacy to play a key role in resolving the conflict, used the EU CFSP diplomatic forum as a means to increase, and reinforce, national influence and diplomatic weight. Foreign Minister Douste-Blazy accordingly commented on the conclusion of the general affairs/external relations council on 1 August that 'this joint message from the Europeans is an important step that backs the draft resolution on Lebanon that France put before the UN Security Council and constitutes a positive sign for a lasting solution to the crisis' (French Foreign Ministry, 11 September 2006). This statement reinforces the notion that for Paris, the EU platform was useful to reinforce French foreign policy aims, and therefore constitutes evidence of policy projection and the export of national preferences onto the EU agenda.

Creating UNIFIL

Given France's considerable efforts in the political response to the war in Lebanon, participation in UNIFIL, if not in a leading then at least a considerable capacity was inevitable. Informally it was soon established that France might provide up to 5,000 troops for a multinational force to Lebanon – although one domestic concern was that a controversial mission to the Middle East might have negative repercussions on the French Muslim community and social cohesion as a result (BBC News, 8 August 2006). However, during the course of the negotiations over putting together the peace-keeping force, France delayed its agreement to send a sizeable force on account of security concerns. President Chirac in particular sought to guarantee security for French troops through requesting clarity about UNIFIL's rules of engagement and the need for a streamlined chain of command before committing more troops. This position was shared by the Ministry of Defence as well as other branches of the French government. Speaking in front of the French Senate, Michèle Alliot-Marie, Minister of Defence emphasized the decisive role played by France in the current UNIFIL as well as the expanded UNIFIL and reviewed the conditions that France had successfully imposed on the deployment of additional troops as a precondition for substantial commitments. These included that orders would come from a single command, that a special defence staff be reserved for this specific operation, that explicit instructions be available in the event of contact with armed elements, and that the use of force may be engaged, particularly if the UNIFIL's freedom of movement were to be compromised. Chairman Vinçon offered the unanimous support of the members of the Foreign Affairs Committee to the action undertaken by the Head of the Government and the ministers involved in both the diplomatic and military management of the Lebanon crisis (French Ministry of Defence, 31 August 2006). As in the case of the policy negotiations, there was broad agreement among different branches of government. But France responded to political pressure from other member states to increase its troop contributions. In the end, France committed 2,000 soldiers to UNIFIL as well as 1,700 as part of the French naval fleet near the Lebanese coast (de Beer, 2006).

Foreign Minister Douste-Blazy subsequently informed the National Assembly Foreign Affairs Committee on French participation in UNIFIL. He highlighted both the importance of the mission – to guarantee the scheduled 'dual process': deployment of the Lebanese army in southern Lebanon and withdrawal of the Israeli troops to the Blue Line – and France's key role in the implementation of UNSCR 1701 in part through taking command over UNIFIL until February 2007. Lastly, he emphasized that France was 'expecting neighbouring countries to contribute wholeheartedly to the implementation of UNSCR 1701. Any violation of its provisions – particularly of the embargo on arms for Hezbollah – would risk jeopardizing the ceasefire' (French Foreign Ministry, 7 September 2006).

Europeanization vs. alliance politics

As in the political negotiations over ending the crisis, there is little evidence of alliance politics. In France's view there was little utility in a transatlantic approach, which is reflected in public statements by government officials. President Chirac in particular was clear on his preference for a multinational force under a UN command rather than a different institutional framework. With respect to NATO, he stated that:

> France does not believe it is NATO's role to set up such a force. For technical reasons but also for political reasons, NATO is not designed for this type of intervention. NATO is perceived, whether we like it or not, as the armed wing of the West in these regions, and consequently, in terms of its image, NATO is not the right organization here. (*Le Monde*, 27 July 2006)

His statement also reinforces the conclusion that France, more so than Britain and Germany, was concerned over, and keen to avoid the emergence, of a renewed conflict of civilizations between the West and the Muslim world.

Given that UNIFIL is a UN rather than a EU force, Europeanization considerations do not have a strong explanatory value in this case, either. To be sure, the European component of UNIFIL was stressed repeatedly, for instance by Chairman Vinçon in the French Senate who stressed that the expanded UNIFIL was predominantly composed of European forces. Minister of Defence Aillot-Marie stated that Chirac's announcement for an increase in French contributions constituted a strong commitment on France's part that served to encourage its European partners to overcome their strong initial reticence. She also held that the announcement of France's participation was a source of motivation for these partners (French Ministry of Defence, 2006). The highlighting of European contributions, and French participation as a source of motivation does serve as evidence of Europeanization in the sense of a general salience of the European agenda – Europe showing flag was important even if this was not under an ESDP label. Similarly, highlighting the French lead in Europe serves to underline not just a French preference in favour of ESDP but also the ability to shape European policy and to project national preferences on to the European agenda. Lastly, adaptation pressures to commit troops in larger numbers than originally intended signal the growing Europeanization pressure exerted by EU institutions, in this case the PSC.

DRC: launching EUFOR RD Congo

As in Lebanon, France played a leading role in the launch of EUFOR RD Congo as well as in the diplomatic activities preceding the mission. Unlike Lebanon, however, the US did not play a political or military role in the region, which means that the transatlantic aspect is missing altogether. Prior to the debate over EUFOR RD Congo, Paris had progressively reinforced its national interest and its position on DRC by means of the UN platform in its concern over pacifying the country and the broader region. Over time this also came to involve also the EU platform, and combined the pursuit of its national interest in DRC with that of pushing the development of ESDP further.

Paris taking the initiative to launch EUFOR RD Congo and its favourable response to the UN's request for support reinforces France's long-standing involvement and interest in the Great Lakes region (French Foreign Ministry, 20 February 2008). France has played a role in supporting the peace process and the national transition processes; and, as part of this bilateral involvement, France has pushed for the progressive involvement of international and regional actors including the United Nations, the European Union and African actors. France had also been in favour of sending a UN peacekeeping force to DRC, and consistently supported the consolidation of MONUC to stabilize the security environment, in particular in the eastern regions (French Foreign Ministry, 20 February 2008).

Given this background, and the progressive internationalization and reinforcement of French bilateral relationships by means of the UN and through the EU, including ESDP through Operation Artemis and EUPOL Kinshasa, French interest in accepting the UN's request was unsurprising. Unlike Artemis, however, where France had acted as framework nation and contributed the bulk of the troops, credibility for ESDP in the case of EUFOR RD Congo required a more diverse European participation. This led to difficulties in Franco-German relations, despite the fact that Chirac and Merkel agreed on the necessity for launching the ESDP operation during Merkel's first meeting with Chirac after her election, including German military contributions (Beer and Schmidt, 2006). France also lobbied for the approval of an opinion paper to express EU support for MONUC in March 2006, which led to the formal agreement to deploy EU military capabilities. As a result, Berlin – the Foreign Ministry in particular – did entertain the suspicion 'that behind-the-scenes dealing between Paris and New York placed Germany in a position in which it could not refuse to take on the leadership role' (Ehrhart, 2007: 8). France was also in favour of extending the time frame of the mission, which further supports the conclusion that France's interests in the DRC context as well as the length of the mission differed considerably from those of Germany. France also suggested the deployment of a Battle Group (in a rotation that would only include a small number of French soldiers), further suggesting that this was a move to export national preferences for an EU operation on to the European agenda. Given German reluctance to contribute the bulk of the operation including a Battle Group, France did agree to contributed 1,090 troops (French Ministry of Defence, 2006) as well as the EU Force Commander, Major-General Christian Damay. In the case of EUFOR RD Congo, therefore, France was not only in favour of launching the mission but also exerted pressure on a second member state – Germany – to assume command over the mission in order to 'Europeanize' a French initiative and fundamental policy preference.

The perception of a French lead in the conceptualization of the mission and the pressure exerted on other member states was reinforced by the fact that, during the planning process of the mission, the UN request sent by UN Under-Secretary General Jean-Marie Guéhenno – a French national – to the British EU Presidency bypassed internal EU consultation mechanisms altogether. This caught other EU member states by surprise and unprepared for the request (see Major, 2008) – and reinforced the impression that this was a French rather than a European or UN initiative, and that Paris was keen to 'lock in' the mission.

Europeanization

French decision-making with respect to the launch of EUFOR Congo demonstrates considerable evidence of Europeanization, understood both as the projection of national preferences as well as a fundamental preference for a stronger EU profile in the region and in ESDP. The preference for a larger role for the EU is evident from the fact that the French Foreign Ministry emphasized that France has encouraged the growth of the European Union's role in the region; the EU has now established itself as a major player in the peace process in the DRC (French Ministry of Foreign Affairs, 20 February 2008). It is also evident from statements from government officials on France's preference to push the European agenda referred to in the context of the operation in FYROM: 'the EU must be ready, Europe must be an actor, when possible it must act. It's the French European method: to push the agenda, and if we can show that the EU is an actor we should show that the EU can do it alone' (Interview with government official, 8 July 2005). The case of EUFOR RD Congo, with French moves to 'Europeanize' the mission and to strengthen EU–UN cooperation in crisis management certainly illustrates this statement. Policy projection, on the other hand, is evident from France backing the mission, from close coordination between (French) UN and EU counterparts, from bypassing of coordination channels, and from French suggestion of not only a non-French/German lead but also the deployment of an EU Battle Group.

Conclusion

Taken together, the focus of the Europeanization of French foreign policy with respect to ESDP has remained regional with the Balkans and sub-Saharan Africa as key areas of operations; and continues to be focused on the export of national policy preferences – with little evidence of Europeanization where this is not the case. At the same time, the institutionalization of CFSP and ESDP has increased adaptation pressures even for France, as the case of UNIFIL demonstrates.

5
Germany: From Bystander to Participant

Introduction: Germany and European foreign and security policy

The fundamentals of German foreign policy in the post-World War II context consist of what has been termed 'reflexive multilateralim' (Katzenstein, 1997), the aversion to the use of force, and strong transatlantic leanings. With respect to ESDP, this historic specificity has led to what has been termed as 'fence-sitting', with Berlin caught between transatlantic commitments and European rhetoric as far as strengthening Europe's foreign policy was concerned. Germany's multilateralism was less an attempt to create a multilateral world order as in the case of France, but more an attempt to increase its action radius after the defeat in World War II and the concurrent taboo against German unilateralism and military rearmament. With the end of the Cold War, but particularly the conflict in the Balkans and Germany's eventual participation in the NATO operation during the war over Kosovo in 1999, the specific historical taboos began to erode. Germany's political leadership increasingly began to push for 'normalcy' and for Germany to assume a more proactive role in defining and in pursuing its national interests. The period between 2001 and 2006 thus demonstrates a more active Germany when it came to military contributions in the NATO, ESDP and UN context; and a more active Germany when it came to increasing national influence through the platform of the EU but also the UN in the case of Afghanistan. However, adaptation pressures with respect to military operations continue to be strong – as a result, it would be an overstatement to speak of 'proactive' participation in terms of policy initiation.

2001: FYROM and Afghanistan

In FYROM, German foreign policy makers favoured the EU CFSP as a key platform in the political process leading to the resolution of the conflict – therefore, empirical evidence supports the Europeanization hypothesis in particular with respect to the high salience of the European agenda and the adherence to common policy objectives in the political solution to the crisis. With respect to military operations Germany had a clear preference for NATO, both because ESDP was not considered ready to carry out a mission in terms of its institutional development, and because utilizing the NATO framework ensured the continued participation of the US. The alliance politics approach, therefore, explains the decision to participate in the NATO operation and the rejection of an early ESDP takeover of the NATO mission. Domestic considerations are an important factor for understanding policy decisions, in particular Schröder's goal for Germany to assume increasing responsibility in the military realm and to become a more credible and influential player. In Afghanistan, German participation and contribution to the war and reconstruction of Afghanistan was significant. Berlin pledged a total of 5,100 of troops to OEF (3,900) and ISAF (1,200). Germany also played a role in the reconstruction efforts by hosting the Bonn Conference on Afghanistan. Germany's commitment was particularly significant with regard to the use of military force, an area where Germany had traditionally been cautious and seen the use of force as *ultima ratio*. Chancellor Schröder in particular regarded military participation in OEF and ISAF – apart from an expression of solidarity with the US – as a means to increase Germany's independence and latitude for action in world politics. Significant evidence of Europeanization can be found in the policies towards the political and economic reconstruction of Afghanistan, where a single voice for the EU and a profile for the EU CFSP was not only of high salience for German policy makers, but also viewed as a vehicle to increase Germany's scope for action and to export national preferences onto the EU level. Berlin's increasing engagement took place through international institutions and reinforces the fundamentally multilateral conception of German foreign policy. However, solidarity with the US and increasing national influence took precedence over considerations of the place of the EU CFSP/ESDP where military participation in the war in Afghanistan was concerned.

FYROM and the support for the EU CFSP in the political negotiations

German policy towards FYROM after the country declared independence in 1991 centred on conflict prevention and was mainly conducted through multilateral channels, particularly the UN, OSCE and the EU. This also included bilateral relations and cooperation in support of these multilateral efforts. Germany was sensitive to the crisis not just on account of previous experiences in the Balkans and the failure on the part of the EU to act, but also as the danger of wider regional destabilization would have meant a threat of refugee flows and instability close to Germany's borders. The conflict in FYROM also threatened to undermine the broader regional framework that had been put in place after the end of the conflict in Kosovo. There was, therefore, a considerable sense of urgency for German policy makers based on the likely detrimental domestic ramifications mentioned above (Interview with German official, 1 September 2005). The EU was already an important platform for the political and economic process of regional post-conflict reconstruction. And given the goal of eventual integration of the countries of the Western Balkans in the EU together with the goal for a greater role for the EU as a regional political actor, the EU CFSP was a natural institutional venue for resolving the crisis from the perspective of German policy makers. For these reasons, success for the EU CFSP in resolving the crisis in FYROM was of high salience.

Whereas elected officials supported the application of instruments located in the EU CFSP/ESDP, the Federal Foreign Office emphasized restoring stability over the application of new instruments. This shows that although the use of EU CFSP instruments in the negotiation of the crisis was supported and deemed important on account of the symbolism for the evolution of the EU as a political actor, this position was not equally shared among all participants in the governmental process. Policy makers, particularly those in the Federal Foreign Office, regarded the Contact Group as an important platform as US involvement was deemed crucial in resolving the conflict, and considered it an effective platform to influence broader policy responses to the crisis among the major powers involved (Interview with German official, 21 November 2005).

Europeanization vs. alliance politics

The analysis of decisions taken with respect to the political negotiations of the crisis as well as press statements, interviews and the parliamentary debates show considerable evidence of Europeanization. The EU CFSP was regarded as an appropriate institution to resolve the crisis. This supports the first conception of Europeanization of policy adaptation, as German support for Javier Solana and EU Special Representative François Léotard in the negotiation of the crisis accommodated the progress of the EU CFSP. The salience of the EU CFSP agenda is reflected in the German government's decision to agree to their mandates as well as German support for the political negotiations.

Chancellor Schröder and Foreign Minister Fischer both publicly supported EU unity and a leading role for the EU CFSP and Solana in the political negotiation of the conflict. Support for the EU CFSP in political negotiations, and for the comprehensive concept instituted in the Western Balkans since 1999 also crossed party lines. Foreign Minister Fischer made several statements to this effect in the press, and his frequent visits to the region and meetings with Macedonian officials served to underline Germany's support for the EU CFSP negotiating positions and the European agenda more generally, rather than separate German interests (Auswärtiges Amt, 11 March 2001; 4 May 2001; 24 May 2001; 7 June 2001). In his address to the government on the situation in FYROM on 6 July, Fischer emphasized the necessity for a political solution to the crisis, and the chance for EUSR Léotard to shape these negotiations.

Statements made in the Bundestag demonstrate that elites favoured the application of CFSP instruments. In addition to the salience of the European agenda, then, evidence of Europeanization also points towards the existence of norms and preferences that favoured the application of EU instruments. This is reflected in public statements by members of the German parliament, which suggest a broad domestic consensus on the goal of a successful role for the EU CFSP in the negotiation efforts. In the debate surrounding German participation in Essential Harvest on 29 August, Fischer explicitly stated that the main weight in the resolution of the crisis was with the Europeans, and was 'about a new role for Europe in the developing common foreign and security policy' (Fischer, Deutscher Bundestag, 29 August 2001, 18179C). Speaking for the Christian Democrats (CDU), Friedrich Merz stated that 'it is undoubtedly valuable that NATO and the EU for the first time have jointly developed and realized a political concept for the negotiations' (Merz, Deutscher Bundestag, 29 August 2001, 18204D). Wolfgang Gerhardt, speaking for the Free Democrats (FDP), stressed 'Germany's responsibility in shaping Europe's security' (Gerhardt, Deutscher Bundestag, 6 July 2001, 18071C) and emphasized that the significance of the negotiations leading to the Ohrid Agreement was that 'for the first time a European component had been placed along the US component in the negotiations' and that this was 'beneficial for European self confidence' (Gerhardt, Deutscher Bundestag, 29 August 2001, 18184B). With the exception of the former socialist party PDS, who argued for the UN and OSCE as the appropriate institutional framework for the solution of the crisis (Deutscher Bundestag, 6 July 2001, 18075A), statements made in the Bundestag support the conclusion that the application of CFSP instruments in the negotiations leading to the Ohrid Agreement were considered appropriate and of high importance for the development of the EU CFSP.

Evidence of Europeanization also extends to the equation of European and national preferences: both Fischer and Schröder framed the crisis in FYROM and future of the region as 'central to European and therefore also German security' (Fischer, Deutscher Bundestag, 6 July 2001, 18065D; Schröder, Deutscher Bundestag, 29 August 2001, 18201D), and members of the ruling coalition termed it 'a test case for the emerging EU CFSP' (Erler, Deutscher Bundestag, 6 July 2001, 18069D). Significantly, one member of the Bundestag stated that the use of the CFSP 'had been a goal for Germany in particularly with regards to the Balkans' (Sterzing, Deutscher Bundestag, 29 August 2001, 18207A).

With respect to the second conception of Europeanization, that of national projection, there is little evidence of Germany attempting to increase national influence through the EU CFSP platform. Given that member states' influence decreased after Javier Solana had been given a mandate to conduct the political negotiations (Interview with German official 30 August 2005), the EU CFSP was not used as a means to project particular national preferences on to the European agenda in this case. If anything, national influence on EU policies decreased on account of the consolidation of the political negotiation under Javier Solana.

While the growing role of the CFSP as well as the need for the EU to make up for past failings in the region was acknowledged (Interview with German official, 8 August 2005), the priority on the part of the Federal Foreign Office was to respond to the conflict in a way that would contain the spread of violence, see the conflict to a speedy and peaceful resolution, and involve the US as one of the vital participants in the peace process and its implementation. The overall approach to the negotiations, therefore, was cautious. In this sense, the EU CFSP represented one, but not the only and not the most important, forum for the political negotiations in the minds of individual officials. And, because Germany participated in the negotiations in the framework of

to prove itself a reliable partner in NATO even after the first substantial military deployment since the end of World War II during the crisis in Kosovo (Maull, 2000). For his part, Chancellor Schröder pushed for an increasing profile for Germany in NATO to demonstrate that Germany was no longer bound by its past. Although this is even more evident in the German response to the war in Afghanistan, considerations with respect to German participation in the NATO Operation Essential Harvest reflect a similar goal on the part of the Chancellor.

US preferences and a fundamentally transatlanticist orientation in German foreign policy (Fischer, 2001) constituted important factors in German decision-making in this case. However, in press statements and domestic debates, international responsibility and solidarity with NATO allies was often portrayed as the necessary precondition for Europe to act. Importantly, however, this has to be understood in a specific domestic context where the use of force remained contested and where a comprehensive European approach was bound to be more attractive and persuasive than military deployment under NATO. Policy officials in the Federal Foreign Office and the Ministry of Defence, however, were clear on the need for a NATO presence, including German participation in a NATO operation, to stabilize FYROM (Interview with German official, 21 November 2005).

Apart from alliance solidarity, participation in the NATO operation was also deemed important in view of Germany's potential weight in the emerging ESDP: if Germany did not pull its weight in NATO in FYROM, Britain and France would continue to dominate. For the government, this created a dilemma between keeping in line with the defence budget and keeping Germany's commitment within NATO and ESDP (*Financial Times Deutschland*, 2 July 2001).

Although Germany did not take the lead in initiating a NATO operation during the multilateral negotiations leading to the resolution of the crisis – this was left to the UK and France – Berlin did make a commitment to contribute troops to NATO Operation Essential Harvest and to its extensions, Operation Amber Fox and Allied Harmony. After the NATO Council had decided on the British-led Operation Essential Harvest on 29 June 2001 (NATO, 15 August 2001), the Bundestag agreed to the participation of 500 troops after a vote on 29 August 2001 (Deutscher Bundestag, 29 August 2001).

Chancellor Schröder was constrained by allies' expectations for Germany to provide troops on the one hand and by domestic reservations toward German deployments on the other. In a classic example of a two-level game (Putnam, 1988), Schröder pushed for Germany to assume increasing responsibility in the field of security and defence by pledging troops to the NATO operation in response to allies' expectations while at the same time having to negotiate domestic support; in particular, winning the support not of the opposition but his own ruling coalition – indicating a lack of support from Schröder's own constituency.

Domestic differences made the question of German military contribution to the NATO mission a significant topic of domestic debate. In particular, this applied to members of the Bundestag, the German parliament, who threatened to vote against a German NATO deployment. Domestic objection to military deployment arose out of two separate positions. The long-held taboo against the use of force was a source of reservations particularly among members of the ruling Red–Green coalition. Members of the Christian Democrats, the leading opposition party, on the other hand, argued that insufficient defence budgets and the resulting military overstretch of Germany's armed forces would prevent Germany from playing the leadership role in Europe advocated by Chancellor Schröder (Rühe, Deutscher Bundestag, 15 March 2001, 15366C). Former Defence Minister Rühe linked consent to the increase of the defence budget by at least 500 million Deutschmark (€250 million) even if other members of the CDU were in favour of the mandate. Rühe's gamble paid off in so far as the CDU fraction in the Bundestag did lift its opposition to the deployment after the government increased the budget for the German contingent in FYROM.

As expected, Schröder could not rely on his own party to carry the vote: 20 SPD members had written an open letter opposing the NATO operation. When Operation Essential Harvest was voted on, of 635 votes, 497 voted in favour, 130 against, and 8 abstained (Deutscher Bundestag, 29 August 2001, 18210A). This gave the government the mandate it needed, but showed that the government's domestic support was weak.

Europeanization vs. alliance politics

Public debates over participation in NATO demonstrate some evidence of Europeanization with respect to the equation of national with European preferences and the rhetorical use of the EU as a cover to pursue national policy preferences and to persuade members of the government to consent to participation in a military operation.

The discussion of a NATO contribution was frequently linked to increasing national influence in the future, also with regard to the nascent ESDP. For instance, Fischer argued on 6 July that a refusal to participate in the NATO operation would have negative implications for the developing ESDP, particularly at a time where the barriers between

NATO and the EU were disappearing (Deutscher Bundestag, 6 July 2001, 18065D). Evidence that EU CFSP was used as a rhetoric device to gain support for German participation in the military operation also points towards evidence of Europeanization understood as the use of the EU as a cover to pursue national policy preferences in addition to adaptational pressures acting on Germany to participate in the NATO operation for solidarity with its allies. This is evident in the linking of the NATO operation to a comprehensive EU conflict prevention strategy towards FYROM. For instance, Peter Struck, the leader of the SPD fraction in the Bundestag argued that the NATO operation was an 'important part of the preventive war – and conflict prevention strategy of the EU towards Macedonia' (Struck, Deutscher Bundestag, 29 August 2001, 18191C). While Germany did not pursue national policy preferences as far as military tools were concerned through the EU CFSP and ESDP in the crisis in FYROM, the argument that participation in the NATO operation would help Europe play a bigger and stronger role in the future played a considerable role in shoring up support for German participation in the NATO operation. The EU represented an important reference point, especially for members of the ruling coalition. For the opposition, which has traditionally focused more on the transatlantic relationship, this was not as important, although the CDU and FDP also favoured European capabilities.

When it comes to the application of military instruments German responses to the crisis support the conclusion that preference was given to NATO out of alliance politics considerations. There is evidence of Germany preferring NATO as a military instrument both for utilitarian reasons, and in order to keep the US involved in European security concerns. In addition to utilitarian considerations, there is also some evidence of Germany giving preference to NATO as an institutional forum out of a transatlantic preference, that it considered NATO as the prime forum for the solution of the crisis, and that Germany preferred NATO over other institutional settings. This is illustrated by the fact that Germany wanted to ensure US support and sound EU–US relations in the handling of the crisis. In addition, the opposition explicitly referred to NATO as a community of shared values that should be strengthened also through this mandate (Merkel, Deutscher Bundestag, 29 August 2001, 18193C), suggesting an inherent preference towards NATO. Importantly, this sentiment was expressed before 11 September.

Evidence of alliance politics as a decisive factor in policy reactions to the crisis supports the conclusion that Germany deemed US involvement of primary importance and aligned with NATO in order to ensure

US participation in the solution of the crisis. Germany did consider US involvement crucial in this particular case as the US was an important political player in the Western Balkans, including in FYROM. Causing a conflict with the US over the handling of the crisis, or over the application of military instruments located in ESDP would have been foolish (Interview with German official, 21 November 2005).

Empirical evidence also supports the conclusion that Germany regarded NATO as the prime forum for the military solution of the crisis. NATO enjoyed greater credibility with especially the Albanian Macedonians and symbolized continued US involvement; when it came to an ESDP takeover of the NATO mandate, the EU had to first convince the Macedonian government to consent to this mandate (Interview with EU official, 21 June 2005). And, the fact that President Trajkovski requested NATO assistance in the solution of the crisis (NATO, 20 June 2001) left no other choice for the institutional venue in the first instance. The political decisions taken with respect to NATO also reflect Germany's traditional foreign policy preference of putting the transatlantic relationship first and the EU second, a tradition that continued under the Red/Green government (Fischer, 2001).

The ESDP takeover from NATO

While German reactions towards the crisis in FYROM demonstrated a preference for a European approach to the resolution of the crisis and the general salience of the European agenda, an ESDP takeover was not considered expedient until much later, when the EU expressed willingness to take over the NATO mission in FYROM at the Copenhagen Council in December 2002 (Council of the European Union, 29 January 2003). This suggests that despite the high profile of the EU CFSP and ESDP in governmental debates, and despite the professed goal on the part of the Chancellor for Europe to play a greater part in matters of security,[1] alliance politics considerations overwhelmingly determined German decision-making with respect to the timing of the handover from NATO to ESDP.

Despite the salience of the EU CFSP in the political resolution of the crisis and the increasing role taken on by Germany in the military management of the crisis as part of the NATO operations, Germany was not in favour of EU Special Representative François Léotard's suggestion of an ESDP takeover of Operation Essential Harvest because it was considered too early. This was on account of timing both where the institutional set-up of ESDP and conditions on the ground in FYROM were concerned. Only when the security situation in FYROM had improved to the point where an ESDP mission was considered safe, and only on the condition that the institutional arrangements between NATO and the EU would be resolved, did Germany support the ESDP takeover of the NATO operation (Interview with German official, 21 November 2005).

However, different players in the German government viewed the matter of the takeover, both on the question of timing and principle, differently. Whereas Chancellor Schröder and Foreign Minister Fischer – along with Javier Solana – were in favour of a handover early on (Interview with German official, 3 November 2005), the Foreign Office itself did not concur with Fischer's position and managed to delay the process. The Federal Foreign Office considered the timing of the initial suggestion premature (Interview with German official, 21 November 2005). The Ministry of Defence, on the other hand, objected to an ESDP takeover for reasons both of principle and of practicality (Interview with former German official, 8 February 2006).

The Federal Foreign Office also did not consider the EU ESDP ready to take on such a mission in terms of its military evolution and considered an ESDP mission as too early, both where the institutional construction and the situation on the ground were concerned. The Balkans and the ESDP departments within the Federal Foreign Office both shared this cautious attitude, but for different reasons: the Balkans department because it considered the situation still too risky for the ESDP to assume responsibility (Interview with German official, 21 November 2005) and was not necessarily in favour of ESDP to begin with (Interview with German official, 3 November 2005), and the ESDP department because it insisted on the conclusion of the Berlin Plus agreement between NATO and the EU before launching an ESDP mission (Interview with German official, 3 November 2005). This reflects both utilitarian and transatlantic preferences within branches of the Federal Foreign Office. The bureaucracy thus acted as a 'retarding element' rather than a ready facilitator of a transition to more responsibility for ESDP (Interview with German official, 3 November 2005). While there was no objection to an ESDP mission in principle, especially given the small size of the mission, it was only when stability in FYROM was guaranteed that the foreign ministry gave the green light for an ESDP mission (Interview with German official, 21 November 2005).

The Ministry of Defence, on the other hand, objected to the utilization of ESDP instruments altogether, primarily on utilitarian grounds: NATO was conducting three active operations in the Balkans at the time, and it was not considered useful to dislodge one of these operations in order to start an ESDP mission when the EU at that point had not even undertaken a crisis management exercise (Interview with former German official, 8 February 2006). What spoke in favour of the ESDP takeover in the minds of defence officials, however, was the chance to improve the working mechanisms with the French by arriving at a formalized agreement between NATO and the EU. This was viewed as a clear advantage because cooperation had been difficult in the past where it had 'always been 14 against 1 where the cooperation with NATO was concerned' (Interview with former German official, 8 February 2006). On account of this reasoning, the Ministry of Defence came to view an ESDP takeover as advantageous.

Europeanization vs. alliance politics

Given the size and the symbolic value of a military operation, the eventual use of ESDP instruments was viewed favourably in principle, but was a question of timing. This is demonstrated by the fact that Germany did push for the application of ESDP instruments in FYROM at the NATO summit in Prague in November 2002 (Overhaus, 2003: 56). This in turn suggests that, along with the early support of the Chancellor and the Foreign Minister for an ESDP mission, policy preferences with regard to the ESDP takeover exhibit some, albeit weak, evidence of Europeanization. This applies with respect to Europeanization understood as policy adaptation as well as changing policy preferences: ESDP came to be supported as the appropriate institution by important decision makers; a key bureaucracy adapted its preference on the use of ESDP instruments, and policy elites generally favoured the application of ESDP instruments.

Although Germany did regard NATO as the prime forum for the solution of the crisis and did inhibit an inherent preference for NATO over the EU setting, early discussions of an ESDP takeover of the NATO mandate show that reservations out of concern over its impact on the transatlantic relationship in this case eroded relatively quickly, particularly as this was an operation of a small enough size – but of significant symbolic value for the EU ESDP – that the EU ESDP could take over without endangering the regional peace, and had US support (Interview with US official, 20 October 2005). The costs of supporting an EU-ization (in the sense of a change in label from NATO to EU ESDP) of the intervention in FYROM, therefore, were low and Germany could and did support the ESDP takeover at relatively low political cost (Overhaus, 2003).

Rather than fundamental transatlantic preferences, German policy makers delayed the application of ESDP instruments out of utilitarian reasons, and on account of US and German preferences for a formalized agreement on EU access to NATO assets prior to the launch of an ESDP operation. Since these two considerations determined German decision-making, the alliance politics framework best explains German policy choices in this case.

Despite the high salience of the EU agenda as it applied to the EU CFSP among the German government particularly the Chancellor and Foreign Minister, an ESDP operation as suggested by François Léotard was considered too early, and of little use except for its symbolism as far as ESDP was concerned and in FYROM generally (Interview with German official, 3 November 2005). Although this symbolism as part of a growing European role was important, it had to be weighed against other factors. To be sure, Fischer had termed the NATO mission in FYROM as a test case for European capacity in crisis management, as Europe carried the main responsibility for developing a regional security structure in the Balkans (Associated Press, 3 September 2001). But deployment was considered risky, as NATO had to rely on the goodwill of the two parties of the conflict to settle the conflict and as there was risk that the conflict could result in new violence. This precluded the application of ESDP instruments in the first instance. This then leads to the overall conclusion that while the crisis of FYROM shows that German policy was Europeanized as far as the political negotiations were concerned, the role afforded to the EU stopped short of an ESDP military operation due to alliance politics consideration. As the next section shows, a similar pattern was at play in military and political responses to the war and subsequent reconstruction efforts in Afghanistan.

Afghanistan: OEF and the war on terror

Following the events of 11 September and the subsequent war in Afghanistan, German foreign policy exhibited potentially contradictory, but essentially interlinked, objectives: to assert Germany's national position in a changed geo-strategic environment, and to push for a greater profile for the EU as well as the UN. This was also reflected in the debates in the Bundestag. In the first address to the Bundestag after the attacks on 19 September, Chancellor Schröder stressed the need for solidarity with the US and Germany's willingness to contribute militarily to the war against terror by stating that 'we as Germans and Europeans aim for unqualified solidarity with the US' adding at the same time that solidarity and gratitude for the US were not a sole basis for the legitimacy of any potential military deployment, but that the goal of any decision would be 'to save the future of our country in a free world, because this is the real issue' (Schröder, Deutscher Bundestag, 19 September 2001,

18302A). Schröder also frequently emphasized Germany's increasing role and international standing, stating that the period of German post-war foreign policy where allies would expect 'something like secondary assistance' had irrevocably passed with the attacks on 11 September. Instead, Germany would have to take seriously its responsibility and commitments to the defence of freedom and human rights, to bring stability and security explicitly including contributions in military operations (Schröder, Deutscher Bundestag, 11 October 2001, 18682C).

The decision to contribute troops to the US-led war on terror created significant unease among the German public and particularly among the ruling coalition, where Schröder faced a potential revolt from members of his own Social Democratic Party and Green coalition partner. While the Cabinet approved the plan for the deployment, which met with the approval from the CDU, CSU and the FDP, members of both the SPD and Green party were against the deployment (Longhurst, 2004: 84). This put the ruling coalition under significant stress. By contrast, for the CDU/CSU the attacks of 11 September had reinforced the parties' transatlantic leanings as well as the conviction that German security interests would have to be protected with political as well as military means – and wherever threats to German security originated geographically (Katsioulis, 2004: 227–52). The PDS, as in the case of the NATO and eventually also ESDP Operations in FYROM, opposed the deployment of Bundeswehr troops. In light of a growing level of dissent within the governing coalition and the prospect of having to rely on opposition votes to secure a parliamentary majority for military support (*Financial Times*, 14 November 2001), Schröder went as far as linking parliamentary approval for the deployment of 3,900 Bundeswehr troops, including special forces (KSK), to a vote of confidence in his government in order to secure the necessary votes in favour of Bundeswehr deployment from his own party on 16 November 2001 (Deutscher Bundestag, 16 November 2001; *Financial Times*, 14 November 2001). He narrowly survived the vote of confidence by a count of 334 (of 662) votes. As had been visible in the case of FYROM, for Schröder the war in Afghanistan presented an opportunity for Germany to play a more assertive role in international politics, but one that posed a not insubstantial risk to his leadership and political survival. Although much of this was done also on account of solidarity with the US, the size of the contribution and the departure from previously held preferences and positions, particularly with respect to the use of military force, supports the conclusion that this was also to increase Germany's international profile and room for manoeuvre, and arose out of national preferences.

Europeanization vs. alliance politics

While the EU agenda was of some salience to German policy makers, this did not apply to military participation in OEF. As a result, evidence that would support the Europeanization hypothesis is limited. However, the application of EU CFSP instruments, or at least an EU special summit and measures to combat global terrorism was important to German policy makers as they did not want to see the EU sidelined completely in the war in Afghanistan. This supports one indicator of Europeanization, that of the salience of the EU CFSP.

Both the chancellor and the foreign minister would have preferred for the EU to play a bigger role, although their position was not shared by other EU member states. Schröder stressed the necessity for a comprehensive approach to the fight against terrorism as well as prevention and management of crises, and emphasized that it was at German insistence that the Belgian EU presidency had called for a special summit of the European Council on 21 September to discuss the EU's stance on the war on terror (Deutscher Bundestag, 19 September 2001, 18302D). Members of the ruling coalition supported and acknowledged Schröder's initiative, stating that 'after 11 September, the European Union has become more important than ever' (Gloser, Deutscher Bundestag, 18 October 2001, 18988A). This shows that the leading coalition supported a growing role for the EU.

While the evidence of Europeanization in this policy area is rather weak, the invocation of Article V of the NATO treaty at the request of the US (*Financial Times*, 3 October 2001), and the use of the NATO Treaty as a legal basis – together with UNSC resolution 1368 and 1373 – for Germany's contribution to OEF points towards the centrality of the alliance in German foreign-policy decisions in this case. There is significant support for the third indicator of alliance politics, that of giving preference to the US and NATO as an institutional forum out of a transatlantic preference. Germany aligned with NATO on the basis of the NATO treaty, and to show solidarity with the US – a point frequently made in public debates and speeches by members of the government as well as the opposition. For instance, speaking for the Christian Democrats, Merz positively acknowledged Schröder's repeated emphasis on unrestricted solidarity with the US and mentioned that 'we from the CDU fraction in the Bundestag had supported you from the start' even when it became clear that 'this solidarity would exceed words' but would include military measures. Merz also stated that 'solidarity with the US cannot be contingent on success of the operation. The solidarity with the US and our own, national interest calls for the deployment of Bundeswehr forces' (Merz, Deutscher Bundestag, 16 November 2001, 19858D).

Transatlantic preference is reflected in a number of domestic decisions also on the part of the ruling coalition, despite reservations voiced with respect to the use of military force by some members of the SPD and the Green Party. With the exception of the PDS, there was broad domestic support for the invocation of Article V and solidarity with the US. The Bundestag voted on 19 September in favour of following up declarations of solidarity with concrete measures. Peter Struck argued that solidarity with NATO and the US was justified on account of NATO's contribution to Germany's post-World War II security; and one could not give up on this constant in German post-war policy 'when for the first time solidarity is requested from us' (Struck, Deutscher Bundestag, 16 November 2001, 19862B). In addition, normative arguments were put forward in Bundestag debates that emphasized NATO as a community of values that made solidarity a matter of more than just a contractual obligation but also a contribution to the defence of values: Schröder stated that the invocation of Article V was 'a decision of great ramifications that commits us not just formally [. . .] the attacks on New York and Washington were not just attacks on the American values, they were attacks on [. . .] the values in our Basic Law [. . .]. We have experienced solidarity over decades. This is why it is simply our duty [. . .] to give back solidarity in this situation' (Schröder, Deutscher Bundestag, 8 November 2001, 19287B).

In conclusion, the decision to deploy troops as part of OEF was not motivated by considerations that would support the Europeanization hypothesis. But neither is the approach of alliance politics suited to fully explain decision-making in this case as domestic considerations of a growing international role for Germany were relevant for understanding policy decisions. The alliance politics approach does not account for the fact that Germany's motivation for military participation in OEF also included increasing Germany's action radius and 'normalcy' in a post-Cold War era. Thus, German participation in OEF is best understood as an expression of transatlantic solidarity in the war against terror, which was largely determined by the preferences and requests made by the Bush administration in addition to efforts by Chancellor Schröder to do away with Germany's post-World War II special status (*Sonderweg*).

The reconstruction of Afghanistan

Germany played a significant role in formulating policies towards Afghanistan's reconstruction after the fall of the Taliban, both by hosting the Bonn Conference on Afghanistan and by initiating the appointment of an EU Special Representative. The EU CFSP agenda was of importance and utility in this case, and presented an important policy platform for reinforcing national preference and for giving the EU a voice. German policy makers early on raised the issue of post-conflict reconstruction of Afghanistan with other relevant actors, and aimed at playing a key role in this area through the auspices of international institutions, notably the UN and the EU. And, unlike military deployment to OEF and ISAF, the German lead and European involvement in the reconstruction of Afghanistan had broad domestic support.

Germany hosted the Afghanistan Conference in late November 2001 at the request of UN Special Representative Lakhdar Brahimi, which signified the substantial stakes and interest for Germany in the international efforts of Afghanistan. Given the positive perception of Germany in Afghanistan, Germany was a natural candidate to host the Conference and to play a leading role in the coordination of international reconstruction efforts (Interview with German official, 30 August 2005). The presence of both Chancellor Schröder and Foreign Minister Fischer at the signing ceremony signified the importance of the policy for the German government. The German concept for the international efforts in Afghanistan included support for the UN in leading the implementation of the Petersberg Agreement, to recognize the EU as one of the pillars for economic reconstruction, and use the existing goodwill of the Afghan people towards Germany, which lent credibility to Germany as playing a leading role (Klaiber, 2003: 12).

Germany's political engagement for the reconstruction of Afghanistan was also due to the fact that Germany had a historically strong interest and connection to Afghanistan, including a close relationship with Afghan exiles in Germany. In addition, echoing the sentiments of increasing Germany's independence and room for manoeuvre, Berlin's political and military engagement in the reconstruction of Afghanistan was also a question of 'no taxation without representation', and the aim to play a significant role through and in EU efforts, given that 'Germany is a net payer in the EU' (Interview with German official, 1 September 2005). This signals that the EU CFSP was perceived as a useful political platform in the reconstruction of Afghanistan on the part of the German government.

The priorities with regard to the CFSP in this case were to both consolidate and make visible the EU's efforts in the reconstruction of Afghanistan, and there were no differences in view among the key participants in the German government. Given the extent of Germany's involvement in the formulation and coordination of reconstruction efforts, the EU represented an important platform through which to pursue German national interests, and to consolidate policy efforts. The extensive use of the EU platform also suggests an inherent preference on the part of German government officials and the foreign office for the use and application of EU CFSP instruments.

Europeanization vs. alliance politics

In the policy decisions surrounding the reconstruction of Afghanistan, there is significant evidence that supports the Europeanization hypothesis particularly with regard to the salience of the European agenda in German foreign policy, as well as using the EU CFSP as a vehicle to export national preferences and to reinforce national policy efforts on the EU level. Policy elites also favoured the application of CFSP instruments, suggesting the existence of norms and preferences that favoured the application of EU instruments over other possibilities.

The European agenda in national foreign policy was salient as far as the EU CFSP was concerned. As mentioned previously, Chancellor Schröder initiated the emergency European Council at Ghent on 19 September, and indicated that he would address the role of Europe and the EU CFSP in the fight against terrorism at the European Council. Foreign Minister Fischer echoed much of these statements and expressed the German preference that this would carry on in a post-Taliban solution for Afghanistan, where the EU could play a visible role and build on its strength in humanitarian issues, economic reconstruction and conflict management (Deutscher Bundestag, 18 October 2001, 18981C–18992B). Germany also pushed for the application of EU political instruments in Afghanistan on 8 October, a proposal that was rejected by the Belgian presidency (*Financial Times*, 9 October 2001). Earlier, Germany had presented what was later termed a 'reflection paper' on the political reconstruction of Afghanistan at a special meeting of Asia experts on 3 October that did not find favour with other EU member states on account of lacking political instruments and a not sufficiently coherent foreign and security policy (Deutscher Bundestag, 18 October 2001, 18981C, 18992B). Still, this demonstrates not only that Germany took an active role in the reconstruction of Afghanistan but attempted to involve EU instruments.

What is more, Berlin actively pushed for a political role for Europe, and this had broad public support. To illustrate, on 18 October in the Bundestag Schröder stated that:

together with the United Nations we will have to define and put into place a long-term concept for Afghanistan's stabilization. Here

Europe, not just the member states as allies of the US, will have to play an important role. Especially in the question of the post-Taliban-process, the voice of Europe must be heard and the activities of Europe must be visible. Europe will support the long-term inclusion of Arab and Islamic states in the anti-terror coalition. (Schröder, Deutscher Bundestag, 18 October 2001, 18983A).

This view was shared by members of the ruling coalition: a member of the Green party stated that 'the UN as well as the EU will be an important factor in the future developments of Afghanistan. It is impor-tant to remember that the EU in cooperation with other international organization has a considerable potential for conflict prevention and cri-sis management, and can support stabilization – as we have seen in the development of Macedonia, (Sterzing, Deutscher Bundestag, 18 October 2001, 19002B).

The EU CFSP also represented a platform through which to pursue national policy preferences and was used as a vehicle to increase Germany's political profile internationally. This supports the second indicator of Europeanization, that of exporting policy preferences on to the EU agenda. The appointment of a German diplomat as the EU's spe-cial envoy to Afghanistan in particular supports this conclusion. It was a German initiative to appoint an EU Special Representative, a German was nominated for the position, Germany drew up the mandate and paid for much of the expenses (Interview with former German official, 9 February 2006).

The theme of German engagement in the framework of a European effort emerged before Klaiber's appointment both in the domestic debates as well as on the international level, as illustrated above. In an interview with Minister of State Dr Volmer on the Afghanistan Confer-ence in Bonn, Volmer stated that Germany would play a role within the EU, particularly in the suggestion of sending an EU-envoy to Kabul so that Europe would gain more visibility (ZDF, 30 November 2001). Berlin was of the view that the EU should have a political representative in Kabul to assist in the political process and to make the EU's efforts in the country visible – in other words, to give the EU a voice (Interview with former German official, 9 February 2006). Klaus-Peter Klaiber was appointed EU Special Representative to Afghanistan on 10 December 2001 and served for six months to coordinate EU actions in the coun-try (Council of the European Union, 10 December 2001). The mandate was drafted by Germany, and there was no other candidate put forward. Funds for the EU Special Representative's salary were made available by Germany as well, suggesting that Klaiber's appointment essentially constituted a national secondment rather than an EU post.

There is no empirical support for considerations of alliance politics having played a role in this case. For one, this was because this particular policy field was not related to military measures where NATO would have been an appropriate institution. More fundamentally, US preferences did not factor significantly in German considerations. Rather, German preferences ran counter to that of the US in formulating policies for Afghanistan's reconstruction, for instance with respect to the question of membership in the Afghan Transitional Authority (ATA) where the US preferred to work with Afghan warlords in the hope of gaining information on terrorists' whereabouts, rather than weakening their political influence in the country (Baraki, 2004). Instead, the initiatives undertaken by Germany with respect to this policy area show significant evidence of Europeanization. The salience of the European agenda was high, the EU CFSP was suggested as an appropriate institution, and Germany used its political and diplomatic weight to raise the EU's profile in this case. This indicates the existence of a genuine German preference for a stronger and more capable EU, at least politically.

German participation in ISAF

Given Germany's high profile in the diplomatic engagement for the peace process in Afghanistan, the contribution to OEF as well as the country's reconstruction, military participation in ISAF followed logically. Germany welcomed the UN Security Council Resolution stationing ISAF for an initial mandate of six months, and regarded it as a legal basis for German participation in ISAF. Moreover, members of the governing coalition such as Klose and head of cabinet Struck indicated early on that Germany should consider a lead nation position (Agence France Presse, 20 December 2001) – although Defence Minister Scharping indicated at the time that the Bundeswehr was 'not yet capable' to do this (*Berliner Zeitung*, 22 December 2001). Germany was also not in favour of an overall US command but insisted on keeping the two operations – ISAF and OEF – separate for reasons of domestic sensibilities. After a meeting of the cabinet on 21 December on the deployment of German forces, defence minister Scharping said that Germany would put at ISAF's disposal the necessary capabilities as soon as possible (dpa, 22 December 2001). Among government officials, both in the Ministry of Defence, the Foreign Ministry as well as the chancellor and foreign minister, participation in ISAF was uncontested. This basic consensus on German participation in ISAF extended to actors in the broader political process as well.

On 22 December 2001 the Bundestag voted in favour of German participation in ISAF, which began in January 2002. The German contingent numbered 1,200 initially and increased up to 2,500 by 2003 when Germany and the Netherlands assumed the lead (Wagener, 2003: 33–49). With the exception of the PDS, the governing coalition as well as the opposition were in agreement on the necessity of military measures to support the reconstruction of Afghanistan – both on the initial deployment as well as the extension of the original mandate beyond 20 June 2002.

Other than in the debates over OEF, the issue of an EU format for the European contributions to ISAF created some discord among EU member states, and was at least informally discussed as a possible option even if no specific plans for a concrete operation followed from these discussions (Interview with former German official, 8 February 2006). Germany did not, however, in the end support these discussions, even if Chancellor Schröder pledged support in an international force as a potential coordinated EU contribution at the close of the Bonn Conference on 5 December (*Financial Times*, 6 December 2001). This demonstrates that a preference for a more visible role for the EU existed on the part of Chancellor Schröder, although this was not appropriate in practice. From the perspective of a former German official interviewed 'the ESDP at that time was still in its infancy and not robust enough to undertake such an operation' (Interview with former German official, 9 February 2006). Fischer subsequently rejected the Belgian claim at Laeken that the ISAF force was created by the EU, stating that it could not be an EU force due to the EU's lack of operational structures, and that the issue would be handled by the UN Security Council instead (*Financial Times*, 14 December 2001).

Europeanization vs. alliance politics

As with the military participation in OEF, there is little evidence to support the Europeanization hypothesis in the case of ISAF. Despite initial discussions about an EU force, and statements of the possibility of an EU coordinated force on the part of the chancellor, the idea was abandoned and not taken up again. This suggests that the application of ESDP instruments did not figure prominently enough in German decision-making in this case to move from policy suggestions to operational planning.

Still, there is evidence that members of government, in particular the foreign minister, in principle supported a strong EU profile in this case; and that the application of EU CFSP instruments was of high salience.

2006: Lebanon and DRC

By 2006, German's international position both with respect to military deployments and general willingness to assume responsibility in the world had changed considerably on account of its military involvement in Afghanistan and the Balkans. While domestic reservations against the use and purpose of military force continued to exist, actions undertaken by the Schröder government had increased the 'normalcy' of German foreign policy. Despite the fact that Chancellor Merkel, following the outcome of the September 2005 elections, was leading a Grand Coalition between the Christian and the Social Democrats, and therefore had to balance both positions, discussions on the deployment of military force were taking place in a less contested atmosphere than those surrounding FYROM and Afghanistan.

Under the leadership of Angela Merkel, the basic coordinates of political action that had guided the previous administration did not change significantly: multilateralism, strengthening Germany's commitment to and position in the European Union, including its CFSP/ESDP, and a strong link with NATO – with more emphasis placed on transatlantic relations and NATO on the part of Merkel (in accordance with CDU preferences). Strengthening both CFSP and ESDP continued to be perceived as being in Germany's best interest; and, Germany preparing for its EU Presidency in the first half of 2007 especially in light of the professed goal to move Europe beyond the constitutional impasse since 2005, meant that the goal of strengthening Europe was a constant theme in political debates as they related to Germany's European foreign policy.

The crisis in Lebanon and the European diplomacy and pressures that followed pitted German domestic reservations against not just the use of force but also the deployment of military force in the Middle East, given Germany's ties with Israel, against its European and multilateral commitments. In DRC on the other hand, adaptation pressures came to act on Berlin with respect to participating in an ESDP operation that demanded of Germany to show face with respect to its professed goal of pushing forward ESDP and to take a seat alongside France and Britain in terms of influence in Europe's security and defence policy. Whereas Lebanon led to the breaking of yet another historical taboo – deploying military force in the Middle East – participation in EUFOR RD Congo highlighted Europeanization pressures and the initially reluctant assumption of responsibility. What had been evident in FYROM – participation in order to shape the ESDP agenda at a future point – continued to apply in the case of DRC as well.

The war in Lebanon: political responses

As in Britain and France, apart from a political solution to the military conflict, a key concern initially was also to evacuate German citizens from the conflict region. Otherwise, Germany's fundamental position towards the conflict, also with respect to calling for a ceasefire, was closer to that of Britain and the US than to France both on account of Berlin's historical links with Israel as well as its transatlantic ties. This position was also reflect in Germany's European diplomacy, when Berlin and London persuaded the EU change its call for an immediate ceasefire in response to a French initiative to a call for the cessation of hostilities instead (*International Herald Tribune*, 1 August 2006).

The objective of transatlantic unity was a policy goal for Merkel; apart from the fact that the Christian Democrats were traditionally more transatlanticist than the Social Democrats, there was also lingering concern over the health of the transatlantic relationship after the split over the war in Iraq. This alignment with the US and reluctance to criticize Israel also put the government, which had otherwise acquired a good reputation in the region as an 'honest broker' without specific national interests like France and Britain in a position where it could not balance these two mutually exclusive positions. Instead, Germany opted for a 'quiet' diplomacy that took place in multilateral fora and that did not push a specific German position but rather attempted to shape the international response from within (*Süddeutsche Zeitung*, 31 July 2006a). Given the size of the conflict, Merkel made no attempt at Berlin assuming or calling for a mediating role in the conflict. Instead the focus was on de-escalation, and on adopting a regional approach by trying to include Syria and Jordan (Taz.de, 17. July 2006).

The Chancellor and Foreign Minister assumed different yet fundamentally complementary political positions towards the crisis. Chancellor Merkel assumed a cautious attitude towards the crisis and focused on transatlantic relations, initially stressing Israel's right to self-defence at the meeting with Bush in Stralsund (faz.net, 13 July 2006). Within the Grand Coalition there were also further differences of opinion: as for the Social Democrats, Minister for Development Heidi Wieczoreck-Zeul called Israel's military reaction 'unacceptable under international law' whereas Foreign Minister Steinmeier emphasized the proportionality of military force (*Süddeutsche Zeitung*, 31 July 2006b). This position, which had also been made clear at the US visit in Stralsund, resulted in Steinmeier facing criticism from the Jewish Council for his perceived critical stance on Israel – the German government was thus under pressure domestically to make clear its support for Israel's right to self-defence (*Der Spiegel*, 14 July 2006). Steinmeier also travelled to the region in support of international efforts and advocated an active inclusion of Syria in the resolution to the crisis (*Süddeutsche Zeitung*, 31 July 2006b).

Apart from political support through the UN, support for a strong EU response and debates over German participation in a multinational peace-keeping force also on account of the historical significance of deploying troops in the Middle East, Germany also undertook bilateral initiatives in the region – Foreign Minister Frank Steinmeier visited the region several times in support of other international efforts (SZ 31 July 2006b), aiming at both showing German initiative and increasing Germany's political weight, and at supporting international efforts. Chancellor Merkel, by contrast, expressed support for international efforts to bring about a ceasefire.

Europeanization vs. alliance politics

Although the EU platform was considered important, also with a view to reinforce national preferences of not calling for an immediate ceasefire, overall German decision-making reflected a similar position to that of the US. However, neither Europeanization or alliance politics considerations fully apply. This is because rather than signifying adjustment to transatlantic preferences, support for Israel reflected Berlin's fundamental policy orientation, which held that Germany had a special relationship and responsibility towards Israel. Increasing domestic criticism of Israel's military operation against Lebanon in light of civilian casualties, notwithstanding, Germany maintained a position closer to that of Israel and the United States that precluded support for the EU Presidency's push for calling for an immediate ceasefire.

Creating UNIFIL

In addition to concerns over regional security and bringing an end to the crisis – while maintaining international unity in the response to it – German reactions to the war in Lebanon were also strongly conditioned by Berlin's historical ties to Israel. This put the idea of stationing German troops in the Middle East – and creating a situation where German soldiers might attack Israelis – in direct conflict with the objective of showing solidarity with the international community by participating in an international peace-keeping force and taking seriously Germany's military ambitions and responsibilities. Thus, during initial calls for a peace-keeping mission, in light of escalating violence, at the G8 summit Merkel stated plainly that German participation in such a force was not on the agenda – and referred to the UN as the forum where such issues would have to be discussed (Handelsblatt, 17 July 2006).

Israel's active consent to an expanded Unifil made German participation less contested, although troop deployments in the end did not include peacekeepers near the Lebanese-Israeli border but instead naval deployment to help police the Lebanese coastline to stop arms smuggling by Hezbollah; this constituted Germany's biggest naval deployment since World War II (*Guardian*, 27 September 2006).

In domestic debates, therefore, at issue was not only a military deployment and its institutional anchoring but also its historical significance – thus, Merkel stated in the Bundestag that 'there is perhaps no other area of the world where Germany's unique responsibility, the unique responsibility of every German government for the lessons of our past, is so clear'; the Israeli request 'is a signal of trust in Germany, the country in whose name the destruction of the Jews and the Second World War began' (*Guardian*, 27 September 2006). Taking responsibility not just for the humanitarian and political, but also the parallel military component of the peace-building process was, for Merkel, a necessity also with a view to the fact that one of the key political causes for the German government (*Staatsraison*) was the right of existence of the state of Israel, and the responsibility to act and participate that derived from that (Deutscher Bundestag, 6 September 2006 4480D). The argument of historical responsibility towards Israel but also German and European history featured strongly in arguments in favour of participating in UNIFIL and in strengthening the EU's capacity to act in foreign policy: with a view to the EU Presidency Merkel stated that 'the necessity for a united Europe acting in foreign and security policy has increased over the past years . . . if one needs justification for a united Europe beyond the common market, it is the interests in peace and freedom, stability and wealth in the world' (4481D). With respect to Germany's multilateral interests, Merkel subsequently stated that 'if we want to serve our interests we cannot accomplish this on our own . . . it is therefore right to act together in security institutions, in the EU and NATO, and to take and share responsibility, (4481D).

Unlike FYROM and Afghanistan five years earlier, the decision in the Bundestag was not equally contested. With the exception of the PDS and part of the Left party, there was broad consensus to participate in the military operation: this shows that the taboo against the use of force had not only weakened, but that the broad consensus among the political elite had developed towards a case-by-case assessment of the necessity to intervene, and towards Germany assuming its part in not just the political but also the military processes in its international interactions. In the end, the government could rely on a sizeable majority who supported the deployment of German naval forces: of 599 votes, 442 were in favour, 152 objected and 5 abstained (Deutscher Bundestag, 20 September 2006 4846A).

Europeanization vs. alliance politics

Despite close coordination with the US in the political resolution of the crisis, there is evidence of the salience of the European agenda in the decision to deploy the military in Lebanon. Importantly, this particular decision was not impacted by alliance politics considerations: the domestic debate and internal decision-making was dominated by historical considerations and Germany's scope for influence both in the region and in European politics. The European agenda was highly salient (adaptation) with a view also to Germany's ambitions for its upcoming EU Presidency (projection), where Germany intended to break the deadlock over the Reform Treaty. Foreign Minister Steinmeier reflected these sentiments in his statements to the Bundestag where he stated that 'ten years ago, nobody would have thought about sending German soldiers alongside soldiers from other European countries ... peacemaking was a task that Europeans left to the United States' (*Guardian*, 27 September 2006). Even if this was not a EU-force, then, Steinmeier's statement reflects the importance attached to the European agenda and therefore supports the salience of the EU in Germany's political considerations.

DRC: Launching EUFOR RD Congo

In response to the UN's request for supporting MONUC during the Congolese elections, Germany participated in EUFOR RD Congo by providing the Headquarters in Potsdam and the Force Commander and by contributing up to 780 soldiers, which made up a third of the overall force – not an insignificant contribution in military terms. Berlin in principle supported this particular ESDP mission both in terms of its design and mandate. However, Germany also had to adapt to French policy entrepreneurship and the resulting Europeanization pressures. While none of the government bureaucracies or leading decision-makers were opposed to the mission per se, inter-European debates coupled with a lack of communication on the broader reason for Germany or European engagement in sub-Saharan Africa, gave the impression of European disunity and made the mission a relatively difficult 'sell' to the German public (Tull, 2007). The analysis of individual decisions and positions on the part of decision-makers subsequently reveals agreement on the subject itself but variations on the size and modalities of German contributions.

Chancellor Merkel, in bilateral meetings with President Chirac, supported the idea and expressed support for the mission as early as January – and it is likely that the decision for Germany to participate in the mission was taken at the bilateral French-German Summit in Versailles on 23 January 2006, although the question of Germany leading the mission was not addressed until later (Tull, 2007). Generally, German officials viewed the December 2005 UN request primarily as a French rather than a UN initiative, mainly as a result of the bypassing of informal channels preceding the official request from the UN. As a result, parts of the government viewed the request rather critically. An overall position, also on the political value of participating in such a mission, had to first be developed, and the mission's feasibility be established.

For the Foreign Office, rather than signalling a change in German political thinking in terms of greater political interest in Africa, German considerations as to the mission were that it was temporally restricted, that it was feasible, and that it was low in risk – and a way to meet political pressure for contributions, with one consideration being that Berlin could opt out on the next occasion (Interview with German official, 27 February 2008). German decision-makers never considered an extension of the mandate – one of the fundamental considerations in agreeing to the operation was that this was an opportunity to showcase that ESDP could take on a temporally restricted mission. Berlin subsequently was not open to any discussion on a prolongation of the mandate, also out of concern for domestic opposition to Germany's military deployment (Tull, 2007).

Political pressure to participate, and to participate in a leading capacity, was extended in the PSC in addition to the bilateral French-German relations. Germany expressed willingness at the PSC meeting in Brussels on 21 February to contribute military forces if other countries were also to contribute troops. One month later, Germany announced that it would provide the Operational Headquarters, and the contribution of one contingent, which constituted a third of the overall force. This was viewed as a compromise solution in light of earlier French requests to send a Battle Group that would have consisted of close to 1,500 Germans and four French military forces (*Der Spiegel*, 21 January 2006).

While there was not fundamental disagreement over EUFOR RD Congo, and while German participation in this force was not contested internally, it nevertheless was not an easy sell as far as the broader public was concerned. The debate in the Bundestag over German participation in EUFOR RD Congo and criticism thereof, rather than focusing on the use of military force per se centred on the absence of a comprehensive concept for Africa as well as the utility of a European presence, given the risks involved. It also exposed a split between members of the Grand Coalition and the Greens on the one hand, and the Free Democrats and the Left on the other. The Greens noted a lack of strategic concept on EU or German policy towards Africa, and stated that the likely effect would be continued ad-hocery in 'stumbling from mission to mission' without an overall strategic or operational concept (Mueller, Deutscher Bundestag, 19 May 2006, 3104 C) – although that did not preclude consent to the mission. The Free Democrats had objected to German participation on account of military risks involved and concerns that the mere presence of European – and German – peacekeepers would not suffice in bringing about a stable environment in which to hold elections (Westerwelle, Deutscher Bundestag, 6 September 2006, 4505C). Chancellor Merkel justified the increasing commitment to sub-Saharan Africa to include a military component on account of Africa's proximity to Europe particularly in light of the number of refugees. Merkel stated that 'we must, in the interest of the Africans but also in the interests of those in Europe who are affected, contribute to a solution of this problem and offer possibilities for development, co-ownership, peace, freedom and prosperity' (Merkel, Deutscher Bundestag, 6 September 2006, 4480D).

The Christian Democrats backed the deployment, given that the necessary preconditions had been fulfilled: the Congolese government had agreed to the mission, there was broad participation of EU member states in the mission, there was a robust UN mandate, there was a temporal limitation of four months, and the mandate restricted the operation geographically (Schockenhoff, Deutscher Bundestag, 19 May 2006, 3106B). Minister of Defence Jung underlined those four conditions and, although alluding to the difficulties in assembling the force within the EU, emphasized that a broad spectrum of contribution from 18 countries was necessary and appropriate (Jung, Deutscher Bundestag, 19 May 2006, 3112A). At the parliamentary vote, 440 voted in favour, 135 against, and 6 abstained; Germany participated in EUFOR with up to 780 soldiers.

Europeanization

The absence of any transatlantic considerations in the decision to deploy troops as part of EUFOR RD Congo make this an ideal case for delineating domestic concerns from those that point towards Europeanization. The indicators of Europeanization relevant are adaptation both in the sense of salience of the European agenda as well as the compromise of national preferences to accommodate (French) proposals towards not only the use of ESDP instruments but also the extent to German involvement in this particular mission; and that of changing preferences as elites favoured the application of ESDP instruments.

With respect to ESDP, there were three motivations for Berlin to participate in this particular operation: it was feasible, it was an opportunity for Germany to move ESDP forward rather than continue with its role of retarding element, and it was in the spirit of effective multilateralism, which Germany supported. In short, the proposed operation in the minds of policy makers was exactly the sort of operation ESDP had been created for in the first place (Interview with German official, 27 February 2008). The value placed on effective multilateralism was also reflected in public debates: Foreign Minister Steinmeier stated that that German engagement in Africa was necessary on account of Germany's multilateral responsibility vis-à-vis the United Nations. He also argued that Germany, not having direct national interest in Congo or Africa more broadly, was also seen as not partial to any particular side (Steinmeier, Deutscher Bundestag, 19 May 2006 3103D).

The emphasis on multilateralism as well as the opportunity to show that Germany was committed to ESDP clearly support the indicators of salience and policy preferences. However, French pressures on Berlin to participate in a leading capacity added adaptation pressures. Initially, reactions to Chirac's suggestion that the EU could send a EU Battle Group, consisting of 1,500 German soldiers were met with disapproval. Government sources cited military overstretch (Deutsche Welle, 27 January 2006), and Defence Minister Jung flatly contradicted French proposals of sending an EU Battle Group or the German-French brigade (Taz.de, 28 January 2006).

While Germany was not opposed to the operation, or to German military participation in some form, French suggestions for using a Battle Group fell on deaf ears for three main reasons: first, a Battle Group could not have carried out all tasks set out in the mandate; second, the mission was not to take place in response to an urgent crisis situation that would have warranted the calling up of a Battle Group but rather was a mission with a six-month lead time; third and most importantly, the costs would have fallen overwhelmingly to Germany as the Battle Group on rotation was staffed primarily by German military. Given the costs lie where they fall principle, this would have been an expensive mission for Germany to undertake (Interview with policy expert, 28 April 2008).

Although Germany achieved a compromise in terms of troop components and forced Paris to commit forces of its own, Berlin nevertheless acquiesced to French preferences in staffing and commanding the mission as well as providing the Headquarters in Potsdam. Although the idea for the mission if not directly originated then at least was supported by Paris, France could not substantially contribute to the mission: given that it had already led Operation Artemis in 2003, a French lead would have put the neutrality of EUFOR RD Congo – and ESDP as a whole – in question. By filling the void, Germany adapted to French pressures in order to accommodate the use of ESDP and the further elaboration of ESDP instruments. However, Berlin's actions also exhibited Europeanized preferences and showed the salience of the European agenda – once a decision on the value of the operation had been arrived at following the UN's request, showcasing ESDP, and acting in the spirit of effective multilateralism were both declared goals for German policy makers.

Conclusion

In conclusion, the evolution of German foreign policy with respect to ESDP evolved towards greater participation in line with Berlin's evolving confidence in exporting national preferences onto the international (and European) stage, and with the further erosion of historical taboos. This does not mean, however, that Germany came to push the ESDP agenda, however – although Berlin used the CFSP platform to reinforce national preferences in the case of Afghanistan, and although it increasingly sought to participate in military operations with a view to be able to either sit out operations in the future or be able to shape the emerging ESDP agenda and to make its weight felt, Germany did not come to actively initiate military operations, or political initiatives, in 2006. While Berlin no longer counts as a passive bystander, then, it is also not quite acting as an agenda setter.

6
From Continuity to Change: an Emerging European Crisis Management Policy?

The Europeanization of national foreign policy? Comparing member states' reactions

The analysis presented in previous chapters has shown that adopting a Europeanization approach that conceptualizes a number of institutional and domestic processes of change and the way in which EU CFSP/ESDP institutions are utilized, strengthened (or sidelined), demonstrates that specific European dynamics exist that influence and shape member states' foreign policy. Focusing on the effects of Europeanization processes on national foreign policy has permitted the delineation of national commitments to the EU CFSP and ESDP from commitments and preferences that lean towards the use of NATO and that privilege the preferences of the US, and those that arise out of a specific domestic context. The analysis has also shown that specific national contexts facilitated or hindered further moves towards Europeanization of national foreign policies, and that some constants in national foreign policy remain. The period between 2001 and 2006, rather than significantly changing national biases and restraints, crystallized some of these, at times conflicting, pressures – this despite the overall rapid growth of ESDP in terms of the number of missions launched as well as the expanding geographical reach of these missions.

Broadly speaking, these enduring national contexts include enduring British reservations on utilizing ESDP unless NATO does not want to be involved; German reluctance to adopt a proactive stance towards ESDP; and French willingness to push the European agenda in the Balkans and sub-Saharan Africa, but not in regions or policy areas that are dominated by transatlantic considerations or in situations where the UN represents a more useful platform to exert national influence. While these national constants remain by and large unchanged, there is some evidence that Brussels-based institutions are exerting increasing adaptation pressures on member states even in the military realm – which means that in specific instances even the 'big three' member states can be constrained in their actions, as the case of increasing member states' military commitments with respect to UNIFIL demonstrates.

This in turn suggests a growing, albeit subtle, shift in the overall pattern of Europeanization in the sense of rising adaptation pressures as a result of increasing institutionalization. For the most part, however, member states' decisions in the individual cases show mostly evidence of either projecting specific national preferences or of adaptation in terms of the salience of the European agenda. This applies both to considerations involving the application of CFSP and ESDP instruments.

Europeanization of foreign policy: preliminary assessments

Applying the concept of Europeanization to policy decisions has yielded some surprising results in terms of member states' willingness to consider CFSP or ESDP as an appropriate platform. Focusing on processes of Europeanization has been valuable in the case of Afghanistan, which at first glance appeared to be determined exclusively by transatlantic considerations. The Europeanization approach has highlighted that the EU CFSP presented a useful political forum for member states in particular with respect to the political and economic aspects of the reconstruction of Afghanistan. It also shows the extent to which one member state, Germany, used the EU CFSP as a political platform for formulating policy. But when it comes to the application of military instruments, Europeanization has shown to be of limited explanatory value. US preferences and member states' aim to utilize NATO, in addition to the nature of the crisis, determined the responses of two of the three countries analysed. The third country, France, resisted NATO assuming command of ISAF in the case of Afghanistan in large part out of concern over the consequences of showing a Western flag in a Muslim country – and did not take a similarly large interest in Afghanistan when it came to matters of political and economic reconstruction as the two other countries analysed in this volume did (Interview with EU official, 11 September 2006).

With respect to the crisis in FYROM, on the other hand, where all three countries were expected to exhibit a European preference based on Europe's previous engagement in the Balkans, adopting the

Europeanization approach yields a less surprising finding – but shows nuances among individual member states. Here, Europeanization high-lighted the extent to which all three countries reacted and adapted to Javier Solana's proactive stance and the recently created office of the SG/HR. While all three countries retained national influence on the negotiations through the Contact Group – in addition to ensuring US support in the negotiations – France in particular used the EU CFSP to project national preferences by lobbying for the appointment of a EUSR. Although this did not lead to institutional change in national systems of governance as a result of voluntary agreements among member states (Olsen, 2002: 923), it does show that member states adapted to existing institutions within the EU CFSP as a major component in the political negotiation of the crisis by either supporting Javier Solana directly, as in the case of Britain, or by adopting a unitary political line with respect to the EU's negotiation position as in the case of France and Germany. Euro-peanization in this case did include the strengthening of the EU CFSP's organizational capacity for collective action (Olsen, 2002; Checkel, 2001) and therefore the development of institutions at the EU level. National policies on FYROM, therefore, confirm the existence of Europeanization processes in national foreign policy.

The limitation of the explanatory value of the Europeanization approach relates to the use of military force under the EU ESDP, and conflicting views among the member states as to the role of the US in European security. Here, the utility of the Europeanization approach – in particular by contrasting Europeanization with alliance politics – lies in the ability to delineate the tension between NATO and transatlantic relations more generally, and the goal to build up the ability for the EU CFSP/ESDP to act. Strengthening the organizational capacity of the EU in FYROM came into conflict with transatlantic preferences and priorities, and the professed wish for both a successful first ESDP mission and the preservation of regional stability on the part of Britain and Germany. This resulted in a delay of the assumption of the military operation under ESDP.

As expected, given the sizeable US interest in the two cases and the influence of transatlantic relations in the individual countries, there are limitations to the explanatory potential of the Europeanization approach. This is particularly the case when it comes to the application of military instruments located in ESDP, where in both cases member states' consideration of US preferences determined policy outcomes. The exception is France in FYROM, although its acquiescence to the appli-cation of NATO in ISAF as well as its transatlantic solidarity in OEF shows that the transatlantic relationship was of importance in France as well.

These findings have implications with respect to the potential contributions of this study formulated in Chapter 1 – the utility of the Europeanization framework to explain national decision-making in foreign security and defence policy. Although the comparison of the four cases has yielded some results that point towards the applicability of the Europeanization framework to explain policy decisions, Europeanization does not serve as an overall explanation for national policy decisions. Integration mechanisms in the sense that existing EU institutions exert influence on national foreign policy that results in policy adaptation were not observed when it came to the application of military instruments under ESDP, with the exception of France's preferences with respect to an ESDP takeover from NATO in FYROM. This means that the utility of the Europeanization framework is limited on account of the influence of the transatlantic alliance in national foreign policy.

Given the tensions surrounding the launch of the first ESDP operation and general US reservations towards ESDP (see Howorth, 2007), the Bush administration adopting a more relaxed attitude towards ESDP (Interview with member state official, 2007) could have been expected to lead towards a greater push for deploying ESDP instruments on the part of the individual member states. The analysis of the two cases of 2006 shows, however, that although alliance politics considerations did not impact national decision-making in 2006 the same way that they did in 2001, this did not automatically result in a greater role for the EU CFSP and ESDP.

The war in Lebanon saw one country, Britain, explicitly aligning itself with the US. France, by contrast, pursued an active diplomacy that run counter to US preferences; whereas a sense of historical responsibility towards Israel as well as attempts at quiet diplomacy were guiding Berlin's reaction to the crisis. This shows that transatlantic relations conditioned British political responses in particular. None of the three countries pursued its policy preferences through the EU platform, although France used the EU to reinforce the outcome of its UN diplomacy. Although all three countries were in favour of a role for the EU and deemed a EU policy towards the Middle East important, this did not lead to advocating, or working towards such a role in the political responses to the war in Lebanon. Although one effect of the war in Lebanon was the suggestion to think about how the EU could play a bigger role in the Middle East more generally, this did not effect a change in national decision-making in this particular crisis.

When it came to putting together UNIFIL, none of the three countries advocated launching a military operation under ESDP despite the fact that the majority of the enhanced UNIFIL peace-keeping force was European. This in turn suggests that reservations with respect to the deployment of military instruments under ESDP originate from feared negative consequences on transatlantic relations as much as they do from national reservations towards pushing for an EU label in high-risk theatres. In the end, then, alliance politics can be a conditioning factor in the decision of when to employ ESDP operations – but does not explain the absence of Europeanization in all cases relating to decisions on military employment. The next sections analyse the findings in more detail.

2001 – FYROM

National decisions towards the crisis in FYROM reveal substantial evidence of Europeanization, particularly regarding the political responses to the crisis. While there is no evidence of Europeanization with respect to the NATO operation, the politics of the ESDP takeover reflects tensions between the EU CFSP/ESDP and NATO/US preferences. Table 6.1 summarizes the findings with respect to the three indicators of Europeanization – adaptation, projection, identity formation – that are analysed in more detail in the sections that follow.

Table 6.1:   Decision-making in FYROM

	Adaptation			Projection			Identity formation		
	UK	F	G	UK	F	G	UK	F	G
Support for the political negotiation of the EU CFSP									
high					x			x	
medium	x	x	x				x		x
low				x		x			
Participation in NATO Operation Essential Harvest									
high									
medium						x		x	x
low	x	x	x	x	x		x		
The politics of the ESDP takeover from NATO									
high					x			x	
medium	x		x						x
low		x		x		x	x		

Support for the EU CFSP in the political negotiations

With respect to the support of the EU CFSP in the political negotiations of the crisis, all three countries exhibited signs of Europeanization, both in the sense of projecting as well as adapting national policies to the EU CFSP. All three countries made efforts to align their statements on the crisis with a common EU line, and all three were explicit that this was a crisis where the EU should take a lead in the political negotiation, which points towards adaptation. Moreover, two of the three countries actively influenced the negotiations. France projected national preferences by successfully lobbying for the appointment of a EU Special Representative, while Britain through its embassy in Skopje played an instrumental part in facilitating Solana's local impact. Germany, although more cautious on account of the geographic proximity of FYROM, also endorsed Solana assuming a role in the negotiation of the crisis. This shows that all three countries viewed the EU CFSP as a legitimate and important tool in the solution of the crisis and means that national foreign policies in the three member states were Europeanized insofar as the EU CFSP was accorded a significant role in the solution of the crisis: Javier Solana had a mandate to negotiate on behalf of the EU member states, and the EU CFSP held a high profile in the national discourse, particularly in France and Germany. The EU CFSP was suggested and supported as the most appropriate institutional platform to deal with the crisis. Of course, the fact that all three member states retained a crucial role in setting the overall political framework through the Contact Group demonstrates that Britain, France and Germany were equally keen to retain national influence in international intervention and shows the importance attached to the inclusion of the US as well as Russia in the solution to the crisis. However, the application of EU CFSP instruments in all three countries was deemed important, and supported through practical measures. This confirms the first hypothesis for the Europeanization proposition formulated in Chapter 1: *in the case of the political negotiation in the crisis in FYROM, there was a significant influence of the EU CFSP on national foreign policy, which resulted in governments advocating a significant role for the EU CFSP.*

Evidence of alliance politics was present in this policy area insofar as the presence of NATO in FYROM and the involvement of the US in the resolution of the crisis were deemed important for a peaceful outcome of the crisis. This in turn points towards the indicator of relying on NATO for utilitarian reasons rather than out of a fundamental transatlantic preference that would have made the application of instruments located in the EU CFSP contentious. The advancement of the EU CFSP and the application of political instruments located within the EU CFSP was uncontested and not regarded as competition to NATO. This in turn supports the conclusion that there is strong evidence of Europeanization with respect to the second hypothesis of alliance politics: *the fact that there was little perceived threat towards the alliance allowed for a significant role afforded to the EU CFSP.* NATO and the EU CFSP were perceived as complementary rather than competing institutions by policy makers in the three countries.

Participation in NATO Operation Essential Harvest

With respect to the decision to launch and participate in NATO Operation Essential Harvest, the Europeanization approach is not relevant as the EU CFSP/ESDP was not suggested in the first place. NATO was considered the relevant military actor both on account of its previous involvement in the area, the trust enjoyed by the local population as well as the continued involvement of the US in the Balkans (Interview with EU official, 21 June 2005), a view that was shared by all three member states. Keeping the US involved in European security, and convincing the US of the continued need for NATO in the region as well as in FYROM, represented a policy goal for the UK in particular (Interview with EU official, 11 September 2006), a view that was shared by France and Germany as well. This in turn confirms the alliance politics hypothesis formulated in Chapter 1: *there was a significant influence of the transatlantic alliance both in terms of the goal of keeping the US involved in European security and utilitarian considerations, and this resulted in a significant role for NATO.* Policy makers in all three countries regarded NATO as the most appropriate forum for supporting the Ohrid Framework agreement following the resolution of the crisis. A degree of variance can be observed in the German case where, although policy makers did not push for military instruments located outside NATO, Europe's capacity to act was frequently invoked to justify German participation in the military operations conducted. This demonstrates that some amount of Europeanization understood as identity formation can be observed in the sense that military participation was linked to the EU rather than national unilateral preferences or NATO and transatlantic ties exclusively; and that this made military participation more easily acceptable domestically.

The politics of the ESDP takeover from NATO

The positions towards the ESDP takeover from NATO revealed the greatest variance between the three countries. France was the only case where the application of ESDP instruments was suggested early on, and the only country that did not consider institutional rather than ad-hoc arrangements between the EU and NATO as necessary to launch an ESDP operation in FYROM. This reflects the underlying attitude towards NATO and the conception of the EU ESDP as autonomous, and an alternative rather than a complementing political and military tool to NATO. The French position also reflects the belief that the operation was small enough for the EU ESDP to take on this challenge without major risk of violence breaking out anew (Interview with French official, 20 June 2005). French decisions in this case therefore reveal strong evidence of Europeanization and confirm the first Europeanization hypothesis: *significant influence of EU security institutions result in governments advocating a significant role for the EU CFSP/ESDP in a particular crisis.*

Britain, by contrast, while not opposed to the eventual application of ESDP instruments in FYROM in principle (Interview with UK official, 29 June 2006), insisted on a prior agreement with NATO. This reflects the privileged position of NATO in British foreign policy thinking as well as strong ties with the US, and therefore confirms the third hypothesis of Europeanization: *EU security institutions exerted some influence on national foreign policy, but this influence was weighed against other factors.* This led to the UK advocating a partial role for the EU that included political, but not military tools in the absence of institutional arrangements between NATO and the EU. The fact that the ESDP as an alternative platform for policy action existed, and the fact that another member state pushed for the application of ESDP instruments means that British policy adapted to consent to an ESDP takeover from NATO. As a result, British policy actions support the alliance politics hypothesis formulated in Chapter 1: *significant influence of the transatlantic alliance, both in terms of US preference against a European role, and pressures to keep NATO in play resulted in a small role afforded to ESDP when it comes to military matters.* The German case, finally, exhibits similar evidence to that of the British case: the eventual application of ESDP instruments was not contested, but the prior agreement with NATO was a precondition for consent to such a mission. In addition, German policy makers also emphasized regional stability: apart from transatlantic relations, then, concern over the impact of an ESDP takeover on regional stability left the Federal Foreign Office cautious on the change from NATO. But the high value placed on the ESDP and Europe's ability to act in national rhetoric demonstrates that domestic norms leaned towards the application of policy tools in ESDP, pointing – in addition to similar adaptation pressures facing the UK – towards Europeanization understood as identity formation, where an ESDP operation was presented as desirable and domestically acceptable. In the case of the UK, there was little evidence that would point towards a shifting preference towards ESDP in general, although the preference for NATO was on account of utilitarian reasons rather than exclusively transatlantic leanings.

2001 – Afghanistan

The analysis of the decisions taken with regard to the war in Afghanistan shows that as in the case of FYROM, the role afforded to the EU was primarily a political one, with the Commission playing a large financial role as well. Importantly there was no fundamental disagreement on this role among the three member states. The role for the EU CFSP stopped short of a military one, however, because the EU ESDP was not considered ready for assuming such a task, and because member states had different conceptions on the appropriate institutional framework to begin with. Britain favoured NATO from early on and Germany likewise preferred NATO. France, finally, did not initially favour the use of NATO in Afghanistan, but adjusted its position in light of allies' preferences. Table 6.2 summarizes the findings along the three indicators of Europeanization.

Table 6.2: Decision-making in Afghanistan

	Adaptation			Projection			Identity formation		
	UK	F	G	UK	F	G	UK	F	G
OEF and the war on terror									
high									
medium									
low	x	x	x	x	x	x	x	x	x
The reconstruction of Afghanistan									
high						x			
medium	x	x							x
low				x	x		x	x	
ISAF and its institutional anchoring									
high									
medium								x	x
low	x	x	x	x	x	x	x		

OEF and the war on terror

The participation in OEF confirms the alliance politics framework in all three countries, but shows little evidence of Europeanization in national foreign policy formulation. Britain, France and Germany regarded the military participation in OEF as a matter of solidarity with the US, with Germany and Britain in particular keen on disposing of the Taliban regime and the opportunity to work towards the elimination of security threats emanating from Afghanistan through the country's reconstruction. As emerged from the analysis in the individual country case studies, both Britain and Germany had attempted to initiate international consensus and a strategy to do more about Afghanistan the year prior to the attacks of 11 September, although the terrorist attacks and the invocation of Article V meant that the US took a pronounced lead on military measures in Afghanistan.

To be sure, leaders used the opportunity for electoral purposes in Paris and to push the country towards assuming more responsibility internationally in Berlin, but the fundamental impulse was transatlantic solidarity in response to the terrorist attacks. This was most apparent in the case of Britain, where Blair seized the occasion to not only get close to the US but also play the role of a mediator between Europe and the US. All three countries also placed a high emphasis on the use of the UN and NATO in terms of the invocation of Article V of the NATO treaty to legitimize the military action in Afghanistan and to place the country's reconstruction on a multilateral footing. Variance in transatlantic solidarity between Britain and France also emerged with respect to the geographic restriction of the war on terror on Afghanistan. Evidence of Europeanization in this case is weak as the application of CFSP instruments was not considered beyond statements of solidarity with the US. British, French and German efforts to coordinate their actions in order to forge a European line does not serve as evidence of Europeanization as this did not result in the application in instruments located in the EU CFSP. Still, this coordination – and the goal for the EU to be a visible platform even if this did not include SG/HR Solana but was confined to the member states – shows that the European agenda, defined as acting in concert rather than through the EU CFSP, was of some salience even in this case. As a result, policy actions in the three member states confirm the following hypotheses for Europeanization and alliance politics formulated in Chapter 1: *there was little influence of EU security institutions on national foreign policy; by contrast, there was significant influence of the transatlantic alliance and US preferences, which resulted in a small role for the EU CFSP.*

The reconstruction of Afghanistan

The analysis of the reconstruction of Afghanistan yields some evidence of Europeanization, but there is variance among the three countries.

Germany successfully projected its national preference for a visible role for the EU CFSP and lobbied for and succeeded in appointing a German national as EUSR. With respect to Germany, then, policy decisions confirm the Europeanization hypothesis: there was a significant influence of EU security institutions on national foreign policy in the sense that the EU CFSP provided a platform through which to enforce national policy preferences for a high political profile for the EU. Britain and France supported this move, indicating that they were in agreement on the need for a visible role for the EU CFSP, and adapted to the preference of another member state. Neither Britain, which was very active in Afghanistan both in the military as well as the political and economic aspects, nor France, which did not take a lead role in Afghanistan or exhibit a strong interest in Afghanistan prior to 11 September (Interview with EU official, 11 September 2006), regarded the EU as a similarly vital platform. This leads to the conclusion that the degree of Europeanization in France and Britain was low. For all three countries, however, the UN was the most important platform to coordinate the reconstruction of Afghanistan. Alliance politics was not applicable in the case, as the UN rather than the US took the lead in shaping the political and economic parameters of the reconstruction of Afghanistan. With respect to Germany, then, the reconstruction of Afghanistan confirms the first Europeanization hypothesis: *significant influence of EU security institutions resulted in advocating a significant role for the EU CFSP in Afghanistan's reconstruction.* With respect to Britain and France, it confirms the second Europeanization hypothesis: *little influence of EU security institutions on national foreign policy resulted in a small role afforded to the EU CFSP.*

ISAF and its institutional anchoring

The participation in ISAF confirms the role of alliance politics rather than Europeanization in two of the three countries. Britain and Germany were in favour of NATO command against initial US preferences (Interview with EU official, 11 September 2006). This was for operational and utilitarian reasons, as NATO command meant that the lead-nation model could be abolished, although multilateral preferences in the case of Germany and the UK constituted a secondary motivation. For France, NATO was not regarded as an appropriate institutional framework, although Paris came to relent on this question in view of allies' pressures and out of the recognition that transatlantic preferences and therefore the US were to prevail. None of the three countries advocated an ESDP operation or a EU label for the European contributions for ISAF. This shows that despite the publicly stated intention for Europe to play a role in the military aspect of Afghanistan's reconstruction on the part of the German chancellor, in the end considerations that reflect the Europeanization hypothesis were not sufficiently strong as to result in a policy proposal to employ ESDP instruments, or to push for a coordinated EU force. Instead, each of the three countries made efforts to coordinate its overall position with the other two as well as the US, although France and Germany attempted to sell this coordination as a European rather than national effort domestically. Still, as in the case of military contributions to the NATO Operation in FYROM, the European rhetoric adopted by French and German leaders points towards a preference if not for the EU ESDP, then at the very minimum for a coordinated European approach subsumed under an EU label. With respect to the institutional anchoring of ISAF, then, member states' foreign policies confirm the following hypotheses formulated in Chapter 1: *while there was little influence of EU security institutions on national foreign policy there was significant influence of the transatlantic alliance and US preferences. This therefore resulted in a negligible role for the EU CFSP/ESDP.*

2006 – Lebanon

Despite the rapid growth of the ESDP in terms of the number of operations launched as well as the expanding geographical reach, significant restraints continued to impact national decision-making in crisis situations in 2006 – with one key difference: whereas in 2001 utilizing the emerging CFSP and ESDP instruments was based to a large extent on national goals to expand the EU's political and eventually also military role at least in the Balkans, by 2006 EU institutions had come to exert pressure on member states to increase their contributions in the case of UNIFIL. Although subtle, this reflects a qualitative shift in the nature of adaptation pressures acting on member states. Rather than member states actively supporting an EU role, or viewing the EU as a platform for policy projections, Brussels-based institutions themselves came to exert adaptation pressures on member states that influenced national decision-making. This does not mean, however, that this resulted in a larger role for the EU in foreign policy: here, national preferences, the UN as a more useful platform to exert international leadership as well as some transatlantic considerations determined decision-making.

2006 also illustrates a marked difference between France and Germany and the UK: whereas in 2001 the UK was an active – albeit, like Germany, on occasions a retarding – actor in formulating EU responses, in 2006 UK political and military interventions as far as the EU CFSP and ESDP was concerned consisted primarily in consenting to ESDP and UN operations but without impacting or substantially driving political decision-making within the EU framework. Due in part to military overstretch elsewhere and to changing (or sharpening) attitudes towards ESDP more generally, it nevertheless shows that Europeanization pressures (or perceived opportunities for projection) have become much weaker in the case of one member state. In the two crises in 2006, however, lacking evidence of Europeanization was not a reaction to pressures emanating from the US or the transatlantic alliance – in the case of EUFOR RD Congo this element was absent altogether, and in the case of Lebanon affected only the political but not the military decisions. Alliance politics, therefore, mattered less, at least where the application of military measures was concerned. Table 6.3 illustrates this in the case of Lebanon.

Table 6.3: Decision-making in Lebanon

	Adaptation			Projection			Identity formation		
	UK	F	G	UK	F	G	UK	F	G
Political responses to the crisis									
high									
medium					x		x	x	x
low	x	x	x	x		x			
Launching UNIFIL									
high									
medium		x				x		x	x
low	x		x	x	x		x		

Political responses to the crisis

In the case of the political responses to the war in Lebanon, alliance politics in the sense that the US position in the region was taken into consideration, certainly impacted the UK; but whereas Berlin's reaction towards the war was determined in large part by its historical ties to Israel, France used the UN as a platform to play a highly visible role – and once that ran counter to that of the US. The EU platform was short-changed as a result: although all three member states were clear that the EU was to play a role, in practice this did not lead to a strengthening of the EU CFSP.

This was due in part to the fact that the position of the EU Presidency – Finland – ran counter to that of Britain and Germany, which left little room for consensus. For France, the EU platform if anything served to reinforce its position and initiatives on the UN level. As a result, the positions of all three countries confirm the following hypothesis: *there is little evidence of an influence of EU security institutions on national foreign policy, which resulted in a small role afforded to the EU CFSP.*

Launching UNIFIL

When it came to participation over the launch of UNIFIL, on the other hand, alliance politics did not impact the decision-making on either the necessity of the force, its institutional anchoring, or the degree of military participation on the part of individual member states. As the US had counted itself out as a neutral political or military actor, the military operation naturally fell to the Europeans – and, on account of its political leadership, to France. Although France was not opposed to leading or substantially contributing to the force, concerns over caveats led to Paris substantially reduce the numbers of troops it was willing to offer. *There is significant influence of EU security institutions – the PSC – on national foreign policy, but this does not result in an operation undertaken under the EU label.*

2006 – Launching EUFOR RD Congo

The case of EUFOR RD Congo reveals evidence of Europeanization in two of the three countries analysed. France projected its national preference for launching the operation onto the EU platform and pressured a second member state, Germany, to participate and to lead the operation, thereby exerting adaptation pressures (see Table 6.4).

Table 6.4:   Decision-making in DRC

	Adaptation			Projection			Identity formation		
	UK	F	G	UK	F	G	UK	F	G
Launching EUFOR RD Congo									
high					x			x	
medium	x		x						x
low		x		x		x	x		

Although French political moves to lock in the mission without prior informal consultations was perceived by Germany as pressure to acquiesce to French preferences, Germany consented to the mission in part because of French pressure and in part because of its own preference towards ESDP. What at first appeared to be a case of Europeanization understood as adaptation as the result of another member state's pressure, then, also reveals political motivations that point towards identity formation as well as the salience of the European agenda in German foreign policy. In the case of the UK, lastly, the fact that London had no objection to this particular mission shows that ESDP was of some salience and that London was happy to give its political consent to the mission. The fact that the UK would not have initiated this particular mission, however, does not indicate that London perceived this particular ESDP operation as valuable for pushing a European agenda (or that London was about to push any particular European agenda) – or that it in any way threatened other foreign policy priorities. This means that decisions taken by Germany but also by France – of course for different reasons – support the Europeanization hypothesis formulated in Chapter 1: *there was a significant influence of EU security institutions on national foreign policy, which resulted in a significant role for the ESDP in this case.* British consent, on the other hand, means that although there is weak evidence of Europeanization considerations based on the lack of opposition to the particular mission (although no moves towards substantial participation) there were also no conflicting interests with a view to alliance politics or domestic reservations that would have precluded London from giving its consent to the launch of EUFOR RD Congo.

On the utility of the Europeanization approach: limitations and opportunities

As the preceding sections have demonstrated, the analysis of member states foreign policies has yielded some insights that refute arguments that 'Europeanization' ought not to be used as an organizing concept to begin with (Kassim, 2000: 238). For one, the Europeanization approach has proven useful in highlighting the influence of the EU on national foreign policy, even if the individual crisis case studies have shown that the influence of the EU security institutions and, by extension, the explanatory value of the Europeanization approach itself, remains limited especially when it comes to the application of military instruments under the EU ESDP and uneven when it comes to crisis decision-making.

Defining and operationalizing the concept has proved challenging for two main reasons. In applying Europeanization to the area of foreign and security policy, precisely defining the term – even if not impossible – nevertheless yielded three, at times overlapping (adaptation and preference formations) and/or contradicting (adaptation vs. projection), definitions. The questions established to guide the empirical analysis established fairly precise evidence of one or more meanings of Europeanization. Nevertheless, even the successful attempts at narrowing the definitions and guiding questions did not significantly ease the complexity of the subject matter, the analytical enterprise, or the empirical results. Processes of Europeanization, in the end, clearly exist but are complex and multifaceted in their influence on national government.

The second challenge in using Europeanization as a guiding concept consisted in the process of delineating Europeanization from other determinants of foreign policy decision-making, and to show the extent to which the European platform is privileged as opposed to bilateral relations between states or policies initiated within the UN format. While it is fairly simple to conclude from public statements and actual policies adopted on the part of the EU or individual decision-makers that Europe matters and that the EU is increasingly active by means of its CFSP and ESDP, establishing the extent to which 'Europe matters' in relations to other foreign policy priorities, such as transatlantic ties or domestic idiosyncrasies, necessitated adopting additional and contrasting perspectives in order to highlight the limits of Europeanization and to expose the tension between European and other priorities in foreign policy decision-making.

Adding the frameworks of alliance politics as well as governmental politics, while useful in analysing conflicting pressures also added significant complexity to the task of collecting and analysing empirical evidence. Charges levelled against Allison's governmental politics model – that researchers need to have a level of understanding of policy-making processes because it is difficult to collect the data without fully immersing oneself in the policy process – also applies to the adoption of the Europeanization and alliance politics framework. Although the question of 'what space for Europe' is a relevant and highly salient one in the light of growing responsibilities and tasks undertaken by the EU CFSP and ESDP, attempting to answer this question in a detailed manner in the first instance required significant data collection and analysis.

Developing a theoretical argument, or aiming for a parsimonious explanation of the drivers of European foreign policy evolution, as a result, is beyond the scope of the Europeanization approach. Although theory development has not been the aim of this particular research undertaking, it must nevertheless be counted among the shortfalls of adopting the Europeanization concept. Although investigations on the drivers of national foreign policy decision-making add research output, they do not move FPA or the analysis of European foreign and security policy beyond the pre-theoretical stage that has frequently been decried in the academic literature (see Ginsberg, 2001). Given the relative youth of both CFSP and ESDP, and the limited time ESDP has been 'out in the field' this seems a somewhat unfair argument in that it might be too soon for abstraction. Nevertheless, the challenge of providing a theory-driven, parsimonious explanation for foreign policy decisions in the CFSP/ESPD context remains for others to explore.

Changing priorities for ESDP

Beyond the Europeanization and alliance politics dichotomy the two cases from 2001 show that the scope of applications of the instruments in CFSP and ESDP was not clearly defined in the minds of member states. Apart from the military limitations of ESDP at the time, resistance on the part of the US/NATO, and member states preferences for avoiding transatlantic conflict, the two cases also highlight that there was no clear conception of where and to what end ESDP instruments should be employed. Whereas the Balkans were uncontested as a terrain for EU civilian and military crisis management instruments on the grounds of previous EU involvement, Afghanistan was not an area where the application of EU military crisis management instruments was perceived to be appropriate for the task of reconstruction, although the EU made substantial commitments to Afghanistan.

Contrasting the two case studies showed that, whereas in the case of FYROM the eventual use of ESDP instruments was not contested in principle and achieving coordination and coherence as part of strengthening the EU's collective action capability (Olsen, 2002: 3) was delayed rather than precluded, the case of Afghanistan has shown that the use of CFSP and ESDP instruments on the part of EU member states was determined by considerations that go beyond considerations of putting the EU on the map as a global security actor. Instead, these considerations included the nature and intensity of the crisis in question; the role of the US and the transatlantic alliance more broadly in the conflict; the geographic scope of the crisis; and considerations over a Western/EU label in a Muslim country.

Events since 2001 have highlighted that questions over the EU's military reach have yet to be resolved: implicitly ESDP appears to be focused on the immediate neighbourhood – the Balkans – as well as sub-Saharan Africa, with most missions launched in those two regions, although the 2003 European Security Strategy (ESS) lists terrorism and failed states among the key threats facing Europe (Council of the European Union, 2003): both are global in nature, and point towards global rather than regional ambitions for the EU as a security actor. Of course, ESDP has gone global with missions ranging from Aceh, Indonesia to the Democratic Republic of Congo (DRC). Geographically, this goes beyond the immediate neighbourhood of potential member states. But the EU's global reach so far has been selective, both geographically as well as in the nature of the missions (Biscop, 2006; Cox, 2006): beyond the Balkans and sub-Saharan Africa, military operations have not been launched and the civilian crisis missions tended to be small in scale. This raises the question of whether the reluctance to deploy military instruments under the EU ESDP is merely a matter of transatlantic friction and the lack of 'Europeanization' of national foreign policy, or whether at bottom this is a matter of ambiguity as to the EU's global role. Events of 2006 showed some resolution of this question – on the short-term mission in DRC there was consensus that this was the sort of mission ESDP was designed for. On the other hand, the Middle East was still considered too dangerous as far as launching a military mission was concerned.

Towards the Europeanization of crisis management?

The analysis of the three member states as well as the evolving views and positions vis-à-vis ESDP suggest that, while aspects of Europeanization can be observed in all three countries, continuity prevailed over change between 2001 and 2006 – and it would be an overstatement to speak of the Europeanization of foreign policy. To be sure, alliance politics is less of a factor in decisions concerning the launch of ESDP operations, and both CFSP and ESDP have matured considerably since ESDP was declared partly operational in 2001. Despite the changing relationship to the US as well as NATO on the part of individual European capitals, however, domestic reservations continue to restrict the geographic and functional scope of ESDP. Beyond the NATO–EU dichotomy, when it comes to military crisis management the period between 2001 and 2006 witnessed a change in views on ESDP, no doubt inspired by the increasing realization on the part of some member states that the value-added of ESDP and European crisis management policies in general was its comprehensive approach that combines security, political and economic policies in one institutional home. Security Sector Reform, and ESDP's contribution to it, has become one of the evolving focal areas that were not part of the original ESDP agenda in 2001 – and is one area where the UK in particular is in favour of. However, when it comes to crisis decision-making in circumstances in which fast unfolding events and the threat of ongoing or escalating violence necessitate fast decisions, such as in

FYROM in 2001 but even more so in Afghanistan in 2001 and Lebanon in 2006, member states fall back on proven parameters in which they can assert national influence – the UN in the case of France; the transatlantic relationship in the case of the UK; and multilateral institutions – either the UN or the EU – in the case of Germany. These tendencies reinforce continuity rather than change in European crisis management. Still, the further institutionalization of European foreign policy as a result of the Lisbon Treaty is likely to lead to greater socialization and adaptation pressures. As the process of putting together UNIFIL has demonstrated, these can be expected to exert an increasing 'Europeanization' pull even in times of crisis. To what extent they offset the transatlantic national and multilateral tendencies outlined above, however, remains to be seen.

Notes

1 The Europeanization of National Foreign Policy?

1 The term 'European foreign policy' is somewhat contested on account of the fact that the EU is not a state and does not implement policies the way states do. However, when adopting a definition of foreign policy as 'the sum of official external relations conducted by an independent actor in international relations' (Hill, 2003: 3), the EU as an independent actor does qualify as has having a foreign policy. As for the specific types of European foreign policy, White (1999) identifies the following: Community foreign policy, Union foreign policy, and national foreign policy.

2 One exception is the concept of 'security communities' that was first explored by Karl Deutsch (1957) and systematically studied in an edited volume by Adler and Barnett (1998).

3 Although Moravcsik does not concern himself with EU foreign and security policy, his theoretical approach has been applied to the analysis of policy-making in EU CFSP/ESDP (see Gegout, 2004).

4 Allison originally called the model 'bureaucratic politics' but changed the name in the 2nd edition of his study, which this research adopts.

5 This is true for Britain and France, where parliamentary consent to the deployment of armed forces is not required.

6 See for instance Forster and Blair (2002) on the impact of European policy-making on the Foreign and Commonwealth Office (FCO) in the UK.

7 In the case of the transatlantic alliance, this applies both to preferences of the US and national policy preferences.

3 Britain: Balancing European and Transatlantic Commitments

1 The EU, represented by the Commission and the Presidency together with the US, Japan and Saudi Arabia co-chaired the Afghanistan Reconstruction Steering Group (ARSG).

4 France: Exporting National Preferences

1 In Operation Artemis France acted as the framework nation and provided the bulk of the personnel with contributions from both EU and non-EU nations. Artemis was the first autonomous EU military mission outside Europe and therefore an important milestone in the development of ESDP (see Gnesotto, 2004).

5   Germany: From Bystander to Participant

1 In an op-ed piece in the *Frankfurter Allgemeine Zeitung* Schröder had written that 'in the future, the EU must be capable of making a contribution to a stable world order that is commensurate with its economic and political potential' (cited in Deutscher Bundestag, 15 March 2001).

Bibliography

Ackermann, A. (2005) 'International Intervention in Macedonia: From Preventive Engagement to Peace Implementation.' In Siani-Davies, P. (ed.), *International Intervention in the Balkans since 1995*. London: Routledge, 105–19.

Adler, E. and M. Barnett (1998) *Security Communities*. Cambridge: Cambridge University Press.

Agence France Presse (2001) France, Britain plan to submit UN resolution on Macedonia, 20 March.

Agence France Presse (2001) Védrine juge plus 'commode' de maintenir une force de l'OTAN en Macedoine, 8 September.

Agence France Presse (2001) EU welcomes fall of Kabul, anxious over what is to follow. 13 November.

Agence France Presse (2001) EU envoy calls for early deployment of UN forces in Afghanistan. 12 December.

Agence France Presse (2001) Blair forces EU climbdown over warning to Washington. 15 December.

Agence France Presse (2001) UN-Sicherheitsrat verabschiedet Resolution für Afghanistan-Mission – Bundeskabinett entscheidet am Freitag über Bundeswehr-Einsatz. 20 December.

Agence France Presse (2002) Blair returns to Britain after South Asian tour. 8 January.

Agence France Presse (2002) EU's Afghan envoy moots broadened mandate for UN forces. 10 January.

Agence France Presse (2002) Germany proposes to share Afghan forces command with Netherlands. 24 September.

Allison, G. (1999) *Essence of Decision: Explaining the Cuban Missile Crisis*. 2nd edition. New York: Longman.

Andreatta, F. (2005) 'Theory and the European Union's International Relations.' In Hill, C. and Smith, M. (eds), *International Relations and the European Union*. Oxford: Oxford University Press: 18–38.

Art, R. (1973) 'Bureaucratic Politics and American Foreign Policy: A Critique', *Policy Sciences* 4: 467–90.

Assemblée Nationale (2001) *Déclaration du gouvernement relative à la situation consécutive aux attentats perpétrés le 11 septembre 2001 aux Etats-Unis d'Amérique par M. Lionel Jospin, Premier Ministre*. Paris, 3 October. www.assemblee-nationale. fr/dg/dg3297.asp

Assemblée Nationale (2001) *Audition de M. Hubert Védrine, Ministre des Affaires Étrangeres, et de M. Alain Richard, Ministre de la Defense, sur la riposte aux attentats.* (Hearing of Mr Hubert Védrine, Foreign Minister and of Mr Alain Richard, Defense Minister on the response to the attacks.) Délégation pour l'Union Européenne. Compte Rendu No. 153. Paris, 9 October.

Assemblée Nationale (2001) *Audition de M. François Léotard, représentant de l'Union européenne en Macedonie.* Commission des affaires étrangères. Compte Rendu no. 8. Paris, 23 October.

Assemblée Nationale (2001) *Déclaration du gouvernement sur la situation en Afghanistan*. (Declaration of the government on the situation in Afghanistan.) Session ordinaire de 2001–2002. Paris, 21 November.

Associated Press (2001) Fischer: NATO-Einsatz in Mazedonien Pruefstein fuer Europa. 3 September.

Auswärtiges Amt (2001) Pressemitteilung 'Bundesminister Fischer fordert zu friedlicher Lösung der Konflikte in Südserbien und im nordmazedonischen Grenzgebiet auf' 11 March. www.auswaertiges-amt.de/www/de/ausgabe_archiv?archiv_id=1303

Auswärtiges Amt (2001) Pressemitteilung 'Bundesminister Fischer fordert Rückkehr zum Dialog in Mazedonien' 4 May 2001. www.auswaertiges-amt.de/www/de/ausgabe_archiv?archiv_id=1490

Auswärtiges Amt (2001) Pressemitteilung 'Bundesminister Fischer fordert Festhalten an der Isolation der albanischen Extremisten in Mazedonien' 24 May. www.auswaertiges-amt.de/www/de/ausgabe_archiv?archiv_id=1576

Auswärtiges Amt (2001) Pressemitteilung. 'Erklärung von Bundesaussenminister Joschka Fischer zur Lage in Mazedonien' 7 June. www.auswaertiges-amt.de/www/de/ausgabe_archiv?archiv_id=1623.

Balaj, B. (2002) 'Der Wiederaufbau Afghanistans: Das Engagement von Weltbank, IWF und EU' (The reconstruction of Afghanistan: the engagement of the World Bank, the IMF and EU), *Internationale Politik* (5): 39–46.

Baraki, M. (2004) 'Afghanistan nach den Taliban', *Aus Politik und Zeitgeschichte* (48): 24–30.

BBC Monitoring Europe (2001) Belgian EU presidency 'disappointed' over French-German-UK pre-summit, 19 October.

BBC News (2001) EU pledges troops for Afghanistan, 14 December http://news.bbc.co.uk/2/hi/world/europe/1709888.stm

BBC News (2002) Q&A: Royal Marines in Afghanistan. 16 April http://news.bbc.co.uk/2/hi/uk_news/1933038.stm

BBC News (2006) France takes lead role on Lebanon. 8 August. http://news.bbc.co.uk/2/hi/middle_east/5257602.stm

Beer, A. and F. Schmidt (2006) Thesen zur Kritik der europäischen Kongo-Politik. http://www.angelika-beer.de/stepone/data/downloads/18/00/00/Thesenpapier_Kongo_von_Angelika_Beer__Frithjof_Schmidt.pdf Accessed on 6 May 2008

de Beer, P. (2006) France in Lebanon: the strength of hesitation. Open Democracy, 29 August. http://www.opendemocracy.net/conflict-middle_east_politics/france_hesitation_3862.jsp Accessed on 10 May 2008.

Berliner Zeitung (2001) Bundeswehr: nach langer Ungewissheit – jetzt ein Auftritt mit leichter Ausrüstung. Berlin, 22 December: 299.

Biscop, S. (2006) *The Ambiguous Ambition: the Development of the EU Security Architecture.* Paper presented at the colloquium The EC/EU: A World Security Actor? An Assessment after 50 Years of the External Actions of the EC/EU, Paris, EU Institute for Security Studies, 15 September.

Biscop, S. (2007) 'The European Security Strategy in Context: a Comprehensive Trend.' In Biscop, S. and Andersson, J.J. (eds), *The EU and the European Security Strategy: Forging a Global Europe.* London: Rouledge: 5–20.

Blair, T. (2001) Speech to the European Research Institute. 21 November. http://europa.eu.int/constitution/futurum/documents/speech/sp231101_en.htm

Blair, T. (2002) Statement to Parliament on NATO Summit. 25 November http://www.pm.gov.uk/output/Page1737.asp

Blair, T. (2003) Doorstep interview by the Prime Minister on the European Union Constitution. 17 October http://www.pm.gov.uk/output/Page4673.asp

Blunden, M. (2000) 'France.' In Manners, I. and Whitman, R. (eds), *The Foreign Policies of European Union Member States*. Manchester: Manchester University Press: 19–43.

Bolton, J. (2007) *Surrender is Not an Option: Defending America at the United Nations*. New York: Threshold Editions.

Börzel, T. (1999) 'Towards Convergence in Europe? Institutional Adaptation to Europeanization in Germany and Spain', *Journal of Common Market Studies* 37 (4): 573–97.

Börzel, T. (2002) 'Pace-Setting, Foot-Dragging, and Fence-Sitting: Member State Responses to Europeanization', *Journal of Common Market Studies* 40 (2): 193–214.

Börzel, T. (2003) 'Shaping and Taking EU Policies: Member States Responses to Europeanization', *Queen's Papers on Europeanization* http://www.qub.ac.uk/ies-old/onlinepapers/poe2-03.pdf.

Brown, C. (2001) *Understanding International Relations*. London: Macmillan.

Bulmer, S. (1998) 'New Institutionalism and the Governance of the Single European Market', *Journal of European Public Policy* 5 (3): 365–86.

Bulmer, S. and M. Burch (1999) 'The Europeanization of Central Government: The UK and Germany in Historical Institutionalist Perspective', Oslo: *ARENA Working Paper* 99/30.

Bull, H. (2002) *The Anarchical Society: a Study of Order in World Politics*. Basingstoke: Palgrave – now Palgrave Macmillan.

Caldwell, D. (1977) 'Bureaucratic Foreign Policy-Making', *American Behavioural Scientist*, 21: 87–110.

Caporaso, J. et al. (2001) *Transforming Europe: Europeanization and Domestic Change*. Ithaca, NY: Cornell University Press.

Checkel, J. (2001) 'The Europeanization of Citizenship?' In Caporaso, J. et al. (eds), *Transforming Europe: Europeanization and Domestic Change*. Ithaca, NY: Cornell University Press.

Chirac, J. (2001) *Conférence de Presse Conjointe de Monsieur Jacques Chirac Président de la République, de Monsieur Lionel Jospin Premier Ministre, et de Monsieur Hubert Védrine Ministre des affaires étrangères lors du Conseil Européen (2001)*. Stockholm, 24 March. http://www.elysee.fr/elysee/root/bank/print/2318.htm

Chirac, J. (2001) *Address by Jacques Chirac, President of France, at the special meeting of the North Atlantic Council NATO HQ*. Brussels, 13 June. http://www.nato.int/docu/speech/2001/s010613c.htm

Chirac, J. (2001) *Intervention televisée de M. Jacques Chirac, president de la republique, a la suite des operations militaires en afghanistan*. (Televised interview following military operations in Afghanistan.) Palais d'Elysee, 7 October.

Chirac, J. (2001) *Conference de Presse de Monsieur Jacques Chirac President de la Republique a l'issue de son entretien avec monsieur Kofi Annan secretaire general de l'ONU* (Press Conference of Jacques Chirac on his meeting with Kofi Annan, Secretary General of the United Nations), New York, 6 November.

Chirac, J. (2001) *Pointe de presse conjoint de M Jacques Chirac président de la république et de M. Lakhdar Brahimi représentant spécial du secrétaire général des nations unies pour l'afghanistan.* (Joint Press Conference of Mr Jacques Chirac and Mr Lakhdar Brahimi, Special Representative of the United Nations to Afghanistan.) Palais de l'Elysée, 8 November.

Chirac, J. (2001) *Intervention télévisée de M. Jacques Chirac, président de la république.* (Television appearance of Mr Jacques Chirac.) Palais de l'Elysée, Paris, 16 November.

Chirac, J. (2001) *Conférence de presse conjointe a l'issue du conseil européen* (Joint conference on the European Council). European Council, Laeken, 15 December.

Chirac (2004) Nato summit press conference (excerpts). Istanbul, 28 June.

Ciuță, F. (2002) 'The End(s) of NATO: Security, Strategic Action and Narrative Transformation', *Contemporary Security Policy* 23(1): 35–62.

CNN.com (2001) EU calls for UN role in Afghanistan. 17 October.

CNN.com (2001) EU links Afghan aid to human rights. 19 November.

Cole, A. and H. Drake (2000) 'The Europeanization of the French Polity: Continuity, Change and Adaptation', *Journal of European Public Policy* 7(1): 26–43.

Council of the European Union (2001) *2338th Council Meeting General Affairs,* Brussels March 19–20 http://www.seerecon.org/Calendar/2001/events/c20010319_ga.htm

Council of the European Union (2001) *Council Joint Action of 29 June 2001 concerning the appointment of the Special Representative of the European Union in the Former Yugoslav Republic of Macedonia* (2001/492/CFSP). Brussels, 29 June.

Council of the European Union (2001) *Conclusion and Plan of Action of the Extraordinary European Council Meeting on 21 September 2001.* SN 140/01. http://ue.eu.int/ueDocs/cms_Data/docs/pressData/en/ec/140.en.pdf. Brussels, 21 September.

Council of the European Union (2001) *Council Joint Action of 10 December concerning the appointment of the Special Representative of the European Union.* 2001/875/CFSP. Brussels, 10 December.

Council of the European Union (2001) *Presidency Conclusions, European Council Meeting in Laeken.* Brussels, 14/15 December. http://ec.europa.eu/governance/impact/docs/key_docs/laeken_concl_en.pdf

Council of the European Union (2002) *28th Council meeting,* Brussels, 27 May http://europa.eu/rapid/pressReleasesAction.do?reference=PRES/02/148&format=HTML&aged=1&language=EN&guiLanguage=en

Council of the European Union (2003) *Council Joint Action on the European Union military operation in the former Yugoslav Republic of Macedonia* 2003/92/CFSP. Brussels, 27 January.

Council of the European Union (2003) *Copenhagen European Council, 12 and 13 December 2002, Presidency Conclusions.* Brussels, 29 January. http://ue.eu.int/ueDocs/cms_Data/docs/pressData/en/ec/73842.pdf

Council of the European Union (2003) *A Secure Europe in a Better World: European Security Strategy.* Brussels, 12 December.

Council of the European Union (2006). *EU military operation in support of the MONUC during the election process in DR Congo: Council adopts Joint Action, appoints Operation and Force Commanders.* 8761/06 (Presse 121), Luxembourg, 27 April.

Council of the European Union (2006) *Extraordinary EU Council Meeting: Conclusions on Lebanon.* Brussels, 25 August.

Cox, M. (2006) *Why ESDP*. Evidence presented at Hearing 'The Security Strategy and the Future of the European Security and Defence Policy' European Parliament, Brussels, 13 July.

Dembinski, M. (2007) 'Europe and the UNIFIL II Mission: Stumbling into the Conflict Zone of the Middle East', *CFSP Forum* 5 (1): 1–4.

Deutsch, K. (1957) *Political Community in the North Atlantic Area*. Princeton: Princeton University Press.

Deutscher Bundestag (2001) 158. Session, 15 March, Plenarprotokoll 14/158.

Deutscher Bundestag (2001) 183. Session, 6 July, Plenarprotokoll 14/183.

Deutscher Bundestag (2001) 184. Session, 29 August, Plenarprotokoll 14/184.

Deutscher Bundestag (2001) 187. Session, 19 September, Plenarprotokoll 14/187.

Deutscher Bundestag (2001) 192. Session, 11 October, Plenarprotokoll 14/192.

Deutscher Bundestag (2001) 195. Session, 18 October, Plenarprotokoll 14/195.

Deutscher Bundestag (2001) 198. Session, 8 November, Plenarprotokoll 14/198.

Deutscher Bundestag (2001) 202. Session, 16 November, Plenarprotokoll 14/202.

Deutscher Bundestag (2001) 210. Session, 22 December, Plenarprotokoll 14/210.

Deutscher Bundestag (2006) 36. Session, 19 May, Plenarprotokoll 16/36.

Deutscher Bundestag (2006) 46. Session, 6 September, Plenarprotokoll 16/46.

Deutscher Bundestag (2006) 50. Session, 20 September, Plenarprotokoll 16/50.

Deutsche Welle (2006) Congo Deployment Meets Muted Response in Germany. 27 January.

DFID (2001) *Afghanistan – Recovery: an emergency plan for the first 100 days*. London, 13 November. http://www.publications.parliament. uk/pa/cm200203/cmselect/cmintdev/84/8402.htm

Downing Street Press Briefing (2001) 25 June.

dpa (2001) Bis zu 1200 deutsche Soldaten nach Kabul. 22 December.

Duke, S. (1999) *The Elusive Quest for European Security: from EDC to CFSP*. Basingstoke: Macmillan – now Palgrave Macmillan.

Dyson, K. and K. Goertz (2003) 'Living with Europe: Power, Constraint, and Contestation.' In Dyson, K. and Goertz, K. (eds), *Germany, Europe and the Politics of Constraint*. Oxford: Oxford University Press.

The Economist (2003) Dealing with the foot-draggers: blame, aim, fire. London, 1 May.

The Economist (2006) Abroad be dangers. London, 24 August.

Ehrhart, H.-G. (2007) 'EUFOR RD Congo: a Preliminary Assessment', *European Security Review* 32 (3): 9–12.

Eldridge, J. L. C. (2002) 'Playing at Peace: Western Politics, Diplomacy and the Stabilization of Macedonia', *European Security* 11(3): 46–90.

European Commission (2003) *Country Strategy Paper (CSP) Afghanistan, 2003–2006*. http://europa.eu.int/comm/external_relations/afghanistan/csp/03_06.pdf

Europe Report (2001) EU/US: Summit fails to resolve climate change row, 16 June.

Everts, S. (2000) Berlin-Paris-London. In Pijpers, A. (ed.) *On Cores and Coalitions in the European Union: The Position of Some Small Member States*. Clingendael Institute: 15–32.

faz.net (2006). Merkel und Bush in Sorge ueber Russland, Nahen Osten und Iran. 13 July http://www.faz.net/s/RubA24ECD630CAE40E483841DB7D16F4211/Doc...4C329074A890AC771F66 ~ ATpl ~ Ecommon ~ Scontent~Afor~Eprint.html

Featherstone, K. and C. Radaelli (eds) (2003) *The Politics of Europeanization.* Oxford: Oxford University Press.

Financial Times (2001) Ethnic Albanian leader pessimistic over talks. London, 6 April.

Financial Times (2001) US wary of committing Nato troops to Macedonia. London, 14 June.

Financial Times (2001) Show of force guards tense path to peace: Britain's role reflects a desire to protect political, military and economic investment in the Balkans. London, 18 August: 5.

Financial Times (2001) Special Envoy seeks EU force for Macedonia: Plan for troops to follow NATO mission. London, 6 September.

Financial Times (2001) Nato enters uncharted waters as it adapts to new environment. London, 3 October.

Financial Times (2001) Europe fails to find united line on Kabul after the Taliban. London. 9 October.

Financial Times (2001) Schröder takes gamble on vote of confidence: troop mobilization – German chancellor forces vote in order to put pressure on dissenting coalition legislators. London, 14 November: 12.

Financial Times (2001) Political change must be quick, say aid donors. London, 6 December: 6.

Financial Times (2001) EU in attempt to forge Afghan policy. London, 14 December.

Financial Times (2001) Peacekeeping dispute mars first day of EU summit. London, 15 December: 7.

Financial Times (2002) UK resists moves to deploy EU force in Macedonia. London, 4 March.

Financial Times (2002) Dispute over defence force links with Nato. London, 30 October.

Financial Times (2003) 'NATO credibility at risk' over call to defend Turkey. London, 10 February: 6.

Financial Times (2006). Rice rules out 'temporary solutions' in Lebanon crisis. 26 July, 3.

Financial Times Deutschland (2001) Bundeswehr vor Nato-Einsatz in Mazedonien. 2 July.

Fischer, J. (2001) 'Die Antwort auf fast alle Fragen ist: Europa', *Die Zeit* http://www.zeit.de/2001/12/Politik/200112_fischer.neu9.3.html.

Foley, M. (2000) *The British Presidency*: Manchester: Manchester University Press.

Foley, M. (2002) *John Major, Tony Blair and a Conflict of Leadership.* Manchester: Manchester University Press.

Foley, M. (2004) 'Presidential Attribution as an Agency of Prime Ministerial Critique in a Parliamentary Democracy', *British Journal of Politics and International Relations* 6(3): 292–311.

Forster, A. and W. Wallace, (2000) 'Common Foreign and Security Policy: From Shadow to Substance?' In Wallace, H. and Wallace, W. (eds) *Policy-Making in the European Union*, 4th edition. Oxford: Oxford University Press.

Forster, A. and A. Blair (2002) 'Trends and Patterns in British European Policy.' In Blair, A. and Forster, A. (eds), *The Making of Britain's European Foreign Policy.* Harlow: Pearson Education Limited: 167–91.

Frankfurter Allgemeine Zeitung (2001) Kämpfe können wieder ausbrechen. Frankfurt, 25 October.

French Foreign Ministry (2006) 'Core Group' Meeting on the Israeli-Lebanese Crisis, Speech by M. Philippe Douste-Blazy, Minister of Foreign Affairs, 26 July. https://pastel.diplomatie.gouv.fr/editorial/actual/ael2/bulletin.gb.asp?liste= 20060727.gb.html&submit.x=17&submit.y=10&submit=consulter Accessed on10 May 2008.

French Foreign Ministry (2006a) Middle East Thirdly Monthly Press Conference given by M. Dominique de Villepin, Prime Minister, Mantes-la-Jolie, 31 July. https://pastel.diplomatie.gouv.fr/editorial/actual/ael2/bulletin.gb.asp? liste=20060801.gb.html Accessed on 11 May 2008.

French Foreign Ministry (2006b) Situation in the Middle East. Statements Made by M. Philippe Douste-Blazy. Beirut, 31 July. https://pastel.diplomatie.gouv.fr/ editorial/actual/ael2/bulletin.gb.asp?liste=20060801.gb.html Accessed on 21 October 2008.

French Foreign Ministry (2006) On the situation in the Middle East and France's involvement in the implementation of UNSCR 1701. Speech by M. Philippe Douste-Blazy, Minister of Foreign Affairs, before the National Assembly Foreign Affairs Committee (excerpts). Paris, 7 September. https://pastel.diplomatie. gouv.fr/editorial/actual/ael2/bulletin.gb.asp?liste=20060908.gb.html Accessed on 11 May 2008.

French Foreign Ministry (2006) UNIFIL: France helps ensure the task of monitoring Lebanon's coastline. Paris, 11 September. http://www.diplomatie.gouv.fr/ en/article-imprim.php3?id_article=5304 Accessed on 21 October 2008.

French Foreign Ministry (2008) France and the Great Lakes Region. 20 February. http://www.diplomatie.gouv.fr/en/article-imprim.php3?id_article=5276 Accessed on 6 May 2008.

French Ministry of Defence (2006) Press Release. Michèle Alliot-Marie, Minister of Defence, speaking before the members of the Committee for Foreign Affairs, Defence and Armed Forces, chaired by Serge Vinçon (UMP – Cher), presents France's role in the implementation of an expanded UNIFIL. Paris, 31 August. http://www.defense.gouv.fr/ministre/prises_de_parole/discours/speeches_and_ communiques/michele_alliot_marie_to_the_senate_30_august_2006 Accessed on 11 May 2008.

Garton Ash, T. (1993) *In Europe's Name: Germany and the Divided Continent*. New York: Random House.

Garton Ash, T. (2001) 'Is There a Good Terrorist?' *The New York Review of Books*, 48.

Gegout, C. (2004) 'An Evaluation of the Making and Functioning of the European Union's Common Foreign and Security Policy (CFSP) System.' PhD Thesis, European University Institute, Florence.

Gegout, C. (2005) 'Causes and Consequences of the EU's Military Intervention in the Democratic Republic of Congo: a Realist Explanation', *European Foreign Affairs Review*, 10(3): 427–43.

Gegout, C. (2007) 'The EU and Security in the Democratic Republic of Congo: Unfinished Business', *CFSP Forum* 5(1): 5–9.

General Affairs Council (2001) Press Release Brussels, 8 October. www.yale.edu/ lawweb/avalon/sept_11/eu_005.htm

Giegerich, B. (2006) *European Security and Strategic Culture*. Baden-Baden: Nomos.

Ginsberg, R. (1989) *Foreign Policy Actions of the European Community: The Politics of Scale*. Boulder, CO: Lynne Rienner.

Ginsberg, R. (2001) *The European Union in International Politics: Baptism by Fire*. Lanham, MD: Rowman & Littlefield.

Gnesotto, N. (ed.) (2004) *EU Security and Defence Policy: the First Five Years (1999–2004)*. Paris: Institute for Security Studies.

Gordon, P. and B. Suzan (2002) 'France, the United States and the War on Terrorism', *U.S.-France Analysis*, The Brookings Institution, 1 January http://www.brook.edu/fp/cuse/analysis/terrorism.htm

Gourevitch, P. (1978) 'The Second Image Reversed: The International Sources of Domestic Politics', *International Organization* 32(4): 881–912.

Government Press Briefing (2001) Tuesday 28 Morning Briefing. London, 28 August. http://www.number10.gov.uk/output/page2147.asp

Gowan, R. (2007) 'The EU's Multiple Strategic Identities: European Security after Lebanon and the Congo', *Studia Diplomatica* 60(1): 59–80.

Grevi, G. (2007) *Pioneering foreign policy: The EU Special Representatives*. Chaillot Paper No. 106. Paris, EU Institute for Security Studies.

Guardian (2001) Troops arrive for Balkans task. London, 18 August: 2.

Guardian (2002) Leaked papers reveal split over Macedonia troops. London, 4 March.

Guardian Unlimited (2006) Abandon your Lebanon policy, former Foreign Office spokesman tells Blair. 1 August. http://politics.guardian.co.uk/foreignaffairs/story/0,,1834931,00.html last accessed on 16 February 2008.

Guardian (2006) Middle East crisis: Diplomacy: Annan sends envoys in effort to contain crisis. 14 July: 5.

Guardian (2006) Middle East: Europe's muted voice. 18 July: 30.

Guardian (2006) Middle East crisis: France pushes UN for action on conflict: Security council move challenged by US and British approach. 20 July: 4.

Guardian (2006) Berlin signals new tack over Middle East. 27 September http://guardian.co.uk/world/2006/sep/27/germany.lebanon.print

Haas, E. (1960) 'International Integration: The European and Universal Process', *International Organization* 4: 607–46.

Haine, J-Y. and B. Giegerich (2006) *In Congo, a cosmetic EU operation. International Herald Tribune*, 12 June.

Handelsblatt.com (2006) Wer sorgt fuer Frieden im Lebanon? 17 July http://www.handelsblatt.com/News/printpage.aspx?_p=200051&_t=ftprint&_b=1109074

Heffernan, R. (2003) 'Prime Ministerial Predominance? Core Executive Politics in the UK', *British Journal of Politics and International Relations* 5 (3): 347–72.

Hill, C. (1993) 'The Capability-Expectations Gap, or Conceptualizing Europe's International Role', *Journal of Common Market Studies* 31(3): 305–28.

Hill, C. (1996) 'United Kingdom: Sharpening Contradictions.' In Hill, Christopher (ed.) *The Actors in Europe's Foreign Policy*. London: Routledge: 68–89.

Hill, C. (1998) 'Closing the Capability-Expectations Gap? A Common Foreign Policy for Europe?' In Peterson, S. and Sjursen, H. (eds), *Competing Visions of the CFSP*. London: Routledge: 18–38.

Hill, C. (2003) *The Changing Politics of Foreign Policy*. New York: Palgrave Macmillan.

Hill, C. (2004) 'Renationalizing or Regrouping? EU Foreign Policy Since 11 September 2001', *Journal of Common Market Studies* 42(1): 143–63.

Hill, C. and M. Smith (2005) 'Acting for Europe: Reassessing the European Union's Place in International Relations.' In Hill, C. and Smith, M. (eds), *International Relations and the European Union*. Oxford: Oxford University Press: 388–406.

Hix, S. and K. Goertz (2000) 'Introduction: European Integration and National Political Systems', *West European Politics* 23(4): 1–26.

Hoffmann, S. (2001) 'Classic Diplomacy in the Information Age; Hubert Vedrine explains French Foreign Policy', *Foreign Affairs*, July/August: 137–41.

House of Commons (2001) *Government policy towards the Former Republic of Yugoslavia and the wider region following the fall of Milosevic*. Select Committee on Foreign Affairs, London, 27 March.

House of Commons (2001) *Examination of Witnesses (Questions 20–39). Major-General Tony Milton, OBE, RM, Director General Joint Doctrine and Concepts*. Select Committee on Defence. London, 7 November 2001.

House of Commons (2001a) *Examination of Witnesses (Questions 1–19), The Rt Hon Jack Straw*. Select Committee on Foreign Affairs London, 20 November.

House of Commons (2001b) *International Development – Minutes of Evidence. Memorandum submitted by The Rt Hon Clare Short MP, Secretary of State for International Development*. Select Committee on International Development. London, 20 November.

House of Commons (2001) *International Development – Written Answers to Questions (23 Nov 2001)*. Commons Hansard vol. 375 no. 58. London, 23 November.

House of Commons (2001) *Examination of Witnesses (Questions 20–40), The Rt Hon Jack Straw*. Select Committee on Foreign Affairs London, 5 December.

House of Commons (2001) *British-US Relations*. Select Committee on Foreign Affairs. London, 18 December.

House of Commons (2002a) *Foreign Policy Aspects of the War Against Terrorism*. Select Committee on Foreign Affairs. London, 12 June.

House of Commons (2002b) *Foreign Policy Aspects of the War Against Terrorism: Memorandum from Mr Paul Bergne*. Select Committee on Foreign Affairs. London, 12 June.

House of Commons (2003) *Afghanistan: The Transition from Humanitarian Relief to Reconstruction and Development Assistance*. London, 14 January.

House of Commons (2006) *European Scrutiny Select Committee, Thirty-First Report*. London, 14 June. http://www.publications.parliament.uk/pa/cm200506/cmselect/cmeuleg/34-xxxi/3402.htm last accessed on 18 May 2008.

House of Commons (2007) *Global Security: The Middle East. Foreign Affairs Committee, Eighth Report*. London, 13 August.

House of Lords (2002) *Eleventh Report: The European Policy on Security and Defence*. European Union Committee. London, 29 January.

Howorth, J. (2000) 'Britain, NATO and CESDP: Fixed Strategy, Changing Tactics', *European Foreign Affairs Review* 5: 377–96.

Howorth, J. (2003–04) 'France, Britain and the Euro-Atlantic Crisis', *Survival* 45(4): 173–92.

Howorth, J. (2005) 'From Security to Defence: the Evolution of CFSP.' In Hill, C. and Smith, M. (eds), *International Relations and the European Union*. Oxford: Oxford University Press: 179–204.

Howorth, J. (2007) *Security and Defence Policy in the European Union.* Basingstoke: Palgrave Macmillan.

Human Rights Watch (2002) *Paying for the Taliban's Crimes: Abuses against ethnic Pashtuns in Northern Afghanistan.* Report 14 (2), April.

Huntington, S. (1960) 'Strategic Planning and the Political Process', *Foreign Affairs* 38: 285–99.

Independent (2001) EU may take over from NATO in Macedonia. London, 7 September.

Independent (2001) War on Terrorism: Diplomacy – foreign ministers beef up statement of support by EU. London, 18 Octobe: 4.

International Crisis Group (2001a) *The Macedonian Question: Reform or Rebellion.* Balkan Report no. 109. Skopje/Brussels, 5 April.

International Crisis Group (2001b) *Macedonia: The Last Chance for Peace.* Balkans Report n. 113. Skopje/Brussels, 20 June.

International Crisis Group (2001c) *Macedonia: Filling the Security Vacuum.* Balkans Briefing. Skopje/Brussels, 8 September.

International Crisis Group (2002) *Moving Macedonia Toward Self-Sufficiency: A New Security Approach for NATO and the EU.* Balkans Report no. 135. Skopje/Brussels, 15 November.

International Crisis Group (2005) *Rebuilding the Afghan State: The European Union's Role.* Asia Report No 107. Brussels, 30 November.

International Crisis Group (2006) *Securing Congo's Elections: Lessons from the Kinshasa Showdown.* Africa Briefing No. 42. Brussels, 2 October.

International Herald Tribune (2002) France upbraids US as 'simplistic'. 7 February.

International Herald Tribune (2006) UN and EU prepare to step in; world leaders discuss new peacekeeping force; Israel says no. 17 July.

International Herald Tribune (2006) Envoy says EU is 'ready to help' end fighting. 19 July.

International Herald Tribune (2006) EU calls for 'cessation of hostilities'. 1 August.

Irish Times (2002) France joins in Afghan bomber attacks. 6 March: 10.

Irish Times (2001) Internment revisited as UK prepares to lead force. 20 December: 9.

Irondelle, B. (2003) 'Europeanisation without the European Union? French Military Reforms 1991–96', *Journal of European Public Policy* 10 (2): 208–26.

ITAR-TASS News Agency (2001) EU special envoy tenders resignation. 10 September.

Janning, J. (1996) 'A German Europe – A European Germany? On the Debate over Germany's Foreign Policy', *International Affairs* 72 (1): 33–41.

Kaarbo, J. (1998) 'Power Politics in Foreign Policy', *European Journal of International Relations* 4(1): 67–97.

Kampfner, J. (2003) *Blair's War.* London: Free Press.

Kassim, H. (2000) 'Conclusion'. In Kassim, H., Peters, B. G. and Wright, V. (eds), *The National Co-ordination of EU Policy.* Oxford: Oxford University Press: 235–64.

Katsioulis, C. (2004) 'Deutsche Sicherheitspolitik im Parteiendiskurs: Alter Wein in neuen Schläuchen.' In Harnisch et al., *Deutsche Sicherheitspolitik: Eine Bilanz der Regierung Schröder.* Baden-Baden: Nomos Verlagsgesellschaft: 227–52.

Katzenstein, P. (ed.) (1997) *Tamed Power: Germany in Europe.* Ithaca, NY: Cornell University Press.

Keatinge, P. (1984) 'The Europeanization of Irish Foreign Policy.' In Drudy, P. and McAleese, D. (eds), *Ireland and the European Community*. Cambridge: Cambridge University Press: 33–57.

Keohane, R. (1984) *After Hegemony: Cooperation and Discord in the World Political Economy*. Princeton: Princeton University Press.

Klaiber, K. (2002) *The European Union in Afghanistan: Impressions of my term as Special Representative*. National Europe Centre Paper No. 44, Australian National University. http://www.anu.edu.au/NEC/klaiber.pdf

Klaiber, K. (2003) 'Political and Economic Reconstruction in Afghanistan', *German Foreign Policy in Dialogue* 4(10): 12–15.

Knill, C. (2001) *The Europeanization of National Administrations: Patterns of Institutional Change and Persistence*. Cambridge: Cambridge University Press.

Krasner, S. (1971) 'Are Bureaucracies Important? (Or Allison Wonderland)', *Foreign Policy* 7: 159–79.

Ladrech, R. (1994) 'Europeanization of Domestic Politics and Institutions: The Case of France', *Journal of Common Market Studies* 32(1): 69–88.

Lansford, T. (2002) 'Whither Lafayette? French Military Policy and the American Campaign in Afghanistan', *European Security* 11 (3): 126–45.

Layne, C. (1993) 'The Unipolar Illusion: Why New Great Powers Will Rise', *International Security* 17 (Spring): 5–51.

Le Monde (2001) L'Union européenne et l'OTAN coordonnent leurs efforts pour soutenir la Macedoine. Paris, 21 March: 3.

Le Monde (2001) We are all American. Paris, 13 September.

Le Monde (2006) Situation in the Middle East: Interview with Jacques Chirac, 27 July.

Lieven, A. (2001) 'The End of NATO', *Prospect*, December.

Light, M. (1994) 'Foreign Policy Analysis.' In Groom, A. and Light, M. (eds), *Contemporary International Relations: A Guide to Theory*. London: Pinter Publishers: 93–108.

Liotta, P. H. (2003) 'Spillover Effect: Aftershocks in Kosovo, Macedonia and Serbia', *European Security* 12(1): 82–108.

Liotta, P. H. and C. R. Jebb (2002) 'Cry, the Imagined Country: Legitimacy and the Fate of Macedonia', *European Security* 11(1): 49–80.

Longhurst, K. (2004) *Germany and the Use of Force*. Manchester: Manchester University Press.

Lucarelli, S. (2000) *Europe and the Breakup of Yugoslavia: A Political Failure in Search of a Scholarly Explanation*. The Hague: Kluwer Law International.

Major, C. (2005) 'Europeanization and Foreign and Security Policy – Undermining or Rescuing the Nation State?', *Politics* 25(3): 175–90.

Major, C. (2008) 'EU–UN cooperation in military crisis management: the experience of EUFOR RD Congo in 2006. Occasional Paper 72. Paris, EU Institute for Security Studies.

Manners, I. and R. Whitman (2000) *The Foreign Policies of European Union Member States*. Manchester: Manchester University Press.

Mastanduno, M. (1999) 'Preserving the Unipolar Moment: Realist Theories and US Grand Strategies after the Cold War.' In Kapstein, E. and Mastanduno, M. (eds), *Unipolar Politics: Realism and State Strategies after the Cold War*. New York: Columbia University Press.

New York Times (2006). Europe pledges a larger force inside Lebanon. 26 August: 1.

Niblett, R. (2001) 'France and Europe at the end of the Cold War: Resisting Change.' In Niblett, R. and Wallace, W. (eds), *Rethinking European Order: West European Responses, 1989–97*. Basingstoke: Palgrave – now Palgrave Macmillan.

Nuttall, S. (1992) *European Political Cooperation*. Oxford: Clarendon Press.

Observer (2001) The Countdown: marching to the brink of battle. London, 23 September: 11.

Observer (2004) Congo death toll up to 3.8m. London, 10 December.

Øhrgaard, J. (2004) 'International Relations or European Integration: is the CFSP *sui generis?*' In Tonra, B. and Christiansen, T. (eds), *Rethinking European Union Foreign Policy*. Manchester: Manchester University Press: 26–44.

Øhrgaard, J. (2004) 'International Relations or European Integration: is the CFSP sui generis?' In Tonra, B. and Christiansen, T. (eds), *Rethinking European Union Foreign Policy*. Manchester: Manchester University Press: 26–44.

Olsen, J. (2002) 'The Many Faces of Europeanization', *Arena Working Paper* 02/02.

OSCE Press Release (2001) Need for intensified dialogue in the former Yugoslav Republic of Macedonia. Vienna, 30 March.

Overhaus, M. (2003) 'Zwischen kooperativer Sicherheit und militärischer Interventionsfähigkeit. Rot-grüne Sicherheitspolitik im Rahmen von ESVP und NATO.' In Harnisch, S., Grund, C. and Maull, H. (eds), *Deutschland im Abseits? Rot-grüne Aussenpolitik 1998–2003*. Baden-Baden: Nomos Verlagsgesellschaft: 49–64.

Peterson, J. (2002) 'Europe, America and 11 September', *Irish Studies in International Affairs* 13: 1–20.

Piana, C. (2002) 'The EU's Decision-making Policy in the Common Foreign and Security Policy: the Case of the Former Yugoslav Republic of Macedonia', *European Foreign Affairs Review* 7(2): 209–26.

Posen, B. (2004) 'ESDP and the Structure of World Power', *International Spectator* 39(1).

Press Association (2001) Cook pledges support in Macedonian borders crisis, 20 March.

Press Association (2001) Blair and Bush discuss Macedonia crisis, 29 June.

Press Association (2001) Four EU countries pledge to go to war. 8 October.

Putnam, R. (1988) 'Diplomacy and Domestic Politics: The Logic of Two-Level Games', *International Organization* 42 (3): 427–60.

Radaelli, C. (2002) 'Whither Europeanization? Concept Stretching and Substantive Change', *European Integration Online Papers* 4(8).

Radaelli, C. (2004) 'Europeanization: Solution or Problem?', *European Integration Online Papers* 8 (16).

Regelsberger, E. (ed.) (1997) *Foreign Policy of the European Union: from EPC to CFSP and Beyond*. Boulder, CO: Lynne Rienner.

Richard, A. (2001) *The European Union: a rising feature on the international stage*. Remarks by H.E. Mr Alain Richard, Minister of Defence of France. 12th Forum Bundeswehr & Gesellschaft, Welt am Sonntag, Berlin, 2 October.

Riddell, P. (2003) *Hug Them Close: Blair, Clinton, Bush and the 'Special Relationship'*. London: Politico's.

Riddell, P. (2005) 'Europe.' In Seldon, A. and Kavanagh, D. (eds), *The Blair Effect 2001–05*. Cambridge: Cambridge University Press: 362–83.

Ripley, B. (1995) 'Cognition, Culture, and Bureaucratic Politics.' In Neack, L. et al. (eds), *Foreign Policy Analysis: Continuity and Change in its Second Generation*. Englewood Cliffs, NJ: Prentice-Hall.

Risse-Kappen, T. (1996) 'Identity in a Democratic Security Community: The Case of NATO.' In Katzenstein, Peter J. (ed.), *The Culture of National Security*. New York: Columbia University Press: 357–99.

Risse, T. (2001) 'A European Identity? Europeanization and the Evolution of Nation-State Identities.' In Caporaso, J. Cowles, M. G., and Risse, T. (eds), *Transforming Europe: Europeanization and Domestic Change*. Ithaca, NY: Cornell University Press: 198–216.

Roberts, N. and P. King (1991) 'Policy Entrepreneurs: Their Activity Structure and Function in the Policy Process', *Journal of Public Administration Research and Theory* 1(2): 147–75.

Rosati, J. (1981) 'Developing a Systematic Decision-Making Framework: Bureaucratic Politics in Perspective', *World Politics* 33: 234–52.

Roy, O. (2004) *Afghanistan: la difficile reconstruction d'un Etat*. Chaillot Paper No. 73, December. Paris, Institute for Security Studies.

Rumsfeld, D. (2001) News Transcript. United States Department of Defense, 23 September.

Sabatier, P. (ed.) (1999) *Theories of the Policy Process*. Boulder, CO: Westview Press.

San Diego Union-Tribune (2003) France wary of expanding NATO peacekeeper role: involvement in Afghanistan raises concerns over mission of alliance. San Diego, 27 February.

San Francisco Chronicle (2003) France makes initial foray into mending its relationship with US – serious negotiations precede leaders' first talk in 2 months. 16 April.

Schilling, W. et al. (1962) *Strategy, Politics, and Defense Budgets*. New York: Columbia University Press.

Schimmelfennig, F. (1998/99) 'NATO Enlargement: A Constructivist Explanation', *Security Studies* 8 (2/3): 198–234.

Schimmelfennig, F. and U. Sedelmeier (eds) (2005) *The Europeanization of Central and Eastern Europe*. Ithaca, NY: Cornell University Press.

Singer, D. J. (1961) 'The Levels of Analysis Problem in International Relations', *World Politics* 14 (1): 77–92.

Smith, M. (1999) *The Core Executive in Britain*. London: Macmillan.

Smith, M. E. (2000) 'Conforming to Europe: the Domestic Impact of EU Foreign Policy Cooperation', *Journal of European Public Policy* 7(4): 613–31.

Smith, M. E. (2004) *Europe's Foreign and Security Policy: The Institutionalization of Cooperation*. Cambridge: Cambridge University Press.

Smith, M. (2006) 'Britain, Europe and the World.' In Dunleavy, P. et al. (eds), *Developments in British Politics* 8. Basing stoke: Palgrave Macmillan: 169–73.

Smith, S. (1994) 'Foreign Policy Theory and the New Europe.' In Carlsnaes, W. and Smith, S. (eds), *European Foreign Policy: The EC and Changing Perspectives in Europe*. London: SAGE: 1–20.

Snyder, G. (1977) *Alliance politics*. Ithaca, NY: Cornell University Press.

Sokalski, H. J. (2003) *An Ounce of Prevention: Macedonia and the UN Experience in Preventive Diplomacy*. Washington, DC: United States Institute for Peace Press.

Spectator (2001) The Great Euroamerican Plot. 27 October, 20–1.

Der Spiegel (2002) Interview mit Bundesaussenminister Joschka Fischer. 21 January.
Der Spiegel (2006) Regierung will Kongo-Einsatz deutscher Soldaten verhindern. 21 January.
Der Spiegel (2006) Zentralrat der Juden kritisiert Steinmeier. 14 July http://www.spiegel.de/politik/ausland/0,1518,druck-426815,00.html
Stavridis, S. (ed.) (1997) *New Challenges to the European Union: Policies and Policy-making*. Aldershot: Dartmouth.
Steiner, M. (1977) 'The Elusive Essence of Decision', *International Studies Quarterly* 21: 389–422.
Süddeutsche Zeitung (2006a) Lavieren aus Klugheit. 31 July http://www.sueddeutsche.de/ausland/artikel/801/81720/print.html
Süddeutsche Zeitung (2006b) Militaerische Gewalt muss verhaeltnismaessig sein. Interview mit dem Aussenminister. 31 July http://www.sueddeutsche.de/deutschland/artikel/802/81721/print.html
Taz.de (2006) Die Kanzlerin erinnert an das Recht Israels zur Selbstverteidigung. Hinter verschlossenen Tueren mahnt sie jedoch zur Maessigung. 17 July. http://www.taz.de/index.php?id=archivseite&dig=2006/07/17/a0048&type=98
Taz.de (2006) Kongo? Nein Danke! 28 January.
The Times (2001) Blair can count on support – for the time being. 18 October.
The Times (2001) Prodi's criticism of solo diplomacy devalues EU. 19 October.
The Times (2001) No. 10 fury as EU claims Afghan role. 15 December.
The Times (2002) Britain picks 'Euro-army' for Afghan peacekeeping mission. 9 January.
Toje, A. (2003) 'The First Casualty in the War against Terror: The Fall of NATO and Europe's Reluctant Coming of Age', *European Security* 12 (2): 63–76.
Tonra, B. (2001) *The Europeanisation of National Foreign Policy: Dutch, Danish and Irish Foreign Policy in the European Union*. Aldershot: Ashgate.
Tonra, B. (2003) 'Constructing the Common Foreign and Security Policy: The Utility of a Cognitive Approach', *Journal of Common Market Studies* 41(4): 731–56.
Torreblanca, J. (2001) *Ideas, Preferences and Institutions: Explaining the Europeanization of Spanish Foreign Policy*. Arena Working Paper 01/26.
Treacher, A. (2001) 'Europe as a Power Multiplier for French Security Policy: Strategic Consistency, Tactical Adaptation', *European Security* 10(1): 22–44.
Treacher, A. (2003) *French Interventionism: Europe's Last Global Player?* Aldershot: Ashgate.
Tull, D. M. (2007) 'Die Führung und Beteiligung der Bundeswehr an EUFOR RD Congo'. In Mair, Stefan (ed.), *Auslandseinsätze der Bundeswehr: Leitfragen, Entscheidungsspielräume und Lehren*. SWP-Studie 27, September, Berlin.
Turkish Daily News (2002) British Opposition worried about British troops stuck in Kabul, 26 February.
UK Ministry of Defence (2001) Military Technical Agreement Between the International Security Assistance Force (ISAF) and the Interim Administration of Afghanistan ('Interim Administration'). http://www.operations.mod.uk/isafmta.pdf
United Nations (1999) Security Council fails to extend mandate of United Nations Preventive Deployment Force in the former Yugoslav Republic of Macedonia. Press Release SC/6648. 25 February http://www.un.org/News/Press/docs/1999/19990225.sc6648.html

United Nations (2001) Agreement On Provisional Arrangements In Afghanistan Pending The Re-establishment Of Permanent Government Institutions (Bonn Agreement), 7 December. http://www.un.org/News/dh/latest/afghan/afghanagree.htm

United Nations (2008) United Nations Interim Force in Lebanon. 24 October. http://www.un.org/Depts/dpko/missions/unifil/index.html

UN High Commissioner for Refugees (UNHCR) (2005) Refugee Statistics, Afghanistan. http://www.unhcr.ch/cgibin/texis/vtx/afghan?page=background.

United Nations Security Council (2006) Resolution 1671 S/RES/1671 (2006). New York, 25 April. http://daccessdds.un.org/doc/UNDOC/GEN/N06/326/70/PDF/N0632670.pdf?OpenElement

United Nations Security Council (2007) Presentation by Javier Solana, EU High Representative for the CFSP, on the Democratic Republic of Congo/EUFOR. S005/07. New York, 9 January. http://ue.eu.int/ueDocs/cms_Data/docs/pressdata/EN/discours/92360.pdf

United Press International (2002) Analysis: All-European force criticized. London, 10 January.

US Department of Defense (2002) International Contributions to the War Against Terrorism, 14 June. http://www.defenselink.mil/news/Jun2002/d20020607contributions.pdf

United States Institute for Peace (2003) *Unfinished Business in Afghanistan: Warlordism, Reconstruction, and Ethnic Harmony.* Special Report No. 105, April.

Védrine, H. (2001) Visit to the United States – Statements made by M. Hubert Védrine during his press conference with Mr Colin Powell, Washington 26 March. http://www.ambafrance-uk.org/article-imprim.php3?id_article=5621 (accessed on 10 December 2008)

Wagener, M. (2003) 'Auslandseinsätze der Bundeswehr. Normalisierung statt Militarisierung deutscher Sicherheitspolitik.' In Maull, H. et al. (eds), *Deutschland im Abseits? Rot-grüne Aussenpolitik 1998–2003.* Baden-Baden: Nomos Verlagsgesellschaft: 33–49.

Wagner, R. H. (1974) 'Dissolving the State: Three Recent Perspectives on International Relations', *International Organization* 28: 435–66.

Wallace, W. (1994) *Regional integration: the West European Experience.* Washington, DC: Brookings Institution.

Wallace, W. (2005) 'The Collapse of British Foreign Policy', *International Affairs* 82(1): 53–68.

Wallace, W. and T. Oliver, (2005) 'A Bridge Too Far: The United Kingdom and the Transatlantic Relationship.' In Andrews, D. (ed.), *Alliance under Stress.* Cambridge: Cambridge University Press.

Walt, S. M. (1987) *The Origins of Alliances.* Ithaca, NY: Cornell University Press.

Walt, S. M. (1997) 'Why Alliances Endure or Collapse', *Survival* 39(1): 156–79.

Walt, S. M. (1999) 'NATO's Future (In Theory).' In Martin P. and Brawley M. (eds), *Alliance Politics, Kosovo, and NATO's War: Allied Force or Forced Allies?* Basingstoke: Palgrave – Now Palgrave Macmillan: 11–26.

Waltz, K. N. (1979) *Theory of International Politics.* New York: McGraw-Hill.

Washington Post (2004) Chirac's multipolar world. Washington, DC, 4 February: A22.

Welch, D. (1992) 'The Organizational Process and Bureaucratic Politics Paradigm', *International Security* 17: 112–46.

Die Welt (2006) Die Europaer werden mit Misstrauen erwartet. 18 May.

White, B. (1999) 'The European Challenge to Foreign Policy Analysis', *European Journal of International Relations* 5(1): 37–66.

The White House, Office of the Press Secretary (1999) Text of a letter from the President to the speaker of the house of representatives and the president of the senate, March 26. Washington, DC. http://www.lib.umich.edu/govdocs/text/pres325.txt

Whitman, R. (1999) *Amsterdam's unfinished business? The Blair government's initiative and the future of the Western European Union*. Occasional Paper 7, Institute for Security Studies, Paris.

Whitman, R. (2004) 'NATO, the EU and ESDP: An Emerging Division of Labour?' *Contemporary Security Policy* 25(3): 430–51.

Williams, M. and I. B. Neumann (1996) 'From Alliance to Security Community: NATO, Russia and the Power of Identity', *Millennium: Journal of International Studies* 29 (2): 357–87.

Wohlforth, W. (1999) 'The Stability of a Unipolar World', *International Security* 24 (Summer): 5–41.

Wong, R. (2005) 'The Europeanization of Foreign policy.' In Hill, C. and Smith, M. (eds), *International Relations and the European Union*. Oxford: Oxford University Press: 134–53.

Wong, R. (2006) *The Europeanization of French Foreign Policy: France and the EU in East Asia*. Basingstoke: Palgrave Macmillan.

ZDF (2001) Interview Volmer. Morgenmagazin, 30 November.

Zielonka, J. (1998) *Explaining Euro-paralysis: Why Europe is Unable to Act in International Politics*. Basingstoke: Macmillan Press – now Palgrave Macmillan.

Index

Afghanistan 38–46, 55, 64, 72–4,
  77–8, 105–6, 123, 137–41,
  162–5, 170
  Bonn Conference 42–3, 77, 123,
    137
  International Security Assistance
    Force (ISAF) 38–9, 43–6, 64,
    80–3, 107–12, 141–4, 164–5
  Operation Enduring Freedom (OEF)
    38, 40–2, 101–2, 108, 123, 134–6,
    162–3
  Petersberg Agreement 138
  Taliban 38–40, 74, 137, 163
Alliance Politics 8–9, 20–4, 27, 64,
  67, 75–7, 82, 97–8, 101, 105,
  111–12, 123, 127, 130, 144
Alliot-Marie, Michèle 117
Allison, Graham 9–11
Amsterdam, Treaty of 4
Annan, Kofi 44, 49, 52, 59

Balkans 1, 22, 29–30, 37, 69, 91,
  109, 124–6, 170–1
Battle Group 119–21, 150, 152
Beckett, Margaret 84
Belgium 39, 41, 61, 64
Bergne, Paul 73, 78, 80
Berlin Plus Agreement, see NATO
Blair, Tony 5, 41, 52, 64, 68, 72–4,
  76–7, 80–1, 84, 90
Bolton, John 50, 85
Brahimi, Lakhdar 44, 77–8, 106, 138
Britain 1, 5, 34, 38, 41, 45, 49, 55,
  63–90, 101, 113, 118, 145–6,
  156–7, 161–2
  Department for International
    Development (DFID) 77–9, 84
  Foreign Office 65–7, 70–1, 73, 77,
    81, 84–6, 89
  House of Commons 69, 76, 85
  Ministry of Defence 70–1, 82
  Position towards ESDP 63, 70–2,
    83–4, 154
Bush, George W. 51, 66, 73, 103

Chirac, Jacques 37, 41, 45, 49, 66,
  88, 92–3, 96–7, 102–6, 109–19,
  150
Common Foreign and Security Policy
  (CFSP) 3–4, 29–34, 61–2, 66–7,
  94–5, 123–7, 137–8, 159–60
Contact Group 32, 35, 66, 93, 95,
  124, 127, 156, 159
Cook, Robin 65–6
Cooper, Robert 50, 73, 78, 81

De Villepin, Dominique 114
Democratic Republic of Congo (DRC)
  2, 47, 55–61, 83–4, 88–9, 118–20
  EUFOR Artemis 29, 47, 57–8, 110,
    112, 119, 153
  EUFOR RD Congo 2, 47, 57–62,
    83–4, 89, 118–20, 145, 149–53,
    167–8
  EUPOL Kinshasa 57, 60, 119
  EUSEC RD Congo 88
  International Committee to Assist
    the Transition (CIAT) 57, 60
  Lusaka Accord 56
  United Nations Mission in the
    Democratic Republic of the
    Congo (MONUC) 2, 56–8, 60–1,
    119
  Pretoria Agreement 56
Dickinson, Mark 33, 65
Douste-Blazy, Philippe 49, 114–17

Effective multilateralism 57, 62, 152
European Security and Defence Policy
  (ESDP) 1–3, 6, 29, 36–8, 70–2,
  83–4, 88–90, 98–101, 119–21,
  131–4, 149–53, 160–2, 170–1
ESDP missions, see respective countries
EU Battle Group, see Battle Group
Eurocorps 109, 112
European Commission 32–3, 42–3,
  57, 79, 106–7, 162
European Political Cooperation (EPC)
  4, 15, 19

European Security Strategy (ESS) 46, 170
Europeanization 1, 3, 8, 13–21, 25–8, 154–8, 168–72
Identity Reconstruction 16
National adaptation 16–17
National projection 16–18

Feith, Pieter 35, 127
Fischer, Joschka 99, 125–6, 129, 132, 134, 138–9, 142–3
Foreign Policy Analysis (FPA) 9–10, 12, 149
Former Yugoslav Republic of Macedonia (FYROM) 2, 3, 29–38, 63–72, 91–102, 123–34, 158–62
Contact Group, *see separate entry*
National Liberation Army (NLA) 31–3, 36
Ohrid Framework Agreement, *see separate entry*
Operation Allied Harmony 36, 128
Operation Amber Fox 36–7, 128
Operation Essential Harvest 34–7, 68–70, 72, 96–8, 101, 125, 127–31, 160
United Nations Preventive Deployment Force (UNPREDEP) 31
France 1, 3–6, 15, 33–4, 41–2, 50–6, 58, 61, 75, 83, 86, 88, 91–121, 128, 146, 155–7, 163–8
Elysée 93
French Ministry of Defence 99, 108, 120
Position towards ESDP 5–6, 91, 98–101, 109–11
Quai d'Orsay 93–94, 108, 120
French-German summits 93, 96, 150

G8 50–1, 148
German political parties
CDU 125, 129–30, 135–6, 143, 145, 146, 151
CSU 135
FDP 125, 130, 135, 137

Green Party 127, 129, 135, 137, 151
PDS 126, 135, 137, 142
SPD 129–30, 130, 135, 137, 146
Germany 3–6, 33–4, 37, 41–5, 53, 58–9, 75, 77, 96, 99, 104, 106–7, 111, 119–20, 122–53, 163–5
Bundestag 125–6, 128–30, 134–7, 139, 142, 148, 151
Bundeswehr 45, 135–6, 141
Federal Foreign Office 124, 126, 128, 132, 150
German Ministry of Defence 128, 132–3, 141
Position towards ESDP 4–6, 122, 131–4, 149–53
Governmental Politics 8–13, 26, 28, 169
Guéhenno, Jean-Marie 57, 120

Helsinki Headline Goal 6
Hezbollah, *see also* Lebanon 48–50, 52, 54, 85, 114, 117, 148
Hoon, Geoff 81–2

Institutionalism 22
Iraq, war in 46, 48, 58, 74, 83–4, 86, 102, 115–16, 146
Israel 48–52, 54–5, 74, 83, 85–7, 115, 117, 145–8, 157, 166
Italy 38, 53–4, 75
UNIFIL, contributions to 53–4

Jospin, Lionel 102–4, 106
Jung, Franz Josef 151–2

Kabila, Joseph 60–1
Karzai, Hamid 42, 44
Klaiber, Klaus-Peter 40, 43–4, 95, 105, 140–1, 143
Kosovo 5, 30–2, 34–5, 65–6, 96, 100, 122, 124, 128
Extraction Force (XFOR) 35, 96
Kosovo Force (KFOR) 35, 68, 96–7

Lebanon 2–3, 47–55, 62, 83–7, 91, 112–18, 145–9
Rome conference 51, 53, 114

Lebanon – *continued*
   UNIFIL   48–9, 51–5, 83–4, 86–8,
      113, 116–18, 121, 147–9, 155,
      158, 165–7, 172
Lehne, Stefan   35, 127
Léotard, François   33–4, 37, 94–5,
      98–100, 125, 131, 134
Liberal Intergovernmentalism   9, 17
Lisbon Treaty   172

Maastricht, Treaty of   4
Merkel, Angela   50, 119, 145–8,
      150–1
Michel, Louis   2, 45
Middle East, EU role in   47–8, 50, 55,
      62, 87
   EU BAM Rafah   47
   EUPOL COPPS   47–8
   Middle East Quartet   47, 49, 83

North Atlantic Treaty Organization
      (NATO)   1–6, 8, 22–4, 35–8, 40,
      45–6, 48, 63–4, 67–72, 75–6,
      80–1, 96–9, 111–12, 122–3,
      127–31, 144, 154–61
   Article V   76, 105, 136–7, 163
   Berlin Plus Agreement   30, 36–8,
      64, 70–1, 100, 132
   North Atlantic Council   46, 96
   Operations, *see respective countries*

Ohrid Framework Agreement, *see also*
      FYROM   32, 34–6, 125, 160
Organization for Security and
      Co-operation in Europe (OSCE)
      32, 36, 98, 124, 126

Pardew, James   33–4
Patten, Chris   32, 65
Petersberg Tasks   6, 52, 70
Political and Security Committee
      (PSC)   46, 48, 51, 53–5, 59, 62,
      83, 87, 118, 150, 167
Powell, Colin   37, 95
Prodi, Romano   74

Rapid Reaction Mechanism
      (RRM)   43
Reflexive multilateralism   90, 112

Rice, Condoleezza   52
Richard, Alain   97
Robertson, George   32–5, 127
Rühe, Volker   129
Rumsfeld, Donald   75
Russia   66, 93, 159

Saint Malo, Anglo-French summit of
      6, 63, 71, 88, 101, 110
Scharping, Rudolf   141
Schröder, Gerhard   96, 123, 125–6,
      128–9, 132, 134–40, 142, 144
Security Sector Reform (SSR)   63,
      89–90, 171
Short, Clare   77, 79, 81
Solana, Javier   2, 6, 32–5, 37, 44–5,
      50, 52–3, 60, 64–5, 82, 95, 110,
      126, 132, 156, 159, 163
Spain, contributions to UNIFIL
      53–4, 59
Steinmeier, Frank-Walter   147, 149,
      152
Straw, Jack   66, 71, 73, 76
Struck, Peter   130, 137, 141, 144

Taliban, *see* Afghanistan
Trajkovski, Boris   33–4, 131
Tuomoija, Erkki   52
Turkey   37, 71, 80—1

United Nations   49, 52, 105–6, 112,
      114
   Operations, *see respective countries*
   UN Department of Peace Keeping
      Operations (UN DPKO)   56
   UN Security Council   50, 54, 86,
      103, 113
United States (US)   3, 8, 22–4, 34,
      37–8, 40–2, 47–51, 66, 69, 72,
      74–7, 80–1, 84–6, 101–3, 115–16,
      123, 126–8, 134–5, 157, 163,
      166

Védrine, Hubert   43, 93, 95–6, 99,
      102–3

Western European Union (WEU)   4, 6